CLASSIC BIBLICAL

BABY NAMES

CLASSIC BIBLICAL BABY NAMES

Timeless Names for Modern Parents

Judith Tropea

Produced by The Philip Lief Group, Inc.

Bantam Books

CLASSIC BIBLICAL BABY NAMES
A Bantam Book / September 2006

Published by Bantam Dell
A Division of Random House, Inc.
New York, New York

Copyright © 2006 The Philip Lief Group, Inc.
Cover illustration by Ben Perini
Cover photos © Penny Gentieu
Cover design by Beverly Leung

Book design by Virginia Norey

LIBRARY OF CONGRESS CATALOGING-IN-PUBLICATION DATA
Tropea, Judith.
Classic biblical baby names: timeless names for modern parents / Judith Tropea;
produced by The Philip Lief Group, Inc.
p.   cm.
ISBN-10: 0-553-38393-0
ISBN-13: 978-0-553-38393-5
1. Names, Personal—Dictionaries.   2. Names in the Bible—Dictionaries.
I. Philip Lief Group.   II. Title.   III. Title: Biblical baby names.
CS2377 .T76 2006   2006042760
929.4′4—dc22

Printed in the United States of America
Published simultaneously in Canada

www.bantamdell.com

BVG   10   9   8   7   6   5   4   3   2   1

CONTENTS

INTRODUCTION

Of all the hundreds of decisions that expectant parents must make, one of the most important is choosing a name for their new baby. "A good name is to be chosen rather than great riches," says Proverbs 22:1. For parents wanting to give their child a name with substance, a name that represents strength and tradition, a name whose enduring meaning will outlast the trends of Brittany, Tiffany, and Tyler, here is *Classic Biblical Baby Names: Timeless Names for Modern Parents*.

Names are an integral part of our identity. A child's name affects his/her self-perception and reflects the parents' beliefs and culture. A name pays tribute to the individual spirit and is one of the first wonderful gifts you can offer your child. Naming your baby is like naming your hopes for the future; the "right" name will shepherd your child into a life of grace, strength, and integrity.

In the beginning, God gave Adam the sacred task of naming every living thing, and the Bible is replete with stories about assigning names. Moses received his name because Pharaoh's daughter "drew him out of the water" (Exodus 2:10) and Leah called her son Asher because she was "happy" (Genesis 30:13). Like Adam, you are given the sacred task of choosing a name for your child—a name that will express your beliefs, your history, and your dreams. With the Bible as a guide, you can be certain that your choice will be underscored by a strong spiritual heritage as well.

For example, naming a girl Bethany, after the village near Jerusalem where Lazarus rose from the dead (John 11:38–44), evokes a spiritual awareness that trendier names such as Madison and Mackenzie may be lacking. It offers her a home in a cherished religious tradition and may even invite her to discover more about her namesake by reading the Bible. Likewise, selecting Tamar instead of Taylor opens a young person to choices that are even more profound and will help give your child a unique sense of self.

For those who are searching for a name that is both meaningful and spiritual, *Classic Biblical Baby Names* offers a myriad of choices. Organized alphabetically by gender, this collection offers hundreds of biblical names culled from both the Old and New Testaments. Each entry includes:

- ✦ The language/cultural origin of the name
- ✦ Pronunciation
- ✦ Concise meaning
- ✦ Spiritual connotation
- ✦ Scriptural story surrounding the name
- ✦ Citation of where the name appears in the Bible
- ✦ Related names and nicknames
- ✦ Alternate names with spelling variations

This book is not intended to be comprehensive. Of the 3,300 names in both the Old and New Testaments, nearly 500 have been selected. The names were chosen with the consideration that they should appeal to contemporary tastes. Others, such as Jezebel and Judas, were excluded because of their association with evil, and Jehoshaphat because of its impracticality.

Unlike some exhaustive name dictionaries, which provide only a one- or two-word definition for thousands of names, *Classic Biblical Baby Names* offers a selection of specifically chosen names that are beautiful and powerful, along with the engaging biblical story of each name's origin. Expectant parents can use this guide to give them background on more-common names and to open up new possibilities of lesser-known names that are classic and unique at the same time. In our multicultural society, unusual names are no longer the exception, and the Bible is a rich resource waiting to be mined.

"A good name is better than precious ointment," says Ecclesiastes 7:1. Take time to peruse these pages and make a choice that will start your precious one off on a distinctive path that will last a lifetime.

CLASSIC BIBLICAL

BABY NAMES

BOYS' NAMES

The angel of the LORD also said to her:
"You are now with child and you will have a son."

—Genesis 16:11

AARON ◆ *(EHR-uhn)* or *(A-ruhn)*

Language/Cultural Origin: Hebrew/Egyptian

Meaning: Mountain of Strength

Spiritual Connotation: Exalted

Related Names/Nicknames: Aaronas, Aharon, Arand, Arend, Ari, Arnie, Erin, Haroun, Harun, Ron, Ronnie, Ronny

Alternate Names: Aaran, Aaren, Aarron, Aaryn, Arin, Aron, Aronne, Arran, Arron

Background Story: When God commanded Moses to lead the Israelites out of Egypt, he sent Aaron—Moses's brother—to help. Aaron served as his brother's mouthpiece because Moses was afraid he was too "slow of speech." Pharaoh wanted proof of God's power before releasing the Israelites, and Aaron and Moses performed numerous "wonders" before him: They transformed a staff into a snake, turned the waters of the Nile into blood, and brought plagues upon Egypt. It was not until the Lord struck down all the firstborn of Egypt that Pharaoh said, "Rise up, go away from my people, both you and the Israelites!" Aaron was a loyal companion to Moses, but when the Lord was giving Moses the Ten Commandments, Aaron gave in to the demands of the Israelites and built an idol for them at the base of the mountain. Thanks to Moses's prayer, however, God forgave Aaron and appointed him the first high priest, with his sons to follow (Exodus 4–40).

Of Interest: From 1970 to 2003, Aaron was one of the fifty most popular names for boys in the United States.

Famous Namesakes: Aaron Burr, U.S. vice president; Aaron Copland, composer; Aaron Neville and Aaron Tippin, singers; Hank Aaron, baseball home-run champion.

ABDIEL ◆ *(AB-dee-ehl)*

Language/Cultural Origin: Hebrew

Meaning: Servant of God

Spiritual Connotation: Faithful Disciple

Related Names/Nicknames: Abdi, Abe, Diel

Alternate Names: None

Background Story: Abdiel was the son of Guni and a descendant of Gad. His own son, Ahi, was "chief in their clan." Abdiel's kin lived in Bashan "and in the pasture lands of Sharon" (1 Chronicles 5:15–16). Abdiel is a name suggesting a man who is true to his beliefs.

Of Interest: Abdiel was the name given to the fictional seraph who withstood Satan in Milton's *Paradise Lost.*

ABDON ◆ *(AB-duhn)*

Language/Cultural Origin: Aramaic

Meaning: Servant

Spiritual Connotation: Worshipper

Related Names/Nicknames: Avda, Avdon

Alternate Names: None

Background Story: There are four men named Abdon in the Bible: a judge of Israel who served for eight years and had forty sons and thirty grandsons (Judges 12:13–14); one of the sons of Shashak, a Benjamite (1 Chronicles 8:23); the firstborn son of Jeiel and Maacah (1 Chronicles 8:29–30); and the son of Micah, sent by King Josiah to the prophetess, Huldah, to determine the fate of his people who had "forsaken" the Lord (2 Chronicles 34:20–28). The name Abdon suggests a man who looks to God for answers.

ABEL ✦ *(AY-buhl)*

Language/Cultural Origin: Hebrew

Meaning: Breath

Spiritual Connotation: Sacred Offering

Related Names/Nicknames: Abe, Abele, Abey, Abhel, Abie, Hebel, Hebhel, Hevel

Alternate Names: Abell, Able, Abyl

Background Story: Adam's son Abel worked as a shepherd, and his older brother Cain tilled the field. One day, each made an offering to the Lord. Cain offered God the "fruit of the ground" while Abel brought him the "firstlings of his flock." God preferred Abel's offering, which filled Cain's heart with rage. He lured Abel into the field and killed him. When God inquired about Abel's whereabouts, Cain rudely replied, "Am I my brother's keeper?" God punished Cain by making him "a fugitive and a wanderer on the earth" (Genesis 4:1–12).

Of Interest: In the New Testament, Abel is considered the first martyr, and Jesus refers to the "blood of righteous Abel" (Matthew 23:35).

ABIEL ✦ *(AY-bee-ehl)* or *(uh-BAI-ehl)* or *(AB-ee-ehl)*

Language/Cultural Origin: Hebrew

Meaning: My Father Is God

Spiritual Connotation: Devoted to the Lord

Related Names/Nicknames: Abi-albon

Alternate Names: Abeel, Abiell, Abyel, Abyell, Ahbiel

Background Story: Two men named Abiel are in the Bible: Kish's father and Saul's grandfather (1 Samuel 9:1, 14:51), and one of the "mighty warriors" who helped David become king (1 Chronicles 11:32). Abiel is a name suggesting a strong faith in God.

Of Interest: Abiel was a popular name among the early Puritan settlers.

ABIRAM ✦ *(uh-BAI-ruhm)*
Language/Cultural Origin: Hebrew
Meaning: High Father
Spiritual Connotation: Dignity
Related Names/Nicknames: Avi, Aviram
Alternate Names: Abhiram

Background Story: Both Abirams in the Bible met unhappy ends. Abiram and his brother, Dathan, accused Moses and Aaron of exalting themselves "above the assembly of the Lord." For questioning God's will, the brothers and their families were swallowed up by the earth (Numbers 16:1–34). The other Abiram was the victim of his father, Hiel, who rebuilt the walls of Jericho "at the cost of" his firstborn son's life (1 Kings 16:34).

ABNER ✦ *(AB-ner)*
Language/Cultural Origin: Hebrew
Meaning: Father of Light
Spiritual Connotation: Believer of Truth
Related Names/Nicknames: Ab, Abbey, Abbie, Abby, Abnar, Abnor, Avnor, Eb, Ebby
Alternate Names: Avner

Background Story: Abner was the chief commander of King Saul's army and also his cousin. It was Abner who introduced David to the king's court following his victory over Goliath. After Saul's death, Abner went to war with David's army to secure the throne for Saul's son, Ishbaal. He lost that fight at the pool of Gibeon and was eventually killed by the commander of David's army, Joab. David sincerely mourned Abner's death, saying, "A prince and a great man has fallen this day in Israel" (2 Samuel 3:38).

Famous Namesakes: Abner Doubleday was a Civil War general at the Battle of Gettysburg and, as legend has it, the inventor of baseball.

ABRAHAM ◆ *(AY-bruh-ham)*

Language/Cultural Origin: Hebrew

Meaning: Father of a Multitude

Spiritual Connotation: Benefactor

Related Names/Nicknames: Abarran, Abe, Abey, Abhiram, Abie, Abrahan, Abram, Abrami, Abramo, Abran, Avi, Avra, Avraham, Avram, Avrom, Avrum, Bram

Alternate Names: Abrahem, Abrahim, Abrahym, Abreham, Abrehem, Abrehym, Abryham, Abryhem, Ebrahim, Ibraheem, Ibrahim

Background Story: Abraham—originally called Abram—lived in Haran with his wife, Sarai, and the rest of his kin. One day, the Lord told Abram to leave his father's country. "I will make you into a great nation," God promised (Genesis 12:1–2). Abram and Sarai traveled from place to place for many years, but they had no children. Finally, Sarai persuaded Abram to have a child with her maid, Hagar, and they named the boy Ishmael. When Abram was ninety-nine, God fulfilled his promise at last. He made a covenant with Abram, changing his name to Abraham and Sarai's name to Sarah, and in her old age "Sarah conceived and bore Abraham a son" named Isaac (Genesis 21:2). Abraham's first son, Ishmael, was sent into the wilderness, where he grew up under God's protection. Then the Lord presented Abraham with his greatest test. He said, "Take your . . . only son Isaac, whom you love, and go to the land of Moriah, and offer him there as a burnt offering." As always, Abraham did as the Lord asked. At the exact moment he raised his knife to kill Isaac, an angel appeared and stopped him. Because of Abraham's faithfulness, God promised to bless him and make his offspring "as numerous as the stars of heaven" (Genesis 22:2–18). At the age of one hundred seventy-five, Abraham died and was buried at Machpelah, where he had also buried his beloved wife Sarah.

Of Interest: God made a covenant with Abraham that he would be the "ancestor of a multitude of nations" (Genesis 17:5). Through Ishmael, he is considered one of the first prophets of Islam, and through Isaac, he is known as the first patriarch of the Jews. His original name, Abram, means "high father" or "exalted father."

Famous Namesakes: Abraham Lincoln was the sixteenth president of the United States.

ABSALOM ✦ *(AB-suh-luhm)*

Language/Cultural Origin: Hebrew

Meaning: Father of Peace

Spiritual Connotation: God's Mercy

Related Names/Nicknames: Abishalom, Absolon, Acke, Aksel, Akseli, Axel, Axelle

Alternate Names: Avsalom, Avshalom

Background Story: Absalom, the son of Maacah, was David's third and favorite son. The trouble began when David's firstborn son, Amnon, violated Absalom's sister Tamar, who was known for her beauty. Absalom killed Amnon and escaped to Geshur, where he found refuge with his grandfather. David grew despondent over the loss of Absalom and, after three years, he allowed him to return to Jerusalem. Absalom, however, had his eye on David's throne and began to gather support. He proclaimed himself king of Hebron, and David fled from Jerusalem. A battle ensued, but Absalom and his supporters were no match for David and his army. Absalom died retreating from the battlefield. Despite his son's rebellious actions, David wept after his death. "O my son Absalom . . . Would I had died instead of you, O Absalom, my son, my son!" (2 Samuel 18:33).

Of Interest: Absalom, Absalom!, written by William Faulkner, is a novel about three families in the South during the time of the Civil War.

ACHAICUS ✦ *(uh-KAY-uh-kuhs)*
Language/Cultural Origin: Greek
Meaning: Sorrowing
Spiritual Connotation: Longing for God
Related Names/Nicknames: Achaia
Alternate Names: Achaikos

Background Story: Achaicus, an early Christian convert, was a leader of the Church in Corinth. With two other converts, Stephanas and Fortunatus, he visited Paul at Ephesus, where they "refreshed" his "spirit." Paul urges the Christians at Corinth to serve these leaders and "everyone who works and toils with them" (1 Corinthians 16:15–18).

ACHIM ✦ *(AY-kihm)*

Language/Cultural Origin: Hebrew

Meaning: Preparing

Spiritual Connotation: Eager for the Lord

Related Names/Nicknames: Ahim, Jachin, Jehoiachin

Alternate Names: Acheim, Acim

Background Story: Achim appears in Matthew's genealogy of Jesus. He is an ancestor of Joseph, the husband of Mary, to whom Jesus was born. The name Achim suggests a man who likes to keep his eye on future possibilities.

Of Interest: Achim is a popular shortened form of the German name Joachim.

Famous Namesakes: Achim Heukemes, German marathon runner, set a new world record for his 4,568-kilometer run through Australia in April of 2005.

ADAM ✦ *(AD-uhm)*

Language/Cultural Origin: Hebrew/Babylonian

Meaning: Red Earth

Spiritual Connotation: Made in God's Image

Related Names/Nicknames: Ad, Adamah, Adamina, Adamo, Adams, Adamson, Adan, Adao, Addams, Addie, Addis, Addison, Addy, Ade, Admon, Adnet, Adnon, Adnot, Akamu

Alternate Names: Addam, Addem, Adem, Adham

Background Story: Adam was the first man in the Bible. God created him "from the dust of the ground" and put him in charge of the garden of Eden. The Lord also created Eve as a partner for him, because it was "not good that the man should be alone." There was only one restriction: The couple were never to eat from the tree of good and evil. But the serpent tempted Eve, who ate from the tree and shared its fruit with Adam. For their disobedience, God threw them out of the garden, and Adam had to "till the ground from which he was taken" (Genesis 2–3). Adam and Eve had many children, but only three are named: Cain, Abel, and Seth.

Of Interest: From 1970 to 2000, Adam was among the top fifty names for boys in the United States.

Famous Namesakes: Adam Clayton Powell Jr., U.S. congressman; Adam Sandler, Adam West, actors; Adam Smith, economist.

ADDI ✦ *(AD-ee)*
Language/Cultural Origin: Hebrew
Meaning: My Witness
Spiritual Connotation: In God's Family
Related Names/Nicknames: None
Alternate Names: Addai, Addei

Background Story: Addi appears in Luke's account of the genealogy of Jesus. He was an ancestor of Joseph, Mary's husband. Addi's father was Cosam and his son was Melchi (Luke 3:28). Addi is a friendly name, suggesting a man who is outgoing and likable.

ADDON ✦ *(AD-uhn)*

Language/Cultural Origin: Babylonian

Meaning: Strong

Spiritual Connotation: Tenacious

Related Names/Nicknames: Adain

Alternate Names: Addan

Background Story: Addon is a family or place name associated with Jews who returned from captivity in Babylon. Because these people were unable to prove their "ancestral houses or their descent," they were unable to participate in the priesthood (Nehemiah 7:61–65). The name Addon suggests a man who handles problems well.

ADIN ✦ *(AY-dihn)*

Language/Cultural Origin: Hebrew

Meaning: Slender

Spiritual Connotation: Promise to God

Related Names/Nicknames: Adena, Adina, Adinu, Aidan, Aiden

Alternate Names: Aden, Adhin

Background Story: Adin was the ancestor of a clan that "returned to Jerusalem and Judah, all to their own towns" after years of captivity in Babylon (Ezra 2:15). The clan numbered in the hundreds and its leaders were among those who signed Nehemiah's covenant with the Lord (Nehemiah 10:16).

Famous Namesakes: Rabbi Adin Steinsaltz has published fifty-eight books on the Talmud, religious thought, sociology, and philosophy.

ADINO ◆ *(uh-DEE-no)*

Language/Cultural Origin: Hebrew

Meaning: Spear

Spiritual Connotation: Defender

Related Names/Nicknames: Dean, Dino

Alternate Names: Adhino

Background Story: Adino the Eznite—also known as Jashobeam—was a "chief among the captains" of David's "mighty men," an elite group of warriors who safeguarded their king. He rose to that high position as a result of killing "eight hundred men at one time" (2 Samuel 23:8). The name Adino suggests a strong, protective man.

ADLAI ◆ *(AD-lay)* or *(AD-lai)*

Language/Cultural Origin: Hebrew

Meaning: God Is Just

Spiritual Connotation: Truthful

Related Names/Nicknames: Ad, Adaliah, Addey, Addie, Addy

Alternate Names: Adlae, Adlay, Adley

Background Story: Adlai was the father of Shaphat, one of David's overseers, who watched "over the herds in the valleys" (1 Chronicles 27:29). The name Adlai suggests a man who is honest and fair in everything he does.

Famous Namesakes: Adlai Stevenson was a U.S. vice president; his grandson, Adlai Ewing Stevenson II, was twice the Democratic candidate for U.S. president; and his great-grandson, Adlai Ewing Stevenson III, was a U.S. senator from Illinois.

ADONAI ✦ *(AH-do-nai)*

Language/Cultural Origin: Hebrew

Meaning: My Lord

Spiritual Connotation: God's Spirit

Related Names/Nicknames: Adonis

Alternate Names: Adhonay, Adoni

Background Story: Adonai is the name for God in the Hebrew Bible, where it appears over six thousand times. It is written in place of "YHVH" or "Jehovah," a name that many Hebrews believed was too sacred to be spoken aloud. Adonai is an excellent name for a boy whose parents wish to instill the spirit of the Lord in him.

Of Interest: "YHVH" is still pronounced Adonai by Jewish people today, while most English-language Bibles translate it as "Lord."

ADRIEL ✦ *(AY-dree-ehl)*

Language/Cultural Origin: Hebrew

Meaning: Of God's Flock

Spiritual Connotation: Nurtured by God

Related Names/Nicknames: None

Alternate Names: Adriell, Adriyel

Background Story: Adriel was married to Saul's daughter, Merab, whom Saul had promised to David for battling the Philistines. Saul used Merab as a "snare . . . that the hand of the Philistines may be against" David. When his plans failed, he gave her to Adriel as a wife (1 Samuel 18:17–19). Later, Adriel and Merab's five sons were killed by the Gibeonites in retribution for Saul's mistreatment of them (2 Samuel 21:1–9).

Of Interest: In one Native American language, Adriel is the word for "beaver" and suggests a person of skill.

Famous Namesakes: Adriel Hampton, journalist; Adriel Heisey, aerial photographer.

AENEAS ✦ *(uh-NEE-uhs)*
Language/Cultural Origin: Greek
Meaning: Praiseworthy
Spiritual Connotation: Honorable
Related Names/Nicknames: Aengus, Angus, Enne
Alternate Names: Aenneas, Aineas, Ainneas, Aneas, Eneas, Enneas, Enneis, Enneiss

Background Story: Aeneas, a man from Lydda, "had been bedridden for eight years, for he was paralyzed." When Peter discovered him he said, "Aeneas, Jesus Christ heals you; get up and make your bed!" With those words, the man was healed. As soon as the people in his town saw him, they embraced the Lord (Acts 9:32–35).

Of Interest: Aeneas—a Trojan hero of Greek and Roman legend—is a character in Homer's epic poem *The Iliad.* He is also the hero of Virgil's *Aeneid,* which tells the story of his journey from Troy to the city that would one day become Rome.

Famous Namesakes: Aeneas Williams, a professional football player for the St. Louis Rams, has appeared in the Pro Bowl eight times.

ALEXANDER ✦ *(al-ihg-ZAN-der)*

Language/Cultural Origin: Greek

Meaning: Defender of Mankind

Spiritual Connotation: Protector

Related Names/Nicknames: Al, Alastair, Alaster, Alcander, Alcinder, Alcindor, Alec, Alek, Alessandro, Alex, Alexan, Alexandra, Alexandros, Alexi, Alexie, Alexis, Alic, Alick, Alik, Alistair, Alix, Allie, Lex, Sacha, Sander, Sandie, Sandro, Sandy, Sascha, Sasha, Saunder, Saunders, Xan, Xander, Zander, Zandro, Zandros

Alternate Names: Aleksander, Aleksandr, Alessandre, Alexandre, Alisander, Alissander, Alissandre, Alixandre

Background Story: There are four Alexanders in the New Testament: the son of Simon of Cyrene, who carried Jesus's cross (Mark 15:21); a relative of Annas, present when the high priest questioned Peter and John (Acts 4:5–7); a man who "suffered shipwreck in the faith" and was excommunicated (1 Timothy 1:19–20); and a Jew in Ephesus, where Paul was converting people. A group of artisans who made shrines for pagan gods feared their trade would "come into disrepute" and incited the crowd against Paul. Alexander "tried to make a defense" for Paul although the crowd refused to listen (Acts 19:24–34).

Of Interest: In 2004 Alexander was the fifteenth most popular name for boys.

Famous Namesakes: Alexander Graham Bell, inventor; Alec Baldwin, Sir Alec Guinness, actors; Alexandre Dumas, Aleksandr Solzhenitsyn, authors; Alexander Haig, U.S. secretary of state; Alexander Hamilton, U.S. secretary of the treasury; Alexander Pope, poet; Alexander Popov, Olympic gold medalist in swimming.

ALLON ✦ *(AL-ehn)*

Language/Cultural Origin: Hebrew

Meaning: Oak Tree

Spiritual Connotation: Tower of Strength

Related Names/Nicknames: Alan, Alona

Alternate Names: Alon

Background Story: Allon was the son of Jedaiah and the father of Shiphi. He was a leader of a Simeonite clan who lived in the valley of Gedor, "where they found rich, good pasture, and the land was very broad, quiet, and peaceful" (1 Chronicles 4:37–40).

Of Interest: Allon-bachuth, or "the oak of weeping," was a famous tree near Bethel, under which Rebekah's nurse, Deborah, was buried (Genesis 35:8).

ALPHAEUS ✦ *(AL-fee-uhs)*

Language/Cultural Origin: Greek

Meaning: Changing

Spiritual Connotation: Open-minded

Related Names/Nicknames: Al, Alfie

Alternate Names: Alfaeus, Alfeos, Alfeus, Alfio, Alphaios, Alpheaus, Alpheus

Background Story: There are two men named Alphaeus in the Bible: the father of James whom Jesus chose as one of his apostles (Matthew 10:3), and the father of Levi, a tax collector with whom Jesus and his disciples dined (Mark 2:14–17). The name Alphaeus is a reminder of the need to be open to change in life.

ALVAN ✦ *(AL-van)*

Language/Cultural Origin: Hebrew

Meaning: Sublime

Spiritual Connotation: Noble

Related Names/Nicknames: Al, Aliah, Alian, Alva, Alvah, Alvie, Alvina, Alwan

Alternate Names: Alven, Alvin, Alvyn, Elvin

Background Story: Alvan was Shobal's firstborn son. His brothers were Manahath, Ebal, Shepho, and Onam. They were the grandchildren of Seir the Horite (Genesis 36:23). The name Alvan suggests a man who always rises to the occasion.

Famous Namesakes: Alvan Adams, basketball player; Alvan Clark, astronomer and maker of astronomical lenses; Thomas Alva Edison, inventor.

AMAL ✦ *(ah-MAHL)*

Language/Cultural Origin: Hebrew

Meaning: Industrious

Spiritual Connotation: Idealist

Related Names/Nicknames: Amali, Amalio, Amel, Amelia, Emil

Alternate Names: Amaal, Amahl

Background Story: Amal, the son of Helem, was from the tribe of Asher. He and his brothers—Zophah, Imna, and Shelesh—were all "heads of their ancestral houses, select mighty warriors, and chief of the princes" (1 Chronicles 7:35–40). Amal is a quiet but powerful name, suggesting a man who knows how to turn his dreams into reality.

Of Interest: Amahl is the name of the young boy in the opera *Amahl and the Night Visitors* by Gian Carlo Menotti.

AMARIAH ✦ *(am-uh-RAI-uh)*

Language/Cultural Origin: Hebrew

Meaning: The Lord Promises

Spiritual Connotation: Covenant

Related Names/Nicknames: None

Alternate Names: Amaria, Amariya, Amariyah, Amarya, Amaryah

Background Story: Amariah was a popular name in the Bible, especially among the Levites. The more prominent were: a Levite from the lineage of Moses whom David assigned to work "in the house of the Lord" (1 Chronicles 23:4, 19); the chief priest who settled religious disputes under Jehoshaphat (2 Chronicles 19:11); one of Hezekiah's priests who distributed the free-will offering (2 Chronicles 31:15); and the prophet Zephaniah's great-grandfather (Zephaniah 1:1). The name Amariah suggests someone who takes his relationship with God seriously.

AMASA ✦ *(uh-MAY-suh)* or *(AM-uh-suh)*

Language/Cultural Origin: Hebrew

Meaning: Bearing a Burden

Spiritual Connotation: Responsible Leader

Related Names/Nicknames: None

Alternate Names: None

Background Story: The name Amasa appears twice in the Bible. The first was the son of Abigail, David's sister. David's son Absalom "appointed Amasa over the army" when he rebelled against his father. After Absalom was killed in battle, David made peace with Amasa by appointing him commander of his army. But David's former commander, Joab, soon retaliated by killing Amasa and regaining his post (2 Samuel 17, 19–20). Amasa was also an Ephraimite chief who "stood up against" making slaves of Judeans captured in battle. Instead, he clothed and fed them—and set them free (2 Chronicles 28:12–13).

Famous Namesakes: Amasa Holcomb, pioneer telescope maker; Francis Amasa Walker, former president of the Massachusetts Institute of Technology (MIT).

AMASAI ✦ *(ay-MA-sai)* or *(ay-MAY-sai)*

Language/Cultural Origin: Hebrew

Meaning: Strong

Spiritual Connotation: Moved by God's Spirit

Related Names/Nicknames: None

Alternate Names: Amasay

Background Story: There are three men named Amasai in the Bible: a Levite priest responsible for the "service of song" in the temple (1 Chronicles 6:31–35); one of Saul's warrior chiefs, who was overcome by the "spirit" and defected to David (1 Chronicles 12:18); and a priest appointed by David "to blow the trumpets before the ark of God" (1 Chronicles 15:24). The name Amasai is mindful of a spirited man who is unafraid to "sing out" God's praises.

AMITTAI ✦ *(uh-MIHT-ai)*

Language/Cultural Origin: Hebrew

Meaning: True

Spiritual Connotation: Faithful

Related Names/Nicknames: Amitan, Tai

Alternate Names: Amitai, Amitay, Amitei, Amittay

Background Story: Amittai was the father of the prophet Jonah and lived in the town of Gath-hepher in Zebulon (2 Kings 14:25). His son, Jonah, prophesied the expansion of Israel by Jeroboam. The name Amittai suggests a man who always stands by his friends.

AMMIEL ✦ *(AM-ee-uhl)*

Language/Cultural Origin: Hebrew

Meaning: God of My People

Spiritual Connotation: Belonging to God

Related Names/Nicknames: None

Alternate Names: Ameiel, Amiel, Amyel

Background Story: Ammiel is the name of four men in the Bible: one of twelve men Moses sent to "spy out the land of Canaan" before he gave it to the Israelites (Numbers 13:1, 12); the father of Machir, who gave aid to David's army during Absalom's rebellion (2 Samuel 17:27); the father of Bathsheba, who was David's wife and Solomon's mother (1 Chronicles 3:5); and a gatekeeper of the tabernacle for David (1 Chronicles 26:5).

Famous Namesakes: Ammiel Alcalay is a poet, critic, essayist, and translator.

AMNON ✦ *(AM-nuhn)* or *(AM-nawn)*

Language/Cultural Origin: Hebrew

Meaning: Faithful and True

Spiritual Connotation: Devoted

Related Names/Nicknames: Aminon, Ammon, Amon

Alternate Names: None

Background Story: A prominent Amnon in the Bible is the son of David and his wife Ahinoam, who "fell in love" with his beautiful half-sister Tamar, a virgin. He tricked her into coming to his house by pretending to be ill and, in spite of her protests, he forced himself on her, then cast her out. Although Tamar was desolate, David refused to punish Amnon, who was his firstborn son. Tamar's brother, Absalom, later had Amnon killed for what he had done to his sister (2 Samuel 13:1–29).

Famous Namesakes: Amnon Lipkin-Shahak, chief of staff of the Israel Defense Forces; Amnon Rubinstein, Israeli politician and scholar; Amnon Wolman, composer.

AMON ✦ *(AY-mahn)*

Language/Cultural Origin: Egyptian/Hebrew

Meaning: Trustworthy

Spiritual Connotation: Reliable

Related Names/Nicknames: None

Alternate Names: Ammon, Amun

Background Story: In the Bible, Amon is a name associated with three men: a governor of Samaria who was ordered by King Ahab to put the prophet Micaiah in prison (1 Kings 22:26); a king of Judah whose servants "conspired against him" and killed him

(2 Kings 21:19–26); and a servant of Solomon and his descendants who returned from captivity in Babylon (Nehemiah 7:59).

Famous Namesakes: Amon G. Carter, Texas newspaper publisher and philanthropist; Amon Gordon, football player for the Cleveland Browns.

AMOS ✦ *(AY-muhs)*

Language/Cultural Origin: Hebrew

Meaning: One Who Is Burdened

Spiritual Connotation: Responsibility

Related Names/Nicknames: None

Alternate Names: Amoss

Background Story: Amos is one of the twelve minor prophets of the Bible. A simple shepherd from the town of Tekoa, he described himself as "no prophet, nor prophet's son; but . . . a herdsman and a dresser of sycamore trees" whom the Lord sent to prophesy to the Israelites. During the reign of Jeroboam, Israel reached its height of wealth and power, and the people grew indifferent to God. Amos's prophecies revealed God's anger at their pride and arrogance—and a promise of punishment if they did not repent. He wrote about God's promise to "shake the house of Israel" as if with a sieve, eliminating its sinners. In the end, however, he would "raise up its ruins and rebuild it," and the fortunes of Israel would be restored (Book of Amos).

Of Interest: The Book of Amos is the oldest prophetic book in the Bible.

Famous Namesakes: Amos Bronson Alcott, educator and father of Louisa May Alcott; Amos Eaton, naturalist; Amos Meller, composer/conductor; Amos Oz, writer.

AMZI ✦ *(AM-zee)*

Language/Cultural Origin: Hebrew

Meaning: My Strength

Spiritual Connotation: Zeal

Related Names/Nicknames: None

Alternate Names: None

Background Story: Amzi is the name of two men in the Bible: one of the Levites David "put in charge of the service of song" in the tabernacle after the ark of the covenant was brought there (1 Chronicles 6:31, 46), and a priest who agreed to live in Jerusalem while Nehemiah was governor (Nehemiah 11:12). The name Amzi suggests a man who goes through life with spirit and enthusiasm.

ANAN ✦ *(AY-nuhn)*

Language/Cultural Origin: Hebrew/Arabic

Meaning: Cloud

Spiritual Connotation: Covenant with God

Related Names/Nicknames: Anani

Alternate Names: Aenon, Hanan

Background Story: Anan was one of the men who signed the written covenant with the Lord created by Nehemiah after the return from Babylonian captivity (Nehemiah 10:26). The name Anan is a reminder that new doors can open when the past is left behind.

ANANIAS ✦ *(an-uh-NAI-uhs)*

Language/Cultural Origin: Greek

Meaning: Gift of the Lord

Spiritual Connotation: Grace

Related Names/Nicknames: Ananiah, Annas, Hananiah

Alternate Names: None

Background Story: Of the three men called Ananias in the Bible, the devout disciple who lived in Damascus is especially notable. In a vision, God commanded Ananias to heal a man named Saul, whom the Lord had blinded on the road to Damascus. Ananias knew that Saul had come to persecute Christ's followers and was afraid. But the Lord told him that Saul was an "instrument" who would bring Christ's message to the world. Ananias went to Saul, laid his hands on him, and said, "Regain your sight and be filled with the Holy Spirit." Saul's vision returned and Ananias baptized him. Saul went on to become the great missionary of the early Church known as Paul (Acts 9:10–19).

Of Interest: Ananias is recognized as a saint in the Catholic Church.

ANDREW ✦ *(AN-droo)*

Language/Cultural Origin: Greek

Meaning: Mighty One

Spiritual Connotation: Courageous

Related Names/Nicknames: Ander, Anders, Anderson, Andie, Andonia, Andor, Andra, Andras, Andre, Andrea, Andreas, Andrei, Andreia, Andres, Andrewes, Andrews, Andrey, Andria, Andriana, Andriel, Andries, Andrija, Andrina, Andris, Andrius, Andros, Andrus, Andy, Deandre, Dre, Drea, Drew, Dru

Alternate Names: Andreu, Andro, Andru

Background Story: Andrew's story began near the Sea of Galilee, where he and his brother, Simon, were fishermen. He was walking with John the Baptist when John saw Jesus and exclaimed, "Look, here is the Lamb of God" (John 1:35–42). Jesus promised to make both Andrew and Simon "fishers of men," so they left their nets and followed him in his ministry. As one of Jesus's apostles, Andrew witnessed his words and miracles with his own eyes. It was Andrew who found the boy with "five loaves and two fish," which Jesus used to feed a crowd of five thousand (John 6:8–9). Andrew was also with the apostles when the Holy Spirit came upon them, giving them the power to preach God's message to the world (Acts 2:1–4).

Of Interest: Andrew is the patron saint of Scotland, Russia, and Greece. The name has ranked among the top ten for boys in the United States since 1990.

Famous Namesakes: Andrew Carnegie, industrialist; Andy Devine, Andy Griffith, Andy Garcia, actors; Andrew Jackson, Andrew Johnson, U.S. presidents; Andy Warhol, Andrew Wyeth, artists; Andrew Lloyd Webber, composer; Prince Andrew, Duke of York.

ANDRONICUS ✦ *(an-DRAWN-uh-kuhs)*

Language/Cultural Origin: Latin

Meaning: Excelling Others

Spiritual Connotation: Incomparable

Related Names/Nicknames: None

Alternate Names: Andronikos

Background Story: Andronicus—together with a man named Junia—was a relative of Paul who lived in Rome. They both became Christians before Paul and were with him in prison. Paul described Andronicus and Junia as being "prominent among the apostles" (Romans 16:7). The name Andronicus implies a man who is an example to other people.

Of Interest: Andronicus is the name of a Catholic saint—a Roman soldier who was martyred for his faith in the early fourth century.

APELLES ✦ *(uh-PEHL-eez)*

Language/Cultural Origin: Greek

Meaning: Separation

Spiritual Connotation: One Who Is Called

Related Names/Nicknames: None

Alternate Names: None

Background Story: Paul greeted Apelles, a fellow Christian, in a letter he sent to the members of the Church in Rome. He described him as someone who was "approved in Christ" (Romans 16:10). The name Apelles suggests an independent thinker.

Of Interest: Apelles—a Greek artist who painted Alexander the Great—was one of the most celebrated artists of the ancient world. None of his works survive.

APOLLOS ✦ *(uh-POL-uhs)*

Language/Cultural Origin: Greek

Meaning: Manly

Spiritual Connotation: Growth toward God

Related Names/Nicknames: Apollo, Apollon, Apollonios, Apollonius

Alternate Names: None

Background Story: Apollos, a Jew born in Alexandria, was one of the first to teach others "the Way of the Lord." Gifted with eloquence and "burning enthusiasm," he studied under Priscilla and Aquila in Ephesus, then journeyed to Corinth, where his knowledge of Jesus's teachings benefited the fledgling Christian community (Acts 18:24–28). When Christ's followers in Corinth divided into factions, Paul reminded them that they did not "belong to" him or Apollos but to Christ. "I planted, Apollos watered, but God gave the growth," Paul said (1 Corinthians 1:12, 3:6).

Of Interest: The name Apollos is closely related to Apollo, the Greek and Roman god of light, music, and poetry.

AQUILA ✦ *(AK-wih-luh)* or *(uh-KWIHL-uh)*

Language/Cultural Origin: Latin

Meaning: Eagle

Spiritual Connotation: Powerful

Related Names/Nicknames: Acquilino, Akilino, Akulina, Aquilina, Aquilino

Alternate Names: Acquila, Acquilla, Akila, Akilla, Aquilla

Background Story: Aquila, a Jew who was exiled from Rome, lived in Corinth with his wife, Priscilla. Paul stayed with him on his first journey, and they practiced their mutual trade of tent-making (Acts 18:1–3). Aquila and his wife traveled with Paul to Ephesus, where they acted as his "helpers in Christ" (Romans 16:3).

In Ephesus, they met Apollos and taught him the accurate "Way of God" (Acts 18:26).

Of Interest: Aquila is also the name of a constellation in the Milky Way.

ARAN ✦ *(AY-ran)*

Language/Cultural Origin: Hebrew

Meaning: Wild Goat

Spiritual Connotation: Adaptable

Related Names/Nicknames: Aaron, Aranne, Aronne

Alternate Names: Aren

Background Story: Aran was the younger son of Dishan and the grandson of Seir the Horite (Genesis 36:28). He was a clan head of the Horites who lived in Edom when Esau settled there. The name Aran suggests a man who can thrive in any situation.

ARCHIPPUS ✦ *(ahr-KIHP-uhs)*

Language/Cultural Origin: Greek

Meaning: Master of the Horse

Spiritual Connotation: Tamer of Souls

Related Names/Nicknames: Archie, Chip

Alternate Names: None

Background Story: Archippus was a "fellow soldier" of Paul in Colosse. He may have been a relative of Philemon and Apphia—

possibly their son (Philemon 1:2). In a letter to the Colossians, Paul offered him words of encouragement: "See that you complete the task that you have received in the Lord" (Colossians 4:17).

Of Interest: In the Catholic Church, Archippus is recognized as a saint, martyred for his religious beliefs.

ARDON ✦ *(AHR-duhn)*

Language/Cultural Origin: Hebrew

Meaning: Descendant

Spiritual Connotation: Beloved Offspring

Related Names/Nicknames: Ard, Arda, Ardie, Ardy

Alternate Names: Arden, Ardin, Arrden

Background Story: Ardon was the youngest son of Caleb "by his wife Azubah." He was a grandson of Hezron and a descendant of Judah and Tamar (1 Chronicles 2:18). The name Ardon suggests a man who feels connected to his past.

Famous Namesakes: Mordecai Ardon was an abstract painter who is considered one of Israel's greatest artists.

ARELI ✦ *(ay-REE-lai)*

Language/Cultural Origin: Hebrew

Meaning: Light of God

Spiritual Connotation: Keeper of the Flame

Related Names/Nicknames: Ari, Ariel

Alternate Names: None

Background Story: When Jacob moved his family to Egypt, Areli was among the many offspring who accompanied him (Genesis 46:16). He was Gad's son and the grandson of Jacob. The Arelites, a clan of the tribe of Gad, were his descendants (Numbers 26:17). Areli is a powerful name, suggesting someone whose faith burns within him.

ARIEL ✦ *(AIR-ee-uhl)* or *(AHR-ee-ehl)*

Language/Cultural Origin: Hebrew

Meaning: Lion of God

Spiritual Connotation: Powerful Leader

Related Names/Nicknames: Ari, Arie, Ariella, Arielle, Arik

Alternate Names: Aeriell, Airiel, Airyel, Airyell, Arel, Ariell, Ariyel, Aryel, Aryell

Background Story: Ariel was one of the leaders of the Israelites whom Ezra led out of captivity in Babylon. When Ezra saw there were no Levite priests among them, he sent Ariel and several other leaders to Casiphia to obtain "ministers for the house of God" (Ezra 8:16–17). Ariel was also a symbolic name for the city of Jerusalem (Isaiah 29:1).

Famous Namesakes: Ariel Sharon is an Israeli political and military leader who was elected prime minister of Israel in 2001. His nickname is Arik.

ARMONI ✦ *(ahr-MO-nai)*

Language/Cultural Origin: Hebrew

Meaning: My Palace

Spiritual Connotation: Favored

Related Names/Nicknames: Armand, Armando, Armen, Armin, Armino, Armon

Alternate Names: None

Background Story: Armoni and his brother, Mephibosheth, were Saul's sons whom David handed over to the Gibeonites because of Saul's "bloodguilt" for killing their people. The Gibeonites "impaled" them, and five of Saul's grandsons, on a "mountain before the Lord." For nearly six months, their mother, Rizpah, stayed with their bodies, preventing them from being defiled by "the birds of the air . . . by day, or the wild animals by night." Moved by her motherly devotion, King David gave Armoni and the others a proper burial in their ancestral tomb (2 Samuel 21:1–14).

ARTEMAS ✦ *(AHR-tih-muhs)*

Language/Cultural Origin: Greek

Meaning: Whole

Spiritual Connotation: Exemplary

Related Names/Nicknames: Art, Artemidorus, Artie, Arty, Diana

Alternate Names: Artemis, Artemus, Artimas, Artimis, Artimus

Background Story: Artemas served Paul as leader of the early Christian Church. In a letter to Titus, Paul considered sending Artemas as a replacement for him in Crete so that Titus could "spend the winter" with Paul at Nicopolis (Titus 3:12).

Of Interest: In the Eastern Orthodox tradition, Artemas was the bishop of Lystra and one of "the seventy disciples" mentioned in Luke's gospel (Luke 10:1).

Famous Namesakes: Artemas Ward was chief commander at the siege of Boston during the American Revolution.

ASA ⬦ *(AY-suh)*

Language/Cultural Origin: Hebrew

Meaning: Healer

Spiritual Connotation: God Restores

Related Names/Nicknames: None

Alternate Names: Aca, Ase

Background Story: Asa—the son of Abijah—was the third king of Judah. During his reign of forty-one years, Asa followed David's example and did "what was . . . right in the sight of the Lord." He "put away" pagan images, broke down their altars, and removed his mother, Maacah, from her position as queen mother, because she worshipped idols. With his faith in God, Asa was able to overcome the army of Zerah the Ethiopian and reign for many years in peace and prosperity. At the end of his life, Asa's faith faltered. Struggling with a "severe" illness, he put his trust in physicians—not in the Lord—and suffered greatly. Asa was succeeded by his son, Jehoshaphat, who walked in his father's "earlier ways" and followed God's commandments (2 Chronicles 14–17).

Of Interest: Asa was a popular name among Puritans in the seventeenth century.

ASAHEL ✦ *(AY-suh-hehl)* or *(A-suh-hehl)*

Language/Cultural Origin: Hebrew

Meaning: Creature of God

Spiritual Connotation: God's Child

Related Names/Nicknames: Asaya, Asa

Alternate Names: Asayel, Asiel

Background Story: Of the four Asahels in the Bible, David's nephew is most prominent. Asahel was a warrior, one of David's thirty mighty men, and "as swift of foot as a wild gazelle." During the battle at Gibeon, he pursued Abner as he retreated. Abner tried to avoid a confrontation, but Asahel "refused to turn away" and Abner was forced to kill him (2 Samuel 2:18–24). Asahel's brother, Joab, later killed Abner in retribution.

Famous Namesakes: Asahel Curtis was a pioneer photographer who documented the Klondike Gold Rush in 1897.

ASAIAH ✦ *(ay-suh-AI-uh)*

Language/Cultural Origin: Hebrew

Meaning: Yahweh Has Made

Spiritual Connotation: God's Creation

Related Names/Nicknames: Asa

Alternate Names: Asahiah

Background Story: There are four biblical Asaiahs: Josiah's trusted servant, sent to consult with the prophetess Huldah when the "book of the law" was found in the temple (2 Kings 22:11–20); the leader of a Simeonite family who "found rich, good pasture" in Gedor (1 Chronicles 4:36–40); a Shilonite, whose family returned to Jerusalem after the "exile in Babylon" (1 Chronicles 9:5); and a Levite who helped to carry "the ark of the Lord" to Jerusalem (1 Chronicles 15:11–12).

ASHER ✦ *(ASH-er)*

Language/Cultural Origin: Hebrew

Meaning: Happy

Spiritual Connotation: Blessed

Related Names/Nicknames: Anshel, Ash, Ashley, Asser, Osher

Alternate Names: Ashor, Ashur

Background Story: When Jacob's wife Leah thought she could bear no more children, she gave her maid, Zilpah, as a wife to Jacob. Asher was Zilpah's second son and Jacob's eighth. After he was born, Leah said, "Happy am I! For the women will call me happy" (Genesis 30:13). Jacob predicted a bright future for his son: "Asher's food shall be rich, and he shall provide royal delicacies" (Genesis 49:20). Asher grew up to become one of the leaders of the twelve tribes of Israel.

AUGUSTUS ✦ *(uh-GUHS-tuhs)* or *(aw-GUHS-tuhs)*

Language/Cultural Origin: Latin

Meaning: Majestic

Spiritual Connotation: Venerable

Related Names/Nicknames: Agostino, Agosto, Aguistin, Agustin, Agustine, Agustino, Augie, August, Augusta, Auguste, Augustin, Augustine,

Augustino, Augusto, Augy, Austen, Austin,
Austyn, Gus, Guss

Alternate Names: Agustus, Augoustos

Background Story: Augustus was the title given to the first Roman emperor. Because of his decree "that all the world should be registered," Joseph and Mary were required to leave Nazareth and go up to Bethlehem, where she gave birth to Jesus (Luke 2:1).

Of Interest: Augustus was the grandnephew of Julius Caesar.

Famous Namesakes: Augustus Busch, beer magnate; Augustus John, artist; Augustus Saint-Gaudens, sculptor; August Strindberg, playwright.

AZAREL ◆ *(AZ-uh-rehl)*
Language/Cultural Origin: Hebrew
Meaning: God Has Helped
Spiritual Connotation: Successful in the Lord
Related Names/Nicknames: None
Alternate Names: Azarael, Azareel

Background Story: Azarel is the name of several Old Testament men: a relative of Saul who defected to David at Ziklag (1 Chronicles 12:6); a chief officer of the tribe of Dan under David (1 Chronicles 27:22); and a priest who played the trumpet at Nehemiah's "dedication of the wall" in Jerusalem (Nehemiah 12:36). Azarel is a confident name, suggesting a man who knows how to achieve his goals, even in the most trying times.

AZARIAH ✦ *(a-zuh-RAI-uh)*

Language/Cultural Origin: Hebrew

Meaning: Helped by God

Spiritual Connotation: Encouragement

Related Names/Nicknames: Abednego, Azarias, Azria, Azriah, Uzziah, Uzziel, Zaria

Alternate Names: Azaria, Azaryah, Azeria, Azeriah, Azorya, Azuria, Azuriah

Background Story: Azariah is a popular name for men in the Bible. Some of the more notable are: a high priest in the days of Solomon (1 Kings 4:2); a king of Judah who "did what was right in the sight of the Lord" (2 Kings 15:1–5); a prophet who encouraged King Asa to initiate religious reform in Judah (2 Chronicles 15:1–8); and one of three young men educated with Daniel in King Nebuchadnezzar's court. The last Azariah, who had his name changed to Abednego, was thrown with his friends into a "furnace of blazing fire" for refusing to worship pagan gods. To the amazement of all, the young men were protected by an angel and walked out unharmed (Daniel 1:6–7, 3:19–27).

Of Interest: In the Prayer of Azariah—included in some versions of the Bible—Azariah thanks and praises God for protecting him and his friends from the fiery furnace.

AZEL ✦ *(A-zuhl)*

Language/Cultural Origin: Hebrew

Meaning: Noble

Spiritual Connotation: Admirable

Related Names/Nicknames: None

Alternate Names: None

Background Story: Azel was a descendant of King Saul through his son, Jonathan. Azel had six sons: Azrikam, Bocheru, Ishmael, Sheariah, Obadiah, and Hanan (1 Chronicles 8:37–38). Azel is a unique name, suggesting a man who has earned the respect of others.

AZZAN ✦ *(AZ-uhn)*

Language/Cultural Origin: Hebrew

Meaning: Very Strong

Spiritual Connotation: Guiding Hand

Related Names/Nicknames: None

Alternate Names: None

Background Story: Azzan was the father of Paltiel, who was a leader "of the tribe of the Issacharites." Azzan's son was chosen by God to help Moses apportion "the land for inheritance" (Numbers 34:16–29). The name Azzan suggests a just man who has strength of character.

BARAK ✦ *(BAY-rak)* or *(ba-RAHK)*

Language/Cultural Origin: Hebrew

Meaning: Flash of Lightning

Spiritual Connotation: Powered by God

Related Names/Nicknames: Barric, Barry

Alternate Names: Barack, Barrak

Background Story: Barak lived at the time of the great prophetess and judge, Deborah. She "summoned" him to raise an army against the Canaanites, who had been oppressing Israel for twenty years. Barak was a reluctant hero and said to Deborah, "If you will go with me, I will go." Deborah agreed, and Barak gathered ten thousand soldiers on the summit of Mount Tabor. When the leader of the Canaanite army approached, the Lord threw his soldiers and chariots "into a panic." Then the Israelites attacked and destroyed the powerful army of Canaan and brought peace to Israel (Judges 4:1–16).

Famous Namesakes: Barack Obama, Illinois state senator; Ehud Barak, former prime minister of Israel.

BARNABAS ◆ *(BAHR-nuh-buhs)*

Language/Cultural Origin: Greek /Aramaic

Meaning: Son of Encouragement

Spiritual Connotation: Comforting

Related Names/Nicknames: Barna, Barnaba, Barnabe, Barnabee, Barnabey, Barnabie, Barnaby, Barney, Barni, Barnie, Barny, Bernabe, Burnaby

Alternate Names: Barnabus, Barnebas, Barnebus

Background Story: Barnabas was a "good man, full of the Holy Spirit and of faith" and an early follower of Christ in Jerusalem. He gave up his possessions for the common good and convinced the apostles to accept the newly converted Paul. When news arrived that the Greeks in Antioch were eager to hear about Jesus, Barnabas traveled there and convinced Paul to join him. They converted "a great many people" in Antioch, where the name "Christian" was first used to describe the disciples. Barnabas then accompanied Paul on his first missionary journey and, although they faced considerable persecution, they brought many believers to the Church (Acts 4, 9, 11, 13–15).

Of Interest: Barnabas is honored as a saint in the Catholic Church and is credited by some as the author of the apocryphal Epistle of Barnabas.

Famous Namesakes: Barney Frank, U.S. congressman from Massachusetts; Barnaby Jones, television detective from 1973 to 1980.

BARTHOLOMEW ✦ *(bahr-THAWL-uh-myoo)*

Language/Cultural Origin: Greek/Aramaic/Hebrew

Meaning: Son of the Furrows

Spiritual Connotation: Humble

Related Names/Nicknames: Bart, Bartal, Bartel, Barth, Bartho, Barthol, Barthold, Bartholoma, Bartholome, Bartholomeo, Bartin, Bartle, Bartlet, Bartlett, Bartolome, Bartolomeo, Bartome, Barton, Bartow, Bartt, Bat, Bates, Bertalan, Bertel, Nathanael

Alternate Names: None

Background Story: Bartholomew was one of the original Twelve Apostles whom Jesus designated "to be with him, and to be sent out to proclaim the message" (Mark 3:18). With the other apostles, he was visited by the Holy Spirit fifty days after the Resurrection of Christ (Pentecost) and baptized so that he could teach God's word to the world.

Of Interest: Tradition has it that Bartholomew brought the gospel to India. He is also a saint in the Catholic Church. Most scholars agree that Bartholomew and Nathanael in the Bible are one and the same apostle.

BARTIMAEUS ✦ *(bahr-tih-MEE-uhs)* or *(bahr-ti-MAY-uhs)*

Language/Cultural Origin: Greek/Aramaic

Meaning: Honorable Son

Spiritual Connotation: Discernment

Related Names/Nicknames: Bart

Alternate Names: Bartimeus

Background Story: Bartimaeus was "a blind beggar . . . sitting by the roadside" when Jesus and his disciples were leaving Jericho. The suffering man heard who was passing and called out, "Jesus, Son of David, have mercy on me!" Although the people around him told him to be quiet, he called out even louder a second time. Jesus stopped and asked, "What do you want me to do for you?" Bartimaeus requested that his sight be restored, and Jesus answered, "Go; your faith has made you well." At that moment, his sight returned and Bartimaeus followed Jesus (Mark 10:46–52).

Of Interest: In Henry Wadsworth Longfellow's epic poem *Christus: A Mystery,* he tells the biblical story of Bartimaeus and his meeting with Jesus.

BARUCH ✦ *(buh-ROOK)* or *(BAY-rook)*

Language/Cultural Origin: Hebrew

Meaning: Blessed

Spiritual Connotation: Dedicated to the Lord

Related Names/Nicknames: Baruchi, Baruj, Benedict, Boruch

Alternate Names: Barouch, Baruk

Background Story: Of the four men named Baruch in the Bible, one is of special note. Baruch was Jeremiah's scribe who "wrote on a scroll" everything the Lord prophesied to Jeremiah about the capture of Judah by Babylon. Baruch read the scroll to the people at the temple and they were "alarmed." When it was given to the king of Judah, he threw it into the fire and demanded the arrest of Jeremiah and Baruch. Jeremiah then dictated an identical scroll to Baruch, adding words about the king's punishment for not listening. Baruch and Jeremiah were eventually imprisoned—and released after Jerusalem fell to the king of Babylon as the Lord had prophesied (Jeremiah 32, 36, 43).

Of Interest: Baruch is considered by some to be an author of the apocryphal Book of Baruch.

Famous Namesakes: Baruch Spinoza, philosopher and theologian; Bernard Baruch, financier and adviser to several presidents.

BELA ✦ *(BEH-luh)*
Language/Cultural Origin: Hebrew
Meaning: Devouring
Spiritual Connotation: Nourishment
Related Names/Nicknames: Albert
Alternate Names: Belah

Background Story: There are three men named Bela in the Bible: the first king who reigned in Edom "before any king reigned over the Israelites" (Genesis 36:32); the oldest son of Benjamin, who was a patriarch of the Belaite clan (Genesis 46:21); and a descendant of Reuben (1 Chronicles 5:1, 8). The name Bela suggests a man who is nourished by love of God and family.

Famous Namesakes: Béla Bartók, composer; Bela Fleck, musician; Bela Lugosi, actor.

BENAIAH ✦ *(bee-NAY-uh)* or *(buh-NAI-uh)*

Language/Cultural Origin: Hebrew

Meaning: The Lord Has Built

Spiritual Connotation: Establishing God's Kingdom

Related Names/Nicknames: Ben

Alternate Names: Benayah

Background Story: Only one of the Benaiahs in the Bible truly stands out. He was a "valiant warrior" and the commander of David's bodyguard. Benaiah was known both for killing a lion and striking down an Egyptian soldier "with his own spear" (2 Samuel 23:20–22). The only quality greater than Benaiah's prowess in battle was his loyalty to David. He refused to side with David's son Adonijah, who proclaimed himself successor to the throne, and supported David's choice of Solomon. When Solomon became king, he rewarded Benaiah's loyalty by appointing him "over the army" (1 Kings 1, 2).

BENJAMIN ✦ *(BEN-juh-muhn)*

Language/Cultural Origin: Hebrew

Meaning: Son of My Right Hand

Spiritual Connotation: Fortunate

Related Names/Nicknames: Ben, Benjamim, Benjamino, Benjee, Benjey, Benji, Benjie, Benjy, Benn, Bennie, Benno, Benny, Benyamin, Benyamino, Yamin, Yamino, Yemin

Alternate Names: Benjaman, Benjamen, Benjamine, Benjamon, Benjiman, Benjimen

Background Story: Benjamin was born on the road between Bethel and Ephrath, the product of "hard labor" that cost his mother, Rachel, her life. Before she died, Rachel named him Ben-oni, or "son of my sorrows," but his father, Jacob, called his youngest son Benjamin (Genesis 35:16–18). Benjamin grew up without his brother Joseph, who had been secretly sold into slavery by his older brothers. When they were reunited years later, Joseph was so moved that he "fell upon his brother Benjamin's neck and wept" (Genesis 45:14). Benjamin was the patriarch of one of Israel's twelve tribes and an ancestor of Saul, the first king of Israel (1 Samuel 9:1–2).

Of Interest: Since 1980, Benjamin has ranked among the top thirty-five names for boys in the United States.

Famous Namesakes: Ben Affleck, Ben Stiller, actors; Benjamin Britten, composer; Benjamin Disraeli, British prime minister; Benjamin Franklin, statesman/inventor; Benny Goodman, musician; Benjamin Harrison, U.S. president; Ben Jonson, playwright; Benjamin Spock, pediatrician.

CAESAR ✦ *(SEE-zer)*

Language/Cultural Origin: Latin

Meaning: Long-haired

Spiritual Connotation: Great Leader

Related Names/Nicknames: Cesare, Cesareo, Cesario, Cesaro

Alternate Names: Caezar, Casar, Ceasar, César, Cezar, Seasar, Sezar

Background Story: Caesar is the title given to several Roman emperors in the New Testament. When Jesus said, "Render to Caesar the things that are Caesar's, and to God the things that are God's," he was referring to Tiberius Caesar, who reigned during his ministry (Mark 12:17). Augustus Caesar was the emperor who decreed "that all the world should be registered" just before Jesus was born (Luke 2:1). Claudius Caesar ruled at the time of the famine in Judea (Acts 11:28), and Paul appealed to Nero Caesar when he was imprisoned (Acts 25:11).

Of Interest: The titles "czar" in Russian and "kaiser" in German are variants of the name Caesar.

Famous Namesakes: Cesar Chavez, labor leader; Cesar Romero, actor.

CALEB ✦ *(KAY-lehb)*

Language/Cultural Origin: Hebrew

Meaning: Faithful

Spiritual Connotation: Unwavering

Related Names/Nicknames: Cal, Cale, Caled, Carmi, Chalebi

Alternate Names: Calib, Calyb, Cayleb, Kaleb, Kayleb, Kaylob

Background Story: After the Exodus, Moses sent Caleb, Joshua, and ten other men "to spy out the land" of Canaan. When the men returned, they reported that the land flowed "with milk and honey," but the people were too powerful. Caleb and Joshua, however, said that Canaan could be taken with the Lord's help. The Israelites "threatened to stone them" but the Lord suddenly appeared and told them only Caleb and Joshua would live to see the Promised Land. Because of their lack of faith, the Israelites would die and their children would suffer forty years in the wilderness before they returned (Numbers 13–14).

Of Interest: The name Caleb has been growing in popularity since 1980. In 2004, it was ranked at thirty-three.

Famous Namesakes: Caleb Carr, novelist; Caleb Deschanel, cinematographer; William Caleb "Cale" Yarborough, champion NASCAR driver.

CARMI ✦ *(KAHR-mai)*

Language/Cultural Origin: Hebrew

Meaning: My Vineyard

Spiritual Connotation: Flourishing

Related Names/Nicknames: Carmee, Carmel, Carmey, Karmey

Alternate Names: Carmie, Karmi, Karmie

Background Story: In the Bible, three different men are called Carmi: Reuben's son who traveled to Egypt with his grandfather, Jacob (Genesis 46:9); the father of Achar, whose actions at Jericho drew the Lord's anger (Joshua 7:1); and a descendant of Judah (1 Chronicles 4:1). The name Carmi suggests a man whose life is rich and productive.

CARPUS ✦ *(KAHR-puhs)*

Language/Cultural Origin: Greek/Latin

Meaning: Fruitful

Spiritual Connotation: My Spirit Thrives

Related Names/Nicknames: Karp

Alternate Names: Karpos

Background Story: Paul spoke of Carpus in a letter he wrote to Timothy from prison. He asked Timothy to visit him soon and added, "When you come, bring the cloak that I left with Carpus at Troas, also the books, and above all the parchments" (2 Timothy 4:9–13). Paul's words imply a close relationship with a man who was probably a convert.

CHILION ✦ *(KIHL-ee-uhn)*

Language/Cultural Origin: Hebrew

Meaning: Complete

Spiritual Connotation: Ideal

Related Names/Nicknames: None

Alternate Names: None

Background Story: Chilion and his brother, Mahlon, were the two sons of Elimelech and Naomi. During a famine, they moved with their parents from Bethlehem to Moab, where they "took Moabite wives." Ruth was Mahlon's wife, and Chilion married Orpah (Ruth 1:1–5). Sadly, the two brothers and their father died in Moab. Ruth returned with her mother-in-law to Bethlehem, but Chilion's wife, Orpah, stayed behind. Chilion is a strong name, suggesting a well-rounded man.

CHRISTIAN ✦ *(KRIHS-chuhn)*

Language/Cultural Origin: Greek/Latin

Meaning: Follower of Christ

Spiritual Connotation: Believer

Related Names/Nicknames: Carsten, Chris, Christan, Christer, Christiano, Christianos, Christiansen,

Christie, Christo, Christon, Christos,
Christy, Cristen, Cristiano, Cristino, Cristos,
Cristy, Karsten, Kerstan, Khristos, Kit, Kris,
Krist, Kristo, Krystiano

Alternate Names: Christiaan, Christion, Cristian,
Khristian, Kristian, Krystian

Background Story: The name Christian—follower of Christ—
only appears three times in the New Testament. Barnabas and
Paul were "first called Christians" when they were teaching in
Antioch (Acts 11:26). Years later, Paul defended himself before
Agrippa and the king responded, "Are you so quickly persuading me to become a Christian?" (Acts 26:28). Finally, Peter said
in a letter, "Yet if any of you suffers as a Christian, do not consider it a disgrace, but glorify God because you bear this name"
(1 Peter 4:16).

Of Interest: The Greeks or Romans were the first to call Christ's
followers "Christians." The early disciples described themselves
as "the faithful" or "believers," but over time the name "Christian" became universally accepted.

Famous Namesakes: Christiaan Barnard, heart surgeon; Christian
Dior and Christian Lacroix, fashion designers; Christian Slater,
actor.

CLAUDIUS ✦ *(KLAW-dee-uhs)*
Language/Cultural Origin: Latin
Meaning: Lame
Spiritual Connotation: Fair and Just
Related Names/Nicknames: Claud, Claudan,
Claude, Claudell, Claudien, Claudino,

Claudio, Claudon, Clodito, Clodo,
Klaudio

Alternate Names: Klaudios

Background Story: Of the two men in the New Testament named
Claudius, one is the fourth emperor of Rome, during whose
reign "a severe famine took place." He was also known for exil-
ing all Jews from Rome (Acts 11:28, 18:2). The other is Claudius
Lysias, a Roman tribune who protected the prisoner Paul from
an overzealous mob planning to ambush and murder him on the
road to Caesarea. Claudius arranged for an envoy of soldiers to
keep Paul safe and wrote to the governor that his fellow coun-
tryman "was charged with nothing deserving death or imprisonment" (Acts 23:12–30).

Of Interest: The meaning of the name Claudius comes from the
fact that the emperor Claudius had a physical disability.

Famous Namesakes: Claude Debussy, composer; Claude Monet,
artist; Claude Pepper, U.S. congressman; Claude Rains, actor.

CLEMENT ✦ *(KLEHM-uhnt)*

Language/Cultural Origin: Latin

Meaning: Mild

Spiritual Connotation: Merciful

Related Names/Nicknames: Clem, Clemence, Clemencio,
Clemens, Clementine, Clementino, Clementius,
Clemmie, Clemmons, Clemmy, Klem, Klemens

Alternate Names: Clemente, Klement, Kliment

Background Story: Clement was one of Paul's fellow Christians in
Philippi. In a letter, Paul wrote that Clement "struggled beside"

him "in the work of the gospel" and that his name was "in the book of life" (Philippians 4:3). The name Clement suggests a kind and gentle man.

Famous Namesakes: Clement Attlee, British prime minister; Clement Clark Moore, poet; Clement Studebaker, manufacturer; Roberto Clemente, baseball player.

CORNELIUS ◆ *(kor-NEEL-yuhs)* or *(kor-NEE-lee-uhs)*

Language/Cultural Origin: Latin

Meaning: Horn

Spiritual Connotation: Power in Faith

Related Names/Nicknames: Con, Connie, Cornel, Cornelia, Cornelie, Cornelio, Cornell, Cornelus, Corney, Kornel, Kornelia, Neal, Neel, Neely, Neil, Niels

Alternate Names: Cornelious, Cornilius, Kornelios, Kornelious, Kornelis, Kornelius

Background Story: Cornelius—a Roman centurion stationed in Caesarea—was "a devout man . . . who prayed constantly to God." One afternoon, an angel appeared and told him to send for Peter, which he did. The next day, a vision also came to Peter as he prayed. The Lord said, "What God has made clean, you must not call profane." Peter was confused by the message, but God told him to return with Cornelius's men to Caesarea. When he met Cornelius—a Gentile—and the crowd who assembled to hear him, Peter realized that God wanted him to ignore the Jewish law forbidding association with them. As he spoke to them about Jesus, suddenly "the Holy Spirit fell upon all who heard the word . . . even the Gentiles." After Peter saw this, he ordered Cornelius and the others to be baptized (Acts 10:1–48).

Of Interest: Cornelius is considered by many to be the first Gentile convert to the faith.

Famous Namesakes: Cornelius Bumpus, musician; Cornelius Vanderbilt, railroad magnate.

CRISPUS *(KRIHS-puhs)*

Language/Cultural Origin: Latin

Meaning: Curled

Spiritual Connotation: Turning to God

Related Names/Nicknames: Chris, Crepin, Crespin, Crispian, Crispin, Crispino, Crispo

Alternate Names: Krispos

Background Story: Crispus was an "official of the synagogue" in the city of Corinth, where Paul was preaching about Jesus. Although many Jews "opposed" Paul's message, Crispus became "a believer in the Lord, together with his household" (Acts 18:6–8). He was one of the few converts baptized by Paul himself (1 Corinthians 1:14).

Famous Namesakes: Crispus Attucks, an African American and the first casualty of the American Revolution; Crispin Glover, actor.

CYRENIUS *(sai-REE-nee-uhs)*

Language/Cultural Origin: Greek/Latin

Meaning: One Who Governs

Spiritual Connotation: Guidance

Related Names/Nicknames: Sy

Alternate Names: None

Background Story: Cyrenius, whose Roman name was Quirinius, was a "governor of Syria" when Augustus Caesar first decreed that everyone in his empire must be taxed. To register, Joseph and Mary went to Bethlehem, a city in Judea where Jesus was later born (Luke 2:1–7). The name Cyrenius suggests a man who has a powerful influence on the people around him.

CYRUS ✦ *(SAI-ruhs)*

Language/Cultural Origin: Persian

Meaning: Heir of the Throne

Spiritual Connotation: Seat of Justice

Related Names/Nicknames: Ciro, Cyra, Kira, Kuros, Kyra, Kyros, Russ, Sy

Alternate Names: Cyris

Background Story: Cyrus was the king of Persia who conquered the Babylonians and freed the exiled Jews, allowing them to return to Israel. Then he declared that the Lord—the source of his power—had commanded him "to build him a house at Jerusalem." Cyrus not only supported the rebuilding of the temple at Jerusalem, he also brought back the holy vessels that the king of Babylon had "carried away" years before. The Israelites saw all this as the fulfillment of Jeremiah's prophecy (Ezra 1:1–11).

Famous Namesakes: Cyrus McCormick, inventor; Cyrus Vance, U.S. secretary of state; Billy Ray Cyrus, country singer.

DAN ✦ *(DAN)*

Language/Cultural Origin: Hebrew

Meaning: Judge

Spiritual Connotation: Mediator

Related Names/Nicknames: Dana, Danai, Danel,
Danette, Dania, Daniel, Daniela, Daniele,
Danilo, Danita, Dann, Dannie, Danny, Danut,
Danuta, Danya

Alternate Names: Daan

Background Story: Dan, the son of Rachel's maid Bilhah, was also
Jacob's fifth son. After Dan was born, Rachel—who could have
no children—said, "God has judged me, and has also heard my
voice and given me a son" (Genesis 30:6). When Jacob was on his
deathbed, he blessed all his sons and said that Dan would "judge
his people" as a tribe of Israel (Genesis 49:16). Dan was, indeed,
a patriarch of one of Israel's twelve tribes and Samson, his
descendant, was a judge.

DANIEL ✦ *(DAN-yuhl)*

Language/Cultural Origin: Hebrew

Meaning: God Is My Judge

Spiritual Connotation: Insight

Related Names/Nicknames: Daan, Dan, Dana,
Danal, Danel, Danell, Danette, Dani, Dania,
Daniele, Danil, Danilo, Danita, Danko, Dann,
Dannel, Dannie, Danny, Dantrell, Danuta,
Danya

Alternate Names: Danail, Daneal, Daneel, Danial,
Daniell, Danyal, Danyel, Deniel

Background Story: As a young man, Daniel and three of his noble friends from Judah were taken to Babylon to be educated and serve King Nebuchadnezzar. All four grew in wisdom, but "Daniel also had insight into all visions and dreams." When the king had a strange dream that none of his "wise men" could understand, the Lord helped Daniel to interpret it, and the king rewarded him with power and a high position. Daniel lived in Babylon for many years, but he never lost his faith in God. Other men were jealous of his position and plotted to bring him down. They tricked another king, Darius, to order that no one could pray to anyone but him for thirty days. Daniel was caught "praying . . . before his God," and Darius was forced to throw him into a "den of lions." But God protected Daniel. The next day he stepped out of the lions' den unharmed. Daniel "prospered" in Babylon and became one of the great prophets of the Old Testament (Book of Daniel).

Of Interest: Daniel has been one of the top ten names for boys in the United States for most of the last twenty-five years.

Famous Namesakes: Danny Aiello, Daniel Day-Lewis, Danny DeVito, Danny Kaye, Daniel Radcliffe, and Danny Thomas, actors; Daniel Boone, frontiersman; Daniel Defoe, writer; Daniel Patrick Moynihan, U.S. senator; Daniel Webster, statesman.

DARIUS ✦ *(duh-RAI-uhs)* or *(DEHR-ee-uhs)*
Language/Cultural Origin: Persian/Greek
Meaning: Wealthy
Spiritual Connotation: Patron
Related Names/Nicknames: Darian, Dariann, Darien, Dario, Darion, Darry, Derry

Alternate Names: Darias, Dariess, Darious, Darrius, Derrius

Background Story: There are three kings named Darius in the Bible, but two are of particular interest. The first Darius was the fourth king of Persia. He supported the rebuilding of the temple in Jerusalem and threatened to punish anyone who stood in the way of its completion (Ezra 6:1–12). Darius the Mede was the ruler of Babylon tricked into throwing Daniel into "a den of lions" for praying to God. To his relief, Daniel returned unharmed and Darius decreed that his people "should tremble and fear before the God of Daniel" because he had saved him (Daniel 6:1–28).

Famous Namesakes: Darius Kasparaitis, hockey player; Darius Danesh and Darius Rucker, singers.

DAVID *(DAY-vihd)* or *(dah-VEED)*

Language/Cultural Origin: Hebrew

Meaning: Beloved

Spiritual Connotation: God's Favorite

Related Names/Nicknames: Dai, Dave, Daveed, Daven, Davena, Daveon, Daveth, Davey, Davi, Davian, Davida, Davidson, Davie, Daviel, Davies, Davin, Davina, Davion, Davis, Davon, Davy, Davyn, Dawson, Devi, Dewey

Alternate Names: Daved, Davidde, Davide, Davood, Davyd, Davydd, Dayvid

Background Story: David, the youngest son of Jesse, is one of the best-known people in biblical history. David "was ruddy, and had beautiful eyes, and was handsome," but he was only a shepherd boy when God anointed him, through Samuel, to be the next king of Israel. King Saul heard that David was "skillful at playing the lyre," so he sent for him to play soothing music whenever he was depressed. The young shepherd proved to be a skillful warrior too and achieved fame by slaying the Philistine Goliath with a single stone from his slingshot. His act of bravery made David popular with the people—but not with Saul, who became jealous and tried to kill him. David, now a great military leader, fled from Saul and took refuge for a while with his enemy, the Philistines. Over the years, he found opportunities to kill Saul but refused to "destroy him; for who can put forth his hand against the Lord's anointed, and be guiltless?" After Saul's death, David was anointed king of Judah and eventually king over Israel. He captured Jerusalem, which came to be known as "the city of David," and planned a temple for the ark of the covenant there. During David's forty-year reign, Israel flourished, but his many wives and children—with their fierce competition for power—caused him much grief. He was eventually succeeded by his son, Solomon, whose mother was Bathsheba. Although David was a man with many faults, he always repented and dedicated his life to God's purpose (1 Samuel, 2 Samuel).

Of Interest: David is considered the author of many psalms in the Bible. His name, which is popular in the United States, has ranked among the top twenty since 1930.

Famous Namesakes: David Beckham, soccer player; David Bowie, musician; David Duchovny, David Niven, David Schwimmer, actors; David Hume, philosopher; David Letterman, television host; David Livingstone, explorer; Dave Winfield, baseball player.

DEKAR ✦ *(DEH-ker)*

Language/Cultural Origin: Hebrew

Meaning: Pierce

Spiritual Connotation: Pioneer

Related Names/Nicknames: None

Alternate Names: Decker, Deker, Dekker

Background Story: Dekar was the father of one of the "twelve officials over all Israel, who provided food for the king and his household" during Solomon's reign (1 Kings 4:7, 9). The name Dekar suggests a man who is bold enough to try something new and challenging.

DELAIAH ✦ *(deh-LAI-uh)*

Language/Cultural Origin: Hebrew

Meaning: God Has Raised

Spiritual Connotation: My Spirit Is Lifted

Related Names/Nicknames: None

Alternate Names: Dalaiah, Delaia, Delayah

Background Story: There are five Delaiahs in the Bible: a descendant of Solomon and David (1 Chronicles 3:24); a man who headed a division of temple priests under David (1 Chronicles 24:18); the head of a clan returning to Jerusalem from captivity in Babylon (Ezra 2:60); the father of a man who tried to stop Nehemiah from rebuilding Jerusalem's walls (Nehemiah 6:10); and an official who tried to convince King Jehoiakim not to burn the scroll containing Jeremiah's prophecies (Jeremiah 36:12). Delaiah is a name that suggests a lively and spirited man.

DEMAS ✦ *(DEE-muhs)*

Language/Cultural Origin: Greek

Meaning: Popular

Spiritual Connotation: Heart of the People

Related Names/Nicknames: Deems, Demarchus,
Demetrius

Alternate Names: Dimas

Background Story: Demas was one of Paul's fellow workers while
he was imprisoned in Rome (Philemon 1:24). The two parted
ways as Paul explains in a letter to Timothy during a low point in
his ministry: "Demas, in love with this present world, has
deserted me and gone to Thessalonica" (2 Timothy 4:10). The
name Demas implies a man who enjoys being surrounded by
friends.

DEMETRIUS ✦ *(dih-MEE-tree-uhs)*

Language/Cultural Origin: Greek

Meaning: Lover of the Earth

Spiritual Connotation: Natural Spirit

Related Names/Nicknames: Demeter, Demetri,
Demetrice, Demetrio, Demetris, Demitri, Demmy,
Dimas, Dimetre, Dimitri, Dimitry, Dimka, Dmitri,
Dmitros, Dmitry

Alternate Names: Dametrius, Demitrios, Demitrius,
Dhimitrios, Dimitrios, Dimitrious

Background Story: Two men are called Demetrius in the New
Testament. The first was a silversmith in Ephesus who made
shrines of the goddess Artemis. Afraid that Paul's teaching
of the gospel would ruin business, he stirred up his fellow

artisans and caused such an uproar that "the city was filled with the confusion" (Acts 19:23–41). The second was a disciple for whom John had high praise. "Everyone has testified favorably about Demetrius," he wrote, "and so has the truth itself" (3 John 1:12).

Of Interest: In Greek mythology, Demeter was the goddess of harvest and fertility.

Famous Namesakes: Dimitri Mendeleev, chemist who developed the periodic table; Dimitri Shostakovich, classical composer.

EBENEZER ✦ *(eh-buh-NEE-zer)*

Language/Cultural Origin: Hebrew

Meaning: Stone of Help

Spiritual Connotation: Gratitude

Related Names/Nicknames: Eb, Eban, Ebbaneza, Eben

Alternate Names: Abenezer, Ebeneezer, Ebeneser, Ebenezar, Eveneser, Evenezer

Background Story: Ebenezer is a place in the Bible where the Israelites "went out to battle against" the Philistines—not once, but three times. At first, the Israelites suffered a terrible defeat. Then they brought the ark of the covenant from Shiloh so that the Lord would protect them, but they lost the ark to the Philistines as well as the second battle (1 Samuel 4:1–11). Years later, the Israelites faced their enemy again. Samuel convinced them to "direct" their hearts to the Lord and he called on God once more. This time the Lord sent the Philistines "into a mighty confusion," allowing the Israelites to defeat them. Samuel erected a stone in the place and called it Ebenezer, saying "Thus far the Lord has helped us" (1 Samuel 7:1–12).

Famous Namesakes: Abba Eban, Israeli statesman; Ebenezer Scrooge, fictional miser who redeems himself in *A Christmas Carol* by Charles Dickens.

EDER ✦ *(EE-der)*

Language/Cultural Origin: Hebrew

Meaning: Flock

Spiritual Connotation: God Watches Over Me

Related Names/Nicknames: Ed

Alternate Names: Adar, Edar

Background Story: There are two men named Eder in the Bible: the son of Beriah, who was an ancestor of Benjamin (1 Chronicles 8:15), and the son of Mushi, a Levite descendant of Merari in the time of David (1 Chronicles 24:30). Eder was also the name of a town in Judah (Joshua 15:21), and "the tower of Eder" is where Jacob "pitched his tent" after burying Rachel (Genesis 35:21).

Of Interest: The "tower of Eder" was probably a watchtower from which shepherds protected their sheep. The name is a symbol of God's watchfulness over his people.

EDOM ✦ *(EE-duhm)*

Language/Cultural Origin: Hebrew

Meaning: Red

Spiritual Connotation: Spirited

Related Names/Nicknames: None

Alternate Names: None

Background Story: Edom, meaning "red," is the name sometimes given to Esau in the Bible. There were two reasons: When Esau was born he "came out red, all his body like a hairy mantle" (Genesis 25:25), and he was so "famished" one day he sold his birthright to his twin brother, Jacob, for some red stew (Genesis 25:29–34). The land of Seir where Esau and his descendants settled came to be known as Edom (Genesis 32:3).

Of Interest: The land of Edom may also have derived its name from its red sandstone cliffs.

ELAH ✦ *(EE-luh)*
Language/Cultural Origin: Aramaic
Meaning: Oak
Spiritual Connotation: Strength
Related Names/Nicknames: None
Alternate Names: None

Background Story: Elah—the name of a king, a tribal chieftan, a clan leader, and several others in the Bible—is most memorable as the site of a battle. The valley of Elah is where young David killed the Philistine Goliath with a stone from his sling and thus began his extraordinary rise to power as the king of Israel (1 Samuel 21:9). The name Elah suggests a man with great personal and spiritual strength.

Of Interest: The valley of Elah derived its name from the Elah tree, a type of oak or terebinth that grew there.

ELAM ✦ *(EE-luhm)*

Language/Cultural Origin: Hebrew/Assyrian

Meaning: Eternity

Spiritual Connotation: Ancient Soul

Related Names/Nicknames: None

Alternate Names: Eilam

Background Story: Elam is best known as the son of Shem and grandson of Noah (Genesis 10:22) and the ancient land that his descendants—the Elamites—inhabited. The name also refers to eight other men in the Bible. Among them were: a gatekeeper of the temple during David's reign (1 Chronicles 26:3); a man who signed the new covenant Nehemiah made with the Lord (Nehemiah 10:14); and a priest present at the dedication of Jerusalem's wall (Nehemiah 12:42).

Of Interest: Elam—one of the oldest civilized areas in world history—was located north of the Persian Gulf in what is now known as southwestern Iran. Its capital was Susa.

ELEAZAR ✦ *(el-ee-AY-zer)*

Language/Cultural Origin: Hebrew

Meaning: God Is My Helper

Spiritual Connotation: Trusted Adviser

Related Names/Nicknames: Elazar, Eleazaro, Elezar, Eli, Elie, Eliezer, Ely, Lazar, Lazare, Lazarus, Lazer, Lazzaro

Alternate Names: Eleasar, Eliazar

Background Story: Three Eleazars stand out in the Bible: Abi-nadab's son, who was consecrated "to have charge of the ark of the Lord" in his father's house (1 Samuel 7:1); one of David's three warriors who braved the camp of the Philistines to bring their leader a "drink from the well of Bethlehem" (1 Chronicles 11:12–19); and Aaron's third son, who succeeded his father as high priest. Eleazar served Moses and Joshua as priest and adviser for over twenty years, taking part in the census and helping to distribute the Promised Land to the tribes of Israel (Numbers 20, 26; Joshua 14:1).

ELI ✦ *(EE-lai)*

Language/Cultural Origin: Hebrew

Meaning: Ascended

Spiritual Connotation: Offering to God

Related Names/Nicknames: Eloi, Eloy, Heli

Alternate Names: Elie, Ely

Background Story: Eli was a man torn between love for his children and devotion to his God. He served as a judge for Israel and as high priest in charge of the tabernacle in Shiloh. It was Eli who raised the prophet Samuel and prepared him for a life of service to the Lord. Eli's sons, however, were not cut of the same cloth. They abused their positions as priests in the temple and "had no regard for the Lord." Because Eli "did not restrain" his sons, the Lord punished him. During a battle with the Philistines, his sons brought the ark of the covenant to Israel's camp. Israel was defeated, the ark was captured, and Eli's sons died. When Eli heard the news, he "fell over backward" and died (1 Samuel 1–4).

Famous Namesakes: Eli Wallach, actor; Eli Whitney, inventor; Elie Wiesel, winner of the Nobel Peace Prize.

ELIAB ✦ *(ee-LAI-ab)*

Language/Cultural Origin: Hebrew

Meaning: God Is My Father

Spiritual Connotation: Child of God

Related Names/Nicknames: Eli

Alternate Names: None

Background Story: Of the several Eliabs in the Bible, three are prominent: the son of Helon, who led "the tribe of Zebulon" in the wilderness (Numbers 2:7); Jesse's oldest son, a soldier in Saul's army, who mocked his brother David until he witnessed him do what no one else could—slay the Philistine Goliath (1 Samuel 17:28); and one of the warriors with "faces of lions" who defected to David at Ziklag (1 Chronicles 12:8–9).

Famous Namesakes: Eliab George Earthrowl, etcher; Eliab Metcalf, portrait artist.

ELIAM ✦ *(ee-LAI-am)*

Language/Cultural Origin: Hebrew

Meaning: People of God

Spiritual Connotation: United in the Lord

Related Names/Nicknames: Elami, Liam

Alternate Names: Ammiel

Background Story: Two men are named Eliam in the Bible: the father of Bathsheba, who was David's wife and Solomon's mother (2 Samuel 11:3), and one of the thirty-seven warrior chiefs who served David (2 Samuel 23:34). The name Eliam suggests a man who experiences a common bond with everyone.

ELIAS ✦ *(ee-LAI-uhs)*

Language/Cultural Origin: Greek

Meaning: My God Is Jehovah

Spiritual Connotation: God's Champion

Related Names/Nicknames: Elia, Elice, Ellice, Ellis, Elyas

Alternate Names: Elijah

Background Story: Elias—the Greek name for the prophet Elijah—is sometimes used in traditional versions of the New Testament. Elias and Moses appeared on the mountain with Jesus when he was "transfigured" before Peter, James, and John (Matthew 17:1–3). The name Elias represents all the prophets of the Old Testament whose word Jesus came to fulfill.

Famous Namesakes: Elias Canetti, Nobel Prize–winning writer; Elias James Corey, Nobel Prize–winning chemist; Elias Howe, inventor of the sewing machine; Elias Wakan, sculptor.

ELIJAH ✦ *(ee-LAI-zhuh)* or *(ih-LAI-zhuh)*

Language/Cultural Origin: Hebrew

Meaning: My God Is Jehovah

Spiritual Connotation: God's Champion

Related Names/Nicknames: Eli, Elia, Elie, Elihu, Elija, Eliot, Eliyahu, Eljah, Elliot, Ellis, Ely, Elyot, Elyott, Ilia, Ilya

Alternate Names: Elias

Background Story: Elijah "the Tishbite" was one of the great prophets of the Old Testament. He dedicated his life to turning the Israelites away from false idols and back to the Lord. Elijah's first prediction—years of drought for King Ahab and his people—

required him to go into hiding. At first, Elijah lived in a ravine, where "ravens brought him bread and meat" every day. Later, he stayed with a poor widow who fed him from her meager supply of food, which miraculously never ran out. "During the third year of the drought" Elijah confronted Ahab again and told him to assemble all the Israelites on Mount Carmel, together with the prophets of Baal. That day, he challenged the prophets to prepare an offering and ask Baal to light it with fire. The false prophets failed, but not Elijah. The Lord created a fire so powerful it "consumed the burnt offering, the wood, the stones, and the dust, and even licked up the water that was in the trench" around it. After this miracle, the drought ended, but Elijah had to go into hiding again. It was during this time that he found and trained Elisha, his successor (1 Kings 17–19). Despite the danger, Elijah continued to prophesy and perform miracles. Even his death was a miracle—the greatest of all—as Elijah "ascended in a whirlwind into heaven" riding in a "chariot of fire" (2 Kings 2:11).

Of Interest: Since 1995, Elijah has been among the top one hundred names for boys in the United States, reaching thirty-one in 2004.

Famous Namesakes: Elijah Allman, singer and son of Cher and Gregg Allman; Elia Kazan, director; Elijah McCoy, inventor; Elijah Wood, actor.

ELISHA ✦ *(ih-LAI-shuh)*

Language/Cultural Origin: Hebrew

Meaning: God Is My Salvation

Spiritual Connotation: True Prophet

Related Names/Nicknames: Eli, Elise, Elisee, Eliseo, Elisher, Eliso, Lisha

Alternate Names: Elishah, Elysha, Elyshah

Background Story: Elisha was a simple farmer when he first met the prophet Elijah and accepted God's call to become his student and successor. Before Elijah's ascent to heaven in a fiery chariot, Elisha asked him for "a double share" of his spirit. The Lord fulfilled his request and Elisha became the leader of Israel's prophets. Like Elijah, he prophesied for the kings of Israel and performed numerous miracles, such as parting the waters of the Jordan, multiplying food during a famine, bringing a young boy back to life, and curing a man of leprosy (1 Kings 19; 2 Kings 2–9).

Famous Namesakes: Elisha Cook Jr., actor; Elisha Otis, inventor of the elevator.

EMMANUEL ✦ *(ih-MAN-yoo-uhl)*

Language/Cultural Origin: Hebrew

Meaning: God Is with Us

Spiritual Connotation: Gift of Salvation

Related Names/Nicknames: Eman, Iman, Imani, Manny, Manual, Manuel, Manuelo

Alternate Names: Emanual, Emanuel, Emanuele, Emmanual, Emmanuelle, Imanuel, Immanuel, Immanuele

Background Story: The name Emmanuel—or Immanuel—appears more than once in the Bible and refers to Jesus. In the Old Testament, Isaiah prophesied this sign from the Lord: "Look, the young woman is with child and shall bear a son, and shall name him Immanuel" (Isaiah 7:14). In the New Testament, Matthew repeated the prophet's words when he wrote about the birth of Jesus: "Look, the virgin shall conceive and bear a son, and they shall name him Emmanuel," meaning "God is with us" (Matthew 1:23).

Of Interest: Most Christians interpret Isaiah's words as a prophecy of Jesus, the Savior.

Famous Namesakes: Emmanuel Ax, classical pianist; Immanuel Kant, philosopher; Emanuel Ungaro, fashion designer.

ENOS ✦ *(EE-nos)* or *(EE-nosh)*

Language/Cultural Origin: Hebrew

Meaning: Mortal Man

Spiritual Connotation: Strength in God

Related Names/Nicknames: None

Alternate Names: Enosh

Background Story: In the New Testament, Enos appears in the genealogy of Jesus as the son of Seth and the grandson of Adam (Luke 3:38). In the Old Testament, he is called Enosh. He was born at a time when "people began to invoke the name of the Lord" and lived for nine hundred five years (Genesis 4:26, 5:11). The name Enos suggests a man who is aware of his imperfections and looks to God for strength.

Famous Namesakes: Enos Slaughter, baseball legend and member of the National Baseball Hall of Fame.

EPHRAIM ✦ *(EE-free-uhm)* or *(EE-fruhm)* or *(EH-fruhm)*

Language/Cultural Origin: Hebrew

Meaning: Fruitful

Spiritual Connotation: Productive

Related Names/Nicknames: Ef, Effie, Effy, Efrain

Alternate Names: Efraim, Efrem, Efrim, Ephraem,
Ephream, Ephrem, Ephrim

Background Story: Ephraim—Joseph's second son with Asenath—
was born in Egypt. Joseph named him Ephraim "for God
has made me fruitful in the land of my misfortune" (Genesis 41:52). When Jacob was near death, Joseph brought his two
sons, Manasseh and Ephraim, to see their grandfather. Jacob
reached out to bless his grandsons and laid his right hand on
Ephraim. Joseph tried to correct his father, insisting that his
older son, Manasseh, should receive his right hand. But Jacob
resisted. He said that Manasseh would become great, but "his
younger brother shall be greater than he, and his offspring
shall become a multitude of nations" (Genesis 48:1–20). With his
blessing, Jacob named Joseph's sons as patriarchs of two of
Israel's tribes.

Famous Namesakes: Ephraim Ellis and Efrem Zimbalist Jr., actors.

EPHRON ✦ *(EE-fron)*

Language/Cultural Origin: Hebrew

Meaning: Fawnlike

Spiritual Connotation: Respectful

Related Names/Nicknames: Ephraim

Alternate Names: Efron

Background Story: Ephron was a Hittite landowner whom Abraham spoke to after Sarah's death. Abraham asked Ephron to sell
him "the cave of Machpelah" so that he could bury his dead.
Ephron responded, "I give you the field, and I give you the cave
that is in it," as a sign of respect. Nevertheless, Abraham paid him
"four hundred shekels of silver" for the land and buried his wife,

Sarah, in the cave. Later, Machpelah became the burial ground for Abraham and many of his descendants (Genesis 23:3–20).

Famous Namesakes: Henry Ephron, writer.

ERAN ✦ *(EHR-an)*
Language/Cultural Origin: Hebrew
Meaning: Watchful
Spiritual Connotation: Attentive
Related Names/Nicknames: Eiran
Alternate Names: None

Background Story: Eran, the son of Shuthelah and the grandson of Ephraim, was the great-grandson of Joseph. The clan of the Eranites are descended from him (Numbers 26:36). The name Eran suggests a thoughtful man who is diligent and attentive to the needs of others.

Famous Namesakes: Eran Tsur, Israeli singer/composer.

ERASTUS ✦ *(ih-RAS-tuhs)*
Language/Cultural Origin: Greek
Meaning: Loved
Spiritual Connotation: Honored Friend
Related Names/Nicknames: Eraste, Rastus
Alternate Names: Erastos

Background Story: Erastus appears three times in the New Testament, as the name of one or more of Paul's Christian companions.

Erastus and Timothy were two of Paul's "helpers" sent ahead to Macedonia while he remained in Asia (Acts 19:22). Erastus was also "the city treasurer" of Corinth who sent greetings to the early Christians of Rome (Romans 16:23). Finally, Paul mentions, in a letter to Timothy, a friend named Erastus who "remained in Corinth" (2 Timothy 4:20).

Famous Namesakes: Erastus Dow Palmer, American sculptor; Erastus Smith, hero of the Texas Revolution.

EREZ ✦ *(eh-REHZ)*

Language/Cultural Origin: Hebrew

Meaning: Cedar

Spiritual Connotation: To Be Firm

Related Names/Nicknames: None

Alternate Names: None

Background Story: In the Old Testament, erez, or cedar tree, is highly regarded as tall, majestic, and excellent (2 Kings 14:9; Song of Solomon 5:15; Amos 2:9). The growth of the cedar is typical of that of the righteous man (Psalms 92:12). In Ezekiel, the admiration and importance of erez is used to convey the Assyrian power: "a cedar in Lebanon with fair branches, and with a forest-like shade, a high stature; and its top was among the thick boughs . . . its stature was exalted above all the trees of the field; and its boughs were multiplied, and its branches became long" (Ezekiel 31:3–5). Also, erez represents not only the righteousness of man but also the strength and endurance of God's love. "The trees of Yahweh are filled with moisture, the cedars of Lebanon, which he hath planted" (Psalms 104:16). This sentiment continues today, as the Syrians refer to erez as "the cedar of the Lord."

ESAU ✦ *(EE-saw)*
Language/Cultural Origin: Hebrew
Meaning: Hairy
Spiritual Connotation: Reconciling
Related Names/Nicknames: None
Alternate Names: Esaw

Background Story: Esau, the oldest son of Isaac and Rebekah, was born mere seconds before his twin brother, Jacob, "all his body like a hairy mantle; so they named him Esau." The brothers' struggle with each other, which began in the womb, continued all their lives. Esau, a hunter, was favored by his father, while Rebekah preferred Jacob, the shepherd. But the Lord told Rebekah that of her two sons "the elder shall serve the younger," and that is exactly what happened. First, Esau sold his birthright to Jacob for a bowl of red stew, which gave him the name Edom or "red." Later, Rebekah tricked the half-blind Isaac into giving his blessing to Jacob instead. Esau was incensed at the deception and planned to kill his brother, but Isaac sent Jacob away to live with Laban, his uncle. For his part, Esau settled in the land of Seir, which came to be known as the land of Edom. Years later, the two brothers reconciled. When Esau saw Jacob he "ran to meet him, and embraced him, and fell on his neck and kissed him, and they wept." Esau had several wives—Adah, Basemath, and Oholibamah—and many children. In time, his descendants became a nation that rivaled Israel (Genesis 25–28, 32–33, 36).

Of Interest: According to the commentaries on Hebrew scripture, Esau is considered a significant character in world history and the forefather of the Roman Empire.

ETHAN ✦ *(EE-than)*

Language/Cultural Origin: Hebrew

Meaning: Enduring

Spiritual Connotation: Steadfast

Related Names/Nicknames: Aitan, Eitan, Etan, Gaithan

Alternate Names: Eathan, Ethen, Eythan

Background Story: There are two notable Ethans in the Bible: Ethan the Ezrahite, a wise man surpassed only by Solomon himself and the author of Psalm 89 (1 Kings 4:31, Psalms 89), and Kish's son, a Levite "in charge of the service of song" during David's reign (1 Chronicles 6:42).

Of Interest: In 2002 and 2004, Ethan ranked as the fifth most popular name for boys in the United States.

Famous Namesakes: Ethan Allen, American Revolution hero; Ethan Hawke, actor.

EZEKIEL ✦ *(ih-ZEE-kee-uhl)* or *(ih-ZEE-kyuhl)*

Language/Cultural Origin: Hebrew

Meaning: God Will Strengthen

Spiritual Connotation: Visionary

Related Names/Nicknames: Haskel, Zeke

Alternate Names: Ezechiel, Ezekial, Ezekyel, Ezikiel, Ezikyel, Ezykiel

Background Story: Ezekiel—one of the great biblical prophets—was an exile living in Babylon when he first received his calling. In his own words, "the heavens were opened, and I saw visions of God" (Ezekiel 1:1–3). His prophecies began with the destruction of Jerusalem, which came at the hands of Nebuchadnezzar several years later (Ezekiel 4–7). Ezekiel, however, was also a prophet of hope for his people. His most dramatic vision took place in a valley of "dry bones." When God commanded Ezekiel to prophesy to the bones, they rattled and came together, "bone to its bone," developing sinews, flesh, and the breath of life. God then told Ezekiel that the bones were "the house of Israel," which he would raise from its grave and bring "back to the land of Israel" (Ezekiel 37:1–14). Ezekiel put everything in writing about himself and his prophecies in the Book of Ezekiel.

Of Interest: Ezekiel has nearly doubled in popularity as a boy's name in the United States since 1994, going from 616 to 316.

EZRA ✦ *(EHZ-ruh)*

Language/Cultural Origin: Hebrew/Aramaic

Meaning: Help

Spiritual Connotation: Spiritual Guidance

Related Names/Nicknames: Azariah, Azur, Esdras, Esera, Ezar, Ezer, Ezera, Ezri

Alternate Names: Esra, Ezrah

Background Story: Ezra was a priest and "a scribe skilled in the law of Moses," who recorded the events of the Israelites' return from exile in Babylon. Ezra himself led the second group to Jerusalem where he "had set his heart to study the law of the Lord" and teach its "statutes and ordinances." The Persian king Artaxerxes sent Ezra with silver and gold for the temple and a letter establishing his authority in Jerusalem (Ezra 7:1–28). After the walls of Jerusalem were completed, the people gathered for a celebration and Ezra read the law of Moses "from early morning until midday . . . and the ears of all the people were attentive to the book of the law" (Nehemiah 8–9).

Famous Namesakes: Ezra Jack Keats, children's writer/illustrator; Ezra Pound, poet.

EZRI ✦ *(EHZ-rai)*

Language/Cultural Origin: Hebrew/Aramaic

Meaning: My Help

Spiritual Connotation: Ready to Serve

Related Names/Nicknames: Ezer, Ezra

Alternate Names: None

Background Story: Ezri lived during the reign of King David. He was the son of Chelub and the king's supervisor "over those who did the work of the field, tilling the soil" (1 Chronicles 27:26). The name Ezri brings to mind a man who is steady and dependable.

FELIX ✦ *(FEE-lihks)*

Language/Cultural Origin: Latin

Meaning: Happy

Spiritual Connotation: Joyful Spirit

Related Names/Nicknames: Fee, Felic, Felice, Felicia, Felician, Feliciana, Feliciano, Felicie, Felicien, Felicio, Felizio, Kalisha, Lisha

Alternate Names: Feliks, Felyx, Phelix

Background Story: Felix is a beautiful name in the Bible, attached to a man with a less than beautiful spirit. He was the Roman governor of Judea, to whom the imprisoned Paul was sent when a faction of Jews plotted to kill him. Although Felix could find no reason to convict Paul, he kept him in prison on the pretense that he would decide his case later. He did allow Paul "some liberty" and sent for him often to "converse." Felix, however, was hoping for a bribe—which he never received. At the end of his term, he left Paul in prison "since he wanted to grant the Jews a favor" (Acts 23–24).

Of Interest: Felix is the name of several saints and popes in the Catholic Church.

Famous Namesakes: Felix Bloch, Nobel Prize winner in physics; Felix Frankfurter, Supreme Court justice; Felix Mendelssohn, composer; Felix Trinidad, champion boxer.

GABRIEL   *(GAY-bree-uhl)*

Language/Cultural Origin: Hebrew

Meaning: God Is My Strength

Spiritual Connotation: Enlightenment

Related Names/Nicknames: Brielle, Gab, Gabbi, Gabbie, Gabby, Gabe, Gabi, Gabian, Gabie, Gabor, Gabrian, Gabriela, Gabriella, Gabriello, Gabrio, Gaby, Gavrel, Gavri

Alternate Names: Gabriele, Gabrielle, Gabriyel

Background Story: Gabriel is an angel of the Lord who appears several times in the Bible. In the Old Testament, he came to Daniel twice: to interpret a vision for him and to communicate a prophecy (Daniel 8:15–16, 9:21). In the New Testament, he brought "good news" to Zechariah that God would answer his prayers and his wife, Elizabeth, would have a son named John. Six months later, he appeared to Elizabeth's cousin, a virgin named Mary, and said, "You will conceive in your womb and bear a son, and you will name him Jesus" (Luke 1:5–38).

Of Interest: In 2003, Gabriel ranked as the thirtieth most popular name for boys in the United States.

Famous Namesakes: Gabriel Byrne, actor; Gabe Kaplan, entertainer; Gabriel Garcia Marquez, Nobel Prize–winning writer.

GAIUS ◆ *(GAY-uhs)* or *(GAI-uhs)*

Language/Cultural Origin: Latin

Meaning: Rejoice

Spiritual Connotation: Praise the Lord

Related Names/Nicknames: Cai, Caio, Caius, Kay, Kaye, Keye, Keyes, Keys

Alternate Names: None

Background Story: Gaius was a popular Roman name among new Christians in the Bible. Some of them are: one of Paul's two "travel companions" who were dragged by the crowd in the riot at Ephesus (Acts 19:29); a disciple "from Derbe" who accompanied Paul on his trip from Greece to Macedonia (Acts 20:4); Paul's host in Corinth when he wrote his letter to the Romans (Romans 16:23); and the recipient of John's third letter, described as "the beloved Gaius, whom I love in truth" (3 John 1:1).

GALLIO ◆ *(GAL-ee-o)*

Language/Cultural Origin: Latin

Meaning: One Who Sucks

Spiritual Connotation: Judgment

Related Names/Nicknames: None

Alternate Names: None

Background Story: Gallio was the Roman proconsul of Achaia during one of Paul's visits to Corinth. On one occasion, the Jews brought Paul before Gallio for "persuading people to worship God in ways that are contrary to the law." Before Paul had a chance to speak in his own defense, Gallio dismissed the complaint as a religious matter and told the Jews to "see to it yourselves" (Acts 18:12–16).

Of Interest: Gallio was the older brother of the famous Roman philosopher Seneca.

GERA ✦ *(GEHR-uh)* or *(ZHEE-ruh)*
Language/Cultural Origin: Hebrew
Meaning: Pilgrimage
Spiritual Connotation: Redemption
Related Names/Nicknames: None
Alternate Names: None

Background Story: In the Old Testament, there are three men called Gera: a son of Benjamin who traveled to Egypt with his grandfather Jacob (Genesis 46:21); the father of Ehud, the "left-handed man" who killed King Eglon and delivered the Israelites from the Moabites (Judges 3:15); and the father of Shimei, who cursed David during the rebellion of Absalom and later asked for his pardon (2 Samuel 16, 19).

GERSHON ✦ *(GER-shahn)*
Language/Cultural Origin: Hebrew
Meaning: Exile

Spiritual Connotation: Guardianship

Related Names/Nicknames: Gersham, Gershoom

Alternate Names: Gershom, Gerson

Background Story: Gershon, Levi's oldest son, was the brother of Kohath and Merari. He had two sons, Libni and Shimei, both patriarchs of their own clans. The members of the Gershonite clan carried out specific functions in the temple. In the wilderness, they were responsible for carrying "the tabernacle, the tent with its coverings," and all of its screens, hangings, and cords (Numbers 3:17–18, 25–26).

Famous Namesakes: Gershon Kingsley, musician.

GIDEON ✦ *(GIHD-ee-uhn)*

Language/Cultural Origin: Hebrew

Meaning: Woodsman

Spiritual Connotation: Triumphant

Related Names/Nicknames: Giddy, Gid, Gidi

Alternate Names: Gedeon, Gideone, Gidon

Background Story: The story goes in the Old Testament that Gideon had a direct call from God to deliver Israel from "the hand of Midian," who had been harassing them for seven years. With ten of his servants, he overthrew the pagan altar of Baal and replaced it with an altar to the Lord. He then rallied an army of thirty-two thousand men. God selected only three hundred of them—against an army of one hundred twenty thousand Midianites—to display the force of his power. Under cover of night, Gideon divided his men, surrounded the enemy, and tricked them into believing he had an enormous army by having them break pottery, wave torches, and blow horns. The Midianites fled in confusion and Israel lived in peace for forty years (Judges 6–8). Gideon is mentioned in the biblical "Hall of Faith" as one of the men who "through faith conquered kingdoms" (Hebrews 11:32–33).

Of Interest: In 1898, two traveling salesmen were asked to share a room in a crowded hotel. They discovered a mutual Christian faith and spent the night reading the Bible, praying, and discussing the idea of a Christian traveling men's association. Within the year, they founded the Gideon Bible, named for Gideon from the Book of Judges, a man who was willing to do whatever God asked of him—including over one hundred years' worth of Bibles in hotel rooms.

Famous Namesakes: Gideon Evans, humorist; Gideon Yago, news correspondent.

GILEAD ✦ *(GIHL-ee-uhd)*
Language/Cultural Origin: Hebrew/Arabic
Meaning: Hill of Testimony
Spiritual Connotation: Monument of God
Related Names/Nicknames: Gil
Alternate Names: Gilad

Background Story: Among others in the Bible, Gilead was the man whose five great-granddaughters were the first to obtain the right for women to inherit their father's property (Numbers 27:10). It is also a mountainous region in the Bible where Elijah once lived, where Laban caught up with Jacob, and where David took refuge from Absalom.

Of Interest: Balm (or balsam) of Gilead comes from a small evergreen tree used for its healing properties. The prophet Jeremiah referred to it when he asked: "Is there no balm in Gilead? Is there no physician there? Why then has the health of my poor people not been restored?" (Jeremiah 8:22). The title of a popular African American spiritual has the answer: "There Is a Balm in Gilead."

GOMER ✦ *(GO-mer)*

Language/Cultural Origin: Hebrew

Meaning: Complete

Spiritual Connotation: Flawless

Related Names/Nicknames: None

Alternate Names: None

Background Story: There are two biblical Gomers: Noah's grandson and Japheth's son (Genesis 10:2), and Hosea's unfaithful wife, who had three of his children (Hosea 1:3). Gomer is a man's name today, suggesting a well-rounded person with many talents.

Of Interest: Noah's grandson, Gomer, is considered the ancestor of the Celtic people.

Famous Namesakes: Gomer Pyle was a lovable character played by Jim Nabors during the 1960s in two television series, *The Andy Griffith Show* and *Gomer Pyle, U.S.M.C.*

HANANIAH ✦ *(han-uh-NAI-uh)*

Language/Cultural Origin: Hebrew

Meaning: Grace

Spiritual Connotation: Mercy

Related Names/Nicknames: Ananias, Annas

Alternate Names: None

Background Story: Hananiah was a common name during biblical times. Among the more memorable were: one of King Uzziah's commanders (2 Chronicles 26:11); an official Nehemiah put in charge of Jerusalem "for he was a faithful man and feared God more than many" (Nehemiah 7:2); and a prince of Judah educated in Nebuchadnezzar's court. The last Hananiah was "called Shadrach" by the palace master. When he and his friends refused to worship the king's pagan gods, they were thrown into "a furnace of blazing fire." Miraculously, an angel appeared to protect the young men, and the fire had no power over them (Daniel 1:6–7, 3:19–27).

Famous Namesakes: Hananiah Harari, abstract artist.

HARAN ✦ *(HAY-ran)*
Language/Cultural Origin: Hebrew
Meaning: Mountaineer
Spiritual Connotation: Endurance
Related Names/Nicknames: None
Alternate Names: None

Background Story: There were two men named Haran in the Bible. One was Abram's youngest brother, who became the father of Lot, Milcah, and Iscah. Haran died before his own father "in the land of his birth" (Genesis 11:26–28). The other was a son of Caleb and his concubine, Ephah (1 Chronicles 2:46). Haran was also the city where Abram lived until his father died and where Jacob lived with Laban. The name Haran is mindful of a man who never gives up.

Of Interest: Haran—an ancient city of Mesopotamia—was an important trading post and a religious center for the Assyrian moon god.

HARIM ✦ *(HAY-rihm)*

Language/Cultural Origin: Hebrew

Meaning: Dedicated to God

Spiritual Connotation: Prayerful

Related Names/Nicknames: None

Alternate Names: None

Background Story: Harim is a family name appearing frequently in the Bible. Harim was a priest appointed to serve in the temple under David (1 Chronicles 24:8); the son of a man who repaired a section of the wall in Jerusalem (Nehemiah 3:11); and the ancestor of two families who returned from captivity in Babylon (Nehemiah 7:35, 42). The name Harim suggests a man who is deeply religious.

HEBRON ✦ *(HEH-brawn)* or *(HEE-bruhn)*

Language/Cultural Origin: Hebrew

Meaning: Community

Spiritual Connotation: Friendship

Related Names/Nicknames: None

Alternate Names: None

Background Story: Hebron was an ancient city in Palestine visited by a number of important biblical figures. Abram pitched his tent "by the oaks of Mamre" in Hebron, Sarah died there, and Abraham, Isaac, Jacob, and their wives found their final resting place in the cave at Machpelah near Hebron (Genesis 23:19). Later, Joshua's spies brought a "cluster of grapes" back from Hebron when they scouted the Promised Land (Numbers 13:22–23). Finally, David was anointed king at Hebron, where he reigned until he captured Jerusalem and made it his capital (2 Samuel 2:11).

Of Interest: Hebron—located on the West Bank south of Jerusalem—is one of the most ancient cities in the Middle East and is considered a sacred site to Jews and Arabs alike.

HERMES ✦ *(HER-meez)*
Language/Cultural Origin: Greek
Meaning: Messenger
Spiritual Connotation: Faithful Follower
Related Names/Nicknames: Hermilio, Hermite, Mercury
Alternate Names: Ermes, Hermas, Hermus

Background Story: Hermes was Paul's disciple and a Christian in Rome during the early days of the Church. Paul greeted him and several other "brothers and sisters" in his letter to the Romans (Romans 16:14).

Of Interest: In Greek mythology, Hermes was the god of eloquence and a messenger for the other gods. During the time of the Old Testament, Hermes was also a common name among household slaves.

Famous Namesakes: Hermes Pan, choreographer.

HEZRON ✦ *(HEHZ-ruhn)*
Language/Cultural Origin: Hebrew
Meaning: Dart of Joy
Spiritual Connotation: A Happy Heart
Related Names/Nicknames: Ron
Alternate Names: None

Background Story: There are two Hezrons in the Bible. One was Reuben's son, Jacob's grandson, and the patriarch of the Hezronites (Numbers 26:5–6). The other was the son of Perez and the grandson of Judah (Numbers 26:21). His sons were Jerahmeel, Caleb, Segub, Ashur, and Ram—a direct ancestor of David. The second Hezron also appears in the genealogy of Jesus (Luke 3:33). The name Hezron suggests a man who always has a smile on his face.

HIRAM ✦ *(HAI-ruhm)*

Language/Cultural Origin: Phoenician/Hebrew

Meaning: Exalted Brother

Spiritual Connotation: Noble Friend

Related Names/Nicknames: Hi, Hy

Alternate Names: Hirom, Horam, Huram, Hurom, Hyram, Hyrum

Background Story: Hiram, the king of Tyre, was a friend and ally of David in the Bible. Hiram showed his respect by sending "cedar trees, and carpenters and masons who built David a house" (2 Samuel 5:11). When Solomon succeeded his father, Hiram supplied him with experienced craftsmen and "cedar and cypress" for the construction of a temple. In exchange, Solomon sent food and oil to Hiram's household (1 Kings 5:8–11). Hiram was also the name of "an artisan in bronze" from Tyre who worked on Solomon's temple (1 Kings 7:13–14).

Famous Namesakes: Hiram Bingham III, explorer and politician; Hiram Leong Fong, first Asian American senator; Hiram Powers, sculptor.

HOSEA ✦ *(ho-ZAY-uh)* or *(ho-ZEE-uh)*

Language/Cultural Origin: Hebrew

Meaning: Salvation

Spiritual Connotation: Forgiveness

Related Names/Nicknames: Joshua

Alternate Names: Hoseah, Hoseia, Hoshea, Hosheia

Background Story: The life of Hosea—a minor Old Testament prophet—mirrored the bittersweet relationship God had with his people in Israel at the time. When God first spoke to Hosea, he told him to "go, take a harlot wife and harlot's children, for the land gives itself to harlotry, turning away from the Lord." Hosea took Gomer as his wife and, although they had three children, she was unfaithful to him, in the same way that Israel had been unfaithful to the Lord by worshipping false gods. But Hosea took his wife back because he could not give up on her, just as Hosea said the Lord would not give up on the people of Israel (Book of Hosea).

Famous Namesakes: Hosea Williams, American civil-rights leader.

ICHABOD ✦ *(IHK-uh-bod)*

Language/Cultural Origin: Hebrew

Meaning: The Glory Is Gone

Spiritual Connotation: Sorrowful

Related Names/Nicknames: None

Alternate Names: Ikabod

Background Story: Ichabod came into the world on a somber note. Before Ichabod's birth, his father died during a battle with the Philistines, who also removed the ark of the covenant from him.

When Ichabod's mother learned about the death of her husband, the loss of the ark, and the subsequent death of her distraught father-in-law, she went into labor and gave birth to her son. Her labor pains were so overwhelming that she also died—but not before she named her child Ichabod, saying, "The glory has departed from Israel, for the ark of God has been captured" (1 Samuel 4:19–22).

Famous Namesakes: Ichabod Crane is a character in Washington Irving's famous story "The Legend of Sleepy Hollow."

IRA ✦ *(AI-ruh)*

Language/Cultural Origin: Hebrew

Meaning: Watchful

Spiritual Connotation: Vigilant

Related Names/Nicknames: None

Alternate Names: Irah

Background Story: Of the three men named Ira in the Bible, two were in the military: Ira, the son of Ikkesh the Tekoite, a captain of the temple guard, and Ira the Ithrite. Both were among "the Thirty" bodyguards sworn to protect David in battle (2 Samuel 23:26, 38). The third was Ira the Jairite, David's priest and, possibly, an adviser (2 Samuel 20:26). The name Ira suggests a man who always keeps his eyes open to possibilities.

Famous Namesakes: Ira Aldridge, actor; Ira Joe Fisher, television weather reporter; Ira Gershwin, lyricist; Ira Levin, writer.

ISAAC ✦ *(AI-zihk)* or *(AI-zuhk)*

Language/Cultural Origin: Hebrew

Meaning: Laughter

Spiritual Connotation: Child of Promise

Related Names/Nicknames: Ike, Ikey, Ikie,
Isa, Isacco, Ishaq, Isi, Itzaak, Itzak, Itzhak,
Itzik, Izzy, Yitzaak, Yitzak, Yitzhak,
Zack, Zak

Alternate Names: Isaak, Isac, Isak, Issac,
Izaac, Izaak, Izak, Izik, Izsak

Background Story: Isaac's birth was nothing short of a miracle.
Although his father, Abraham, had a son named Ishmael,
God promised him another son with whom he would establish "an everlasting covenant." Abraham and his wife, Sarah,
were so elderly at the time that Isaac's birth was a test of faith.
Then, when Isaac was a boy, God tested his father again. He
told Abraham to take his son "to the land of Moriah and offer
him there as a burnt offering." Abraham obeyed. At the last
minute, fortunately, God stopped him and provided a ram for
the offering instead. Isaac went on to marry Rebekah, who
was "fair to look upon," and together they had twin boys,
Esau and Jacob. As Isaac grew older, he decided to bestow his
blessing on his older son, Esau, but Rebekah had other plans.
God had said that of her two sons "the elder shall serve the
younger," so she had Jacob trick Isaac into giving him his
blessing instead. After years of bitterness, Isaac's two sons
reconciled, and when Isaac finally "breathed his last . . . Esau
and Jacob buried him" together (Genesis 17, 21–28, 35). Jacob
became the ancestor of all the Israelites.

Of Interest: Isaac was so named because Abraham "fell on his face
and laughed" when God told him that he, at the age of one hundred, and Sarah, who was ninety, would have a child. Isaac, a

popular name for boys in the United States, was among the top fifty from 2001 to 2004.

Famous Namesakes: Isaac Asimov, writer; Isaac Bruce, football player; Isaac Hanson, musician; Isaac Hayes, songwriter; Sir Isaac Newton, scientist; Itzhak Perlman, violinist; Isaac Bashevis Singer, writer; Izaak Walton, writer/angler.

ISAIAH ✦ *(ai-ZAY-uh)* or *(ai-ZAI-uh)*

Language/Cultural Origin: Hebrew

Meaning: Salvation of God

Spiritual Connotation: God Will Prevail

Related Names/Nicknames: Esa, Esaias, Isa, Isai, Isaias, Isais, Isay, Isayas

Alternate Names: Essaiah, Isaia, Isia, Isiah, Issiah, Izaiah, Izeyah, Iziah

Background Story: Isaiah, the son of Amos, may be the greatest of the Old Testament prophets. What little is known about his personal life comes from his own writings. He was married to a woman he called "the prophetess," had two sons, was probably of high rank, and prophesied during the reigns of four kings of Judah. Isaiah is well known for his work with King Hezekiah, for whom he prophesied the destruction of the Assyrian king and his army. His prophecies frequently attacked social injustice in Judah and urged the Jews to put their trust in the Lord. Isaiah's most famous prophecy—the coming of the Messiah—was a response to King Ahaz, who was fearful that Judah would fall to the Assyrians. Isaiah repeated God's promise that his people would prevail in the end and said, "The Lord himself will give you this sign: the virgin shall be with child, and bear a son, and shall name him Immanuel" (Book of Isaiah).

Of Interest: Isaiah was among the top fifty names for boys in the United States from 2000 to 2004.

Famous Namesakes: Sir Isaiah Berlin, philosopher; Isaiah Horowitz, rabbi and mystic; Isiah Thomas, basketball player; Isaiah Washington, actor; Isaiah Zagar, artist.

ISHMAEL ✦ *(ISH-may-ehl)*

Language/Cultural Origin: Hebrew/Arabic

Meaning: God Hears

Spiritual Connotation: Marked by God's Favor

Related Names/Nicknames: Ishmaiah

Alternate Names: Esmail, Ishmeil, Ismael, Ismail, Yishmael, Ysmael, Ysmail

Background Story: One man stands above all the other Ishmaels in the Bible. He was Abraham's first son, whose mother was Hagar, Sarah's servant, since Sarah was unable to have children of her own. There were problems between the two women from the start, and Hagar ran away while she was still pregnant. But an "angel of the Lord" coaxed her back, saying, "I will so greatly multiply your offspring that they cannot be counted." At thirteen, Ishmael was circumsized, as was his father, because of a covenant made with God. God also promised Abraham a son with Sarah in their old age. Isaac was born and, before long, Sarah wanted Ishmael and Hagar gone. Abraham was distressed, but God comforted him. "I will make a nation of him also," God said, and Abraham sent them away. They wandered the desert until, lacking water, Hagar waited for both of them to die. Once again, an angel appeared and said, "Do not be afraid; for God has heard the voice of the boy." Ishmael grew up in the wilderness "and became an expert with the bow." He married an Egyptian woman and had twelve sons. After Abraham's death, Ishmael joined his half-brother, Isaac, to bury their father in the cave of Machpelah (Genesis 16–17, 21:1–20, 25:9).

Of Interest: Ishmael is considered the ancestor of the Arab people.

Famous Namesakes: Ishmael Reed, writer; Ishmael, narrator of Herman Melville's classic novel *Moby-Dick*.

ISRAEL ✦ *(IHZ-ree-uhl)* or *(IHZ-ray-ehl)* or *(IHZ-rah-ehl)*

Language/Cultural Origin: Hebrew

Meaning: Wrestled with God

Spiritual Connotation: Prevailing Spirit

Related Names/Nicknames: Iser, Isi, Issur, Issy, Izzy

Alternate Names: Isreal, Isreel, Izrael, Izreal, Yisrael, Ysrael

Background Story: God himself gave Jacob the name "Israel" after wrestling with him all night long. "You shall no longer be called Jacob, but Israel, for you have striven with God and with humans and have prevailed," God said (Genesis 32:28). At Bethel, God again called him Israel and gave his blessing: ". . . be fruitful and multiply; a nation and a company of nations shall come from you" (Genesis 35:10–12). The nation that descended from Jacob and his sons was Israel, and his people were called Israelites.

Famous Namesakes: Israel Horovitz, playwright; Israel Houghton, songwriter; Israel Shenker, writer.

JACHIN ✦ *(JAY-kihn)*

Language/Cultural Origin: Hebrew

Meaning: God Will Establish

Spiritual Connotation: Steadfast and Firm

Related Names/Nicknames: Jay

Alternate Names: Jacan, Jakin

Background Story: Jachin, the son of Simeon and grandson of Jacob, was one of the family members who accompanied Jacob into Egypt (Genesis 46:10). Jachin was also the name of two priests in the Old Testament: one who returned from captivity in Babylon (1 Chronicles 9:10), and one who was appointed to serve in "the house of the Lord" under David (1 Chronicles 24:17).

Of Interest: Jachin was the name given to one of the two pillars that stood at the entrance to Solomon's temple in Jerusalem.

JACOB ✦ *(JAY-kuhb)*

Language/Cultural Origin: Hebrew

Meaning: Supplanter

Spiritual Connotation: In God's Plan

Related Names/Nicknames: Cob, Cobb, Cobby, Giacamo, Giacobo, Giacomo, Hamish, Iago, Iakob, Iakov, Jack, Jackie, Jacko, Jacky, Jaco, Jacobi, Jacobo, Jacobus, Jacoby, Jacques, Jago, Jaime, Jake, Jakie, James, Jamesie, Jamey, Jamie, Jamsey, Jay, Jayme, Jim, Jimmie, Seamus, Shamus, Yakov

Alternate Names: Jaccob, Jakob, Jakov, Jakub

Background Story: Jacob was the younger of Isaac and Rebekah's twin sons, but God ordained that he would be the stronger.

Before he was born, the Lord said to his mother that her older son, Esau, "shall serve the younger," and when Jacob came out, his hand was already "gripping Esau's heel." Esau was a skillful hunter, but Jacob—a quiet shepherd—was clever and managed to exchange his brother's birthright for a bowl of stew. He also tricked his blind father into believing he was Esau and received Isaac's blessing in his older brother's place. To avoid Esau's rage, Jacob left home to find work with his uncle, Laban. On the way, he had a dream of a ladder that reached to heaven and of God saying that he and his offspring would one day inherit the land where he was resting. Jacob married Laban's two daughters, Rachel and Leah, with whom he had eight sons. He also had four sons with their two maids, Bilhah and Zilpah. After twenty years, Jacob left with his family for his homeland. On the way back, he had two more dreams. In one dream, he wrestled with God and, in the other, God changed his name to Israel and said, ". . . be fruitful and multiply; a nation and a company of nations shall come from you, and kings shall spring from you." Jacob reconciled with Esau and settled in Canaan. Later, he moved his family to Egypt, where he was reunited with his son, Joseph, before he died. Jacob's dreams came true, and his sons and grandsons became the ancestors of Israel's twelve tribes (Genesis 25, 27–37, 42, 45–49).

Of Interest: From 1999 to 2004, Jacob was the most popular name for boys in the United States.

Famous Namesakes: Jacob Adler, Yiddish actor; Jakob Bernoulli, mathematician; Jacob Grimm, writer; Jake Gyllenhaal, actor; Jacob Javits, U.S. senator; Jacob Needleman, writer/philosopher; Jacob Riis, photographer; Jacob Shubert, producer.

JADON ✦ *(JAY-duhn)*

Language/Cultural Origin: Hebrew

Meaning: God Has Heard

Spiritual Connotation: Speaks to the Lord

Related Names/Nicknames: Jade, Jader

Alternate Names: Jaden, Jadyn, Jadynn, Jaedon, Jaiden, Jaidyn, Jaidynn, Jayden, Jaydon, Jaydyn, Jaydynn

Background Story: Jadon assisted Nehemiah and Eliashib on the walls of Jerusalem after the return from captivity in Babylon. "Repairs were made" by Jadon, together with "the men of Gibeon and of Mizpah." According to the Bible, they were all "under the jurisdiction of the governor of the province beyond the river" (Nehemiah 3:7).

Of Interest: The name Jadon has undergone a surge in popularity in the United States over the past few years, going from seldom used in 1997 to the rank of 372 in 2003.

Famous Namesakes: Jadon Lavik, singer/songwriter.

JAHLEEL ✦ *(JAH-lee-ehl)*

Language/Cultural Origin: Hebrew

Meaning: Waiting for God

Spiritual Connotation: Hope in the Lord

Related Names/Nicknames: Jalal, Jay

Alternate Names: Jaleel, Jalil

Background Story: Jahleel was the third and youngest son of Zebulun and a grandchild of Jacob. With the rest of Jacob's family, he accompanied his grandfather into the land of Egypt

(Genesis 46:14). It is from Jahleel that "the clan of the Jahleelites" are descended (Numbers 26:26). The name Jahleel suggests a man who is both patient and confident.

JAIR ✦ *(JAY-er)*
Language/Cultural Origin: Hebrew
Meaning: Enlightener
Spiritual Connotation: Shining Light
Related Names/Nicknames: Jairo, Jairus, Yair
Alternate Names: None

Background Story: There are four Jairs in the Bible: a descendant of Manasseh who captured the villages of Bashan and renamed it Havoth-jair, which means "the villages of Jair" (Deuteronomy 3:14); a wealthy man in Gilead who judged Israel for twenty-two years and had "thirty sons who rode on thirty donkeys and . . . had thirty towns" (Judges 10:3–5); the father of Elhanan who "killed Lahmi the brother of Goliath" (1 Chronicles 20:5); and the father of Mordecai, Esther's cousin who helped her deliver the Jews from destruction during their captivity (Esther 2:5).

Famous Namesakes: In 1996, Jair Lynch was the first African American gynmnast to medal in the Olympics.

JAIRUS ✦ *(JAY-uh-ruhs)* or *(JEHR-uhs)*
Language/Cultural Origin: Hebrew/Greek
Meaning: God Enlightens
Spiritual Connotation: Believing

Related Names/Nicknames: Jair, Jairis, Jairo,
Jay, Jayrus, Yair

Alternate Names: None

Background Story: Jairus, "a leader of the synagogue," begged
Jesus to heal his only daughter, who was dying. Jesus followed
him to his house. But, on the way, news came that it was too late;
the little girl had died. Jesus's reply was, "Do not fear, only
believe, and she will be saved." When they arrived, Jesus asked
why everyone was "weeping and wailing" when the child was
only "sleeping." They laughed at him, but he took the girl's hand
and said, "Child, get up!" To her parents' astonishment, the girl
immediately came to life and began to move around (Luke
8:41–56).

Of Interest: The Jairus Agency in Massachusetts provides men-
toring relationships for at-risk teens and connects them with
volunteer jobs so they can "discover the rewards of giving to
others."

JAKIM ✦ *(JAY-kihm)* or *(ya-KEEM)*

Language/Cultural Origin: Hebrew/Arabic

Meaning: God Lifts Up

Spiritual Connotation: Chosen

Related Names/Nicknames: Joachim,
Yachim, Yakim

Alternate Names: Jakeem

Background Story: Of the two Jakims in the Bible, one was
Shimei's oldest son and a descendant of Benjamin (1 Chronicles
8:19–21). The other was a priest appointed to serve in the temple
during David's reign, "according to the procedure established"

by Aaron (1 Chronicles 24:12–19). The name Jakim implies a man who lives his life as an example to other people.

JAMES ✦ *(JAYMZ)*

Language/Cultural Origin: Hebrew/Greek/Latin/English

Meaning: Supplanter

Spiritual Connotation: In God's Plan

Related Names/Nicknames: Diego, Jacob, Jago, Jaime, Jaimie, Jame, Jamesina, Jameson, Jamey, Jami, Jamie, Jamieson, Jamison, Jamsey, Jay, Jayma, Jayme, Jem, Jemmy, Jems, Jim, Jimbo, Jimi, Jimmie, Jimmy, Jims, Kimo, Santiago, Seamus

Alternate Names: Jaimes, Jammes, Jaymes, Jayms

Background Story: All the men named James in the Bible played an important role in Christ's life, but James, the son of Zebedee, was the most prominent. He was not only one of Jesus's apostles but also part of his inner circle. With his brother John and Peter, James saw Jesus raise Jairus's daughter from the dead, witnessed his transfiguration, and was present in the garden of Gethsemane. Jesus called James and John "sons of thunder," probably because of their bold defense of him, a defense that made James the first apostle to be martyred (Matthew 10, 17; Mark 3, 5, 14; Acts 12). James, the son of Alphaeus, was another of the apostles with whom Jesus shared his ministry (Matthew 10:3). The third James, a "brother" or relative of Jesus, was present when Jesus appeared to the apostles after the Resurrection, was a leader of the early Church in Jerusalem, and is possibly the author of his own letter in the Bible. He may also be the second apostle named James (Matthew 13:55; Acts 15:13).

Of Interest: James, which is derived from the Hebrew name for Jacob, has been a popular name for centuries. There were seven kings of England and Scotland named James—the King James Bible is named for James I—and six U.S. presidents. From 1940 to 1959, it was the number one name for boys in the United States and has never fallen below nineteen over the last 105 years.

Famous Namesakes: James Buchanan, James Earl Carter, James Garfield, James Madison, James Monroe, James Polk, U.S. presidents; Captain James Cook, explorer; James Dean, James Gandolfini, James Garner, James Mason, Jimmy Stewart, actors; Jimmy Durante, entertainer; Jimi Hendrix, musician; James Joyce, writer; James Taylor, singer; James Watt, inventor.

JAMIN ✦ *(JAY-mihn)* or *(yah-MEEN)*

Language/Cultural Origin: Hebrew

Meaning: Right Hand

Spiritual Connotation: Strong and Skillful

Related Names/Nicknames: Jamian, Jamiel

Alternate Names: Jamon, Jaymin

Background Story: Three Jamins can be found in the Bible: the second son of Simeon, who went into Egypt with his grandfather Jacob and his family (Genesis 46:10); Ram's son from the tribe of Judah (1 Chronicles 2:27); and a Levite who "helped the people to understand the law" of Moses, which Ezra read to them after the wall in Jerusalem was completed (Nehemiah 8:7). The name Jamin suggests a man who knows the hand of God is guiding him.

JARED ✦ *(JEHR-ihd)* or *(JAY-rehd)*

Language/Cultural Origin: Hebrew

Meaning: Descent

Spiritual Connotation: Favored by God

Related Names/Nicknames: Jareth, Jordan

Alternate Names: Jarad, Jarid, Jarod, Jarrad, Jarred, Jarrid, Jarrod, Jaryd, Jerad, Jered, Jerod, Jerrad, Jerred, Jerrod

Background Story: Jared—a descendant of Adam and ancestor of Noah—was the son of Mahalalel and the father of Enoch. "All the days of Jared were nine hundred sixty-two years" (Genesis 5:15–20). He is also mentioned in one of the genealogies of Jesus (Luke 3:37). Jared is a name that implies a sense of connectedness to the rest of the world.

Famous Namesakes: Jared Diamond, Pulitzer Prize–winning writer; Jared Leto, Jared Padalecki, actors.

JASHER ✦ *(JASH-er)*

Language/Cultural Origin: Hebrew

Meaning: Righteous

Spiritual Connotation: Just

Related Names/Nicknames: None

Alternate Names: Jashar

Background Story: The Book of Jasher is probably an ancient songbook, celebrating Israel's heroes. Only two excerpts can be found in the Bible. The first excerpt is Joshua's words to the Lord during his battle with the Amorites: "Sun, stand still at

Gibeon, and Moon, in the valley of Aijalon" (Joshua 10:12). The other is David's lamentation over Saul's death—the Song of the Bow—which begins with, "Your glory, O Israel, lies slain upon your high places! How the mighty have fallen!" (2 Samuel 1:17–19).

Of Interest: The Book of Jasher literally means "the book of the righteous one."

JASON ✦ *(JAY-suhn)*

Language/Cultural Origin: Hebrew/Greek

Meaning: Healer

Spiritual Connotation: Benevolent

Related Names/Nicknames: Jace, Jacek, Jase, Jay, Jayce, Joshua

Alternate Names: Jacen, Jaisen, Jaison, Jasen, Jasin, Jasun, Jaysen, Jayson

Background Story: Jason lived in Thessalonica, where he was converted by Paul and Silas. Some of "the Jews became jealous" of the disciples' success and "formed a mob" to search for them. They went to Jason's house and, when they could not find Paul and Silas, they "dragged Jason and some believers before the city authorities," complaining that Paul and Silas had been guests in his home. Jason was required to pay bail before he was released (Acts 17:1–9). In a letter to the Romans, Paul refers to a "relative" named Jason, who is probably the same man (Romans 16:21).

Of Interest: The name Jason is derived from the Hebrew Joshua. In Greek mythology, Jason was the leader of the Argonauts. During the 1970s, Jason was the third most popular name for boys in the United States. Since then it has ranked in the top fifty.

Famous Namesakes: Jason Alexander, Jason Biggs, Jason Priestley, Jason Robards, actors; Jason Arnott, Jason Elam, football players; Jason Bay, baseball player; Jason Fodeman, writer; Jason Kidd, basketball player; Jason Kreis, soccer player; Jason Miller, actor/playwright; Jason Moran, jazz pianist; Jason Mraz, singer/ songwriter.

JASPER ✦ *(JAS-per)*

Language/Cultural Origin: Greek

Meaning: Treasure Holder

Spiritual Connotation: Splendid

Related Names/Nicknames: Caspar, Cass, Gaspar, Gasper, Jaspis, Kasper, Kass

Alternate Names: Jaspar, Jesper

Background Story: Jasper is a precious stone in the Bible and a symbol of splendor to the Israelites and Jews. It was the twelfth and final stone embedded in the breastplate of the high priest, Aaron (Exodus 39:13), and John described "the holy city of Jerusalem" in Revelation as having "a radiance like a very rare jewel, like jasper, clear as crystal" (Revelation 21:10–11).

Of Interest: Jasper is an opaque quartz stone, usually red, yellow, brown, or green in color. Some scholars believe that the biblical jasper—because of its description as crystallike—may have actually been diamond.

Famous Namesakes: Jasper Carrott, actor/comedian; Jasper Conran, fashion designer; Jasper Johns, artist.

JAVAN ✦ *(JAY-van)*

Language/Cultural Origin: Hebrew

Meaning: Greece

Spiritual Connotation: Ancestor

Related Names/Nicknames: None

Alternate Names: Jahvon, Jaivon, Jayven, Jayvon

Background Story: Javan—Japheth's fourth son and Noah's grandson—was born after the flood. "The coastland peoples spread" throughout the ancient world from Javan and his sons Elishah, Tarshish, Kittim, and Dodanim (Genesis 10:1–5).

Of Interest: In Jewish mythology, Javan is considered the ancestor of ancient Greece, whose people were once referred to as Javan.

JEDAIAH ✦ *(juh-DAI-uh)* or *(jih-DAY-uh)*

Language/Cultural Origin: Hebrew

Meaning: The Hand of the Lord

Spiritual Connotation: Guided

Related Names/Nicknames: Jada, Jediah

Alternate Names: None

Background Story: The name Jedaiah appears several times in the Old Testament, especially among the priestly class. Some of the more noted are: a priest responsible for the second division of service to the temple during David's reign (1 Chronicles 24:7); a man who helped Eliashib repair the temple in Jerusalem (Nehemiah 3:10); a leader of priests who returned from captivity in Babylon (Nehemiah 12:7); and one of three men in charge of Joshua's crown at his coronation (Zechariah 6:9–15).

JEDIDIAH ✦ *(jehd-uh-DAI-uh)*

Language/Cultural Origin: Hebrew

Meaning: Beloved of the Lord

Spiritual Connotation: Cherished

Related Names/Nicknames: Jed, Jedaiah, Jedd, Jedi, Jediah, Yedidiah, Yedidyah

Alternate Names: Jedadiah, Jedediah, Jedidia

Background Story: Jedidiah was a name given to Solomon at his birth. David's first child with Bathsheba had died because of his father's sins. The Lord was angry because David had "struck down Uriah the Hittite . . . and taken his wife" as his own. Bathsheba then had another son with David, and they named him Solomon. God sent a message through the prophet Nathan that he loved this new child, "so he named him Jedidiah, because of the Lord" (2 Samuel 12:9–25).

Famous Namesakes: Jed Harris, producer/director; Jedidiah Morse, author of the first American geography textbook; Jedediah Smith, explorer; Jed Weaver, football player.

JEHIEL ✦ *(jee-HAI-uhl)*

Language/Cultural Origin: Hebrew

Meaning: God Lives

Spiritual Connotation: Inspired

Related Names/Nicknames: Jehiah, Jehieli

Alternate Names: None

Background Story: The Bible mentions a number of Jehiels, each with his own story. Some interesting ones are: a musician appointed to play the harp in celebration of the ark's removal to Jerusalem (1 Chronicles 15:18–20); a tutor who "attended the king's sons" during David's reign (1 Chronicles 27:32); the treasurer in charge of the free-will offerings for the temple in Jerusalem (1 Chronicles 29:8); and one of King Jehoram's brothers assassinated by Jehoram after he "ascended the throne" (2 Chronicles 21:2–4).

JEREMIAH ✦ *(jehr-uh-MAI-uh)*

Language/Cultural Origin: Hebrew

Meaning: The Lord Exalts

Spiritual Connotation: Consecrated

Related Names/Nicknames: Dermot, Dermott, Jem, Jemmie, Jeramie, Jeramy, Jere, Jereme, Jeremias, Jeremie, Jeremija, Jeremy, Jeri, Jermyn, Jerri, Jerrie, Jerry, Yeremia, Yeremiya, Yeremiyah

Alternate Names: Geremia, Jeramaya, Jeramiah, Jeremia, Jeremiya

Background Story: Of all the Jeremiahs in the Bible, none compares to the great prophet of the Old Testament. God came to Jeremiah at an early age and appointed him "a prophet to the nations." During the reigns of Judah's last kings, Jeremiah became unpopular for warning that Jerusalem was facing imminent destruction for the sins of its people. "So will I break this people and this city, as one breaks a potter's vessel," God told him. But Jeremiah also spoke of the "new covenant" the Lord would make with his people. His scribe Baruch read a scroll with his prophecies to the people, but the king of Judah threw it into the fire. During the Babylonian invasion, Jeremiah was thrown into prison, but he was released after the fall of Jerusalem by the Babylonians themselves. When he died, he left behind an impressive body of written work, which is an integral part of the Bible today (Book of Jeremiah).

Of Interest: Jeremiah is considered the author of the Book of Jeremiah and the Book of Lamentations. His prophecy about God's new covenant—"I will put my law within them, and I will write it on their hearts; and I will be their God, and they shall be my people"—is an inspiration for modern Judeo-Christian religions (Jeremiah 31:33).

Famous Namesakes: Jeremiah Birnbaum, Jerry Lee Lewis, singers/songwriters; Jeremy Brett, Jeremy Irons, Jerry Lewis, Jerry O'Connell, Jerry Orbach, actors; Jeremiah Dixon, surveyor/astronomer; Jeremiah Trotter, football player.

JERIAH ✦ *(jeh-RAI-uh)*
Language/Cultural Origin: Hebrew
Meaning: Taught by Yahweh
Spiritual Connotation: Student of the Lord
Related Names/Nicknames: Jarah, Jerah, Jerry
Alternate Names: None

Background Story: Jeriah was a descendant of Hebron and "chief" of a Levitical house placed in charge of the temple when David handed his power over to Solomon (1 Chronicles 23:19). The name Jeriah suggests a thoughtful man who believes in the value of tradition.

JERIEL ✦ *(JEHR-ee-ehl)* or *(jee-RAI-ehl)*

Language/Cultural Origin: Hebrew

Meaning: Fear of God

Spiritual Connotation: Reverence

Related Names/Nicknames: Jerry

Alternate Names: Jerriel

Background Story: Jeriel was Tola's son from the tribe of Issachar. He and his brothers were "heads of their ancestral houses" and "mighty warriors" (1 Chronicles 7:1–2). Jeriel is a strong name, suggesting a man who knows when to give his power over to the Lord.

JESHER ✦ *(JEE-sher)*

Language/Cultural Origin: Hebrew

Meaning: Upright

Spiritual Connotation: Principled

Related Names/Nicknames: None

Alternate Names: None

Background Story: Jesher was a descendant of Judah, the son of Jacob. He was the first son of his father, Caleb, and his mother, Azubah (1 Chronicles 2:18). The name Jesher implies a man who stands up for his beliefs.

JESSE ✦ *(JEHS-ee)*

Language/Cultural Origin: Hebrew

Meaning: God's Gift

Spiritual Connotation: Fulfillment

Related Names/Nicknames: Jesiah, Jess, Joshua, Yishai

Alternate Names: Jesee, Jessee, Jessey, Jessie, Jessy, Jessye

Background Story: Jesse—the grandson of Ruth and Boaz—lived in Bethlehem. He had eight sons, the youngest of whom was David. When God rejected Saul as king of Israel, he told Samuel, "I will send you to Jesse the Bethlehemite, for I have provided for myself a king among his sons" (1 Samuel 16:1). David was often called "the son of Jesse," and Isaiah spoke of him in his prophecy about the Messiah: "A shoot shall come out from the stump of Jesse, and a branch shall grow out of his roots" (Isaiah 11:1). Jesse's name in the genealogy of Jesus is proof that Isaiah's prophecy was fulfilled (Matthew 1:5).

Of Interest: Jesse has ranked among the top one hundred names for boys in the United States since 1970.

Famous Namesakes: Jesse Chisholm, explorer; Jesse Cook, musician; Jesse Jackson, human-rights activist; Jesse Malin, Jesse McCartney, vocalists; Jesse Owens, Olympic gold medalist in track and field; Jesse Ventura, former governor of Minnesota.

JESUS ✦ *(JEE-zuhs)*

Language/Cultural Origin: Hebrew/Greek

Meaning: Savior

Spiritual Connotation: Son of God

Related Names/Nicknames: Isa, Issa, Jehoshua, Jeshua, Jesusa, Josh, Joshawa, Joshua, Josu, Josue, Jozsua, Jozua

Alternate Names: Jesous

Background Story: Jesus—the son of God—is the central figure of the New Testament. The gospels say he was conceived by the Virgin Mary "from the Holy Spirit," born in Bethlehem, and raised by Mary and her husband, Joseph. When Jesus was twelve, his parents found him in Jerusalem's temple, "sitting among the teachers, listening to them and asking them questions," and "were astounded at his understanding" (Luke 2:46–47). His promise came to fruition eighteen years later, when he was baptized by John and selected the men who were to become his apostles. For three full years, Jesus traveled the countryside, teaching God's message and performing such miracles as feeding a crowd of five thousand with five loaves of bread and two fish (Matthew 14:19), healing the sick (Mark 7:36), and bringing the dead back to life (John 11:1–44). Although he attracted numerous followers, the people in power were threatened by his claim that he was the Messiah, and he was turned over to the Roman authorities, who tortured and "crucified him." Three days after his body was buried, his followers found his tomb empty and marveled that he had risen from the dead, as he had prophesied. Jesus appeared to the apostles a few more times before "he blessed them . . . and was carried up into heaven" (Luke 24:50–51).

Of Interest: Christians believe that Jesus is the Messiah who came to redeem the world for its sin, as prophesied in the Old Testament. The name is common in Hispanic cultures, where it is pronounced "hay-SOOS."

Famous Namesakes: Jesús Blasco, writer/illustrator; Jesus Bonilla, actor; Jesus Franco, film director; Jesus Guridi, composer.

JETHRO ◆ *(JEHTH-ro)*

Language/Cultural Origin: Hebrew

Meaning: Excellence

Spiritual Connotation: Wise Counsel

Related Names/Nicknames: Hobab, Jeth, Raguel, Reuel

Alternate Names: Jethroe

Background Story: Jethro was a Midianite priest whose daughter, Zipporah, was married to Moses. While Moses was freeing the Israelites from Egypt, he sent Zipporah and his sons to live with Jethro. After Moses's success, Jethro brought Moses's wife and sons to join him in the wilderness. Aware of the burden Moses had undertaken, Jethro also counseled his son-in-law to set up a system of judges to help him resolve legal disputes. "Let them bring every important case to you, but decide every minor case themselves," Jethro said. "So it will be easier for you, and they will bear the burden with you" (Exodus 3, 18).

Of Interest: Jethro is also called Reuel in the Bible, giving rise to the theory that "Jethro" was Reuel's title and not his name.

Famous Namesakes: Jethro Burns, musician/comedian; Jethro Tull, progressive rock band; Jethro Tull, agriculturist/inventor.

JOACHIM ◆ *(JO-uh-kihm)* or *(wah-KEEM)*

Language/Cultural Origin: Hebrew

Meaning: Founded by God

Spiritual Connotation: Established

Related Names/Nicknames: Akim, Hakim, Jachim, Jakim, Joaquin, Josquin, Yakim

Alternate Names: Ioakim, Joacheim, Joakim, Joaquim

Background Story: The story goes that Joachim and his wife, Anna, had not been blessed with children. Joachim went into the desert for forty days "without food and drink" and prayed that God would give him a child. At the same time, Anna "lamented" that she was not only without child but now a "widow," so she also prayed to the Lord. An angel appeared to both of them and told them that Anna had conceived. Anna gave birth to a girl—Mary—who became the mother of Jesus (Gospel of James).

Of Interest: The name Joachim appears in the apocryphal Gospel of James. It is also the shortened version of the name for two kings of Judah: Jehoiakim and Jehoiachin.

Famous Namesakes: Josquin des Prez, Renaissance composer; Joaquin Miller, poet; Joaquin Phoenix, actor.

JOASH ✦ *(JO-ash)*
Language/Cultural Origin: Hebrew
Meaning: God Has Given
Spiritual Connotation: Sustained by God
Related Names/Nicknames: Joe
Alternate Names: None

Background Story: The most interesting Joash in the Bible was a man of royalty. King Joash of Judah was rescued as an infant from his grandmother Athalia, who held on to the throne by killing all the male heirs. His aunt Jehosheba hid him until he was seven, at which time he was revealed to the palace guards, who "proclaimed him king" and had Athalia killed. Influenced by Jehosheba's husband, who was the high priest, Joash began his rule by destroying the altars of Baal and repairing the temple (2 Kings 11–12).

JOB ✦ *(JOB)*

Language/Cultural Origin: Hebrew

Meaning: He Who Weeps

Spiritual Connotation: Patience

Related Names/Nicknames: Joab, Joby

Alternate Names: Jobe

Background Story: The story of Job in the Bible is the story of human suffering. It all began with an argument between God and Satan. God said about Job, "There is no one like him on the earth, a blameless and upright man who fears God and turns away from evil." Satan argued that Job's goodness was the result of his blessings and challenged God to remove them. Job was faced with a series of trials: His children died, he lost his wealth, and he developed sores all over his body. Job faced his suffering with patience, however, and never lost his faith. It was not possible, he conceded, to truly understand the ways of God. Having made his point, God restored Job's wealth, gave him more children, and allowed him to live to a ripe old age (Book of Job).

JOEL ✦ *(JO-uhl)*

Language/Cultural Origin: Hebrew

Meaning: The Lord Is God

Spiritual Connotation: God's Herald

Related Names/Nicknames: Jole, Shaul, Yoel

Alternate Names: Joell, Joelle

Background Story: One of the many Joels in the Bible was a minor prophet of the Old Testament whose prophecies took place after a plague of locusts in Judah. He called the people to repent and "return to the Lord," who would surely have "pity on his people." In the future, he said, God would see to it that "Judah shall be inhabited forever, and Jerusalem to all generations . . . for the Lord dwells in Zion" (Book of Joel).

Famous Namesakes: Joel Coen, Joel Schumacher, filmmakers; Joel Grey, Joel McCrea, actors; Joel Chandler Harris, writer.

JOHANAN ✦ *(jo-HAY-nuhn)* or *(jo-HAH-nuhn)*

Language/Cultural Origin: Hebrew

Meaning: God Is Gracious

Spiritual Connotation: Gift of Compassion

Related Names/Nicknames: Johann, Johannes, John, Yohanan

Alternate Names: None

Background Story: Johanan was a popular name in the Bible, belonging to a prince, a warrior, a priest, and a hero. Johanan was the oldest son of King Josiah (1 Chronicles 3:15) and one of the "mighty warriors" who defected to David at Ziklag (1 Chronicles 12:4). He was also the leader of an "ancestral house" of Levite priests who returned from captivity in Babylon (Nehemiah 12:23). The last and most heroic Johanan pursued the man who killed the governor of Judah after the Babylonian invasion and saved the people who had been carried off as captives (Jeremiah 40–43).

Of Interest: John is a variation or shortened version of the Hebrew Johanan.

Famous Namesakes: Johann Sebastian Bach, composer; Johanan Herson, painter; Johanan Peltz, World War II Jewish Brigade veteran; Johanan ben Zakkai, Jewish sage.

JOHN ✦ *(JON)* or *(JAHN)*

Language/Cultural Origin: Hebrew/Greek/Latin/English

Meaning: God Is Gracious

Spiritual Connotation: Loved by God

Related Names/Nicknames: Ean, Evan, Ewan, Gianni,
Giovanni, Hank, Hans, Hansel, Ian, Ivan, Ivann, Iwan,
Jack, Jackie, Jackson, Jacky, Jake, Janecek, Janek, Jean,
Johan, Johanan, Johann, Johannes, Johnnie, Johnny,
Jona, Jonathon, Jonnie, Jonny, Jovanni, Juan,
Juanito, Juwan, Sean, Seann, Shane, Shaughn,
Shaun, Shawn, Vanya, Yanni, Zane

Alternate Names: Gian, Gjon, Jaan, Jahn, Jan, Janne,
Jian, Johnn, Jon

Background Story: There are two Johns in the Bible whose stories
are memorable. John the Baptist was Jesus's cousin, a rugged
man who "wore clothing of camel's hair with a leather belt
around his waist" and survived on "locusts and wild honey."
John called for people to "repent" their sins and baptized them
in the Jordan River. When he baptized Jesus, "he saw the Spirit
of God descending like a dove" on him and John knew that
Jesus was the son of God. Later, John's outspoken manner got
him into trouble, and he was imprisoned for criticizing Herod
and his wife. She retaliated by having her daughter ask for
John's head "on a platter" as a reward for dancing before Herod
and his guests (Matthew 3, 14). The second John was the brother
of James and one of Jesus's apostles. Jesus called the brothers
"sons of thunder" because of their zeal and fiery tempera-
ments. John had a special relationship with Jesus and is frequently referred to as "the disciple he loved." He witnessed
Christ's transfiguration, was present for many of his miracles,
and even stood by at the crucifixion. As Jesus was dying, he saw
John standing next to Mary, his mother, and said, "Woman,
here is your son," and John took Mary "into his own home." He

was an early leader of the Christian Church in Jerusalem, where he worked with Peter (Matthew 10, 17; Mark 3; John 19, 21; Acts 3:1; Galatians 2:9).

Of Interest: Tradition has it that John the Apostle is the author of the fourth gospel, three epistles, and the Book of Revelation. Some authorities credit John the Evangelizer, and others believe they are one and the same man. For the last century, the name John has ranked from one to seventeen in popularity as a name for boys in the United States.

Famous Namesakes: John Adams, John Quincy Adams, John Kennedy, John Tyler, U.S. presidents; John Barrymore, John Cusack, Johnny Depp, John Gielgud, John Wayne, actors; John Donne, John Milton, poets; John Elway, football player; John Grisham, novelist; John Lennon, John Williams, composers; John Locke, philosopher.

JONAH ✦ *(JO-nuh)*

Language/Cultural Origin: Hebrew

Meaning: Dove

Spiritual Connotation: Peaceful

Related Names/Nicknames: Jonas, Jonasco, Jonie, Yonah

Alternate Names: Jona

Background Story: Jonah was a prophet in Galilee during the reign of Jereboam (2 Kings 14:25). When he tried to avoid God's command to "cry out against" the city of Nineveh by taking a ship in the other direction, a violent storm arose. The sailors threw Jonah overboard and he was swallowed by an enormous fish, in whose belly he prayed for three days and nights. The fish eventually "spewed Jonah out on dry land," and he went to Nineveh to prophesy its destruction. To Jonah's surprise, the people of Nineveh repented and God decided not to destroy them. When Jonah criticized God for having mercy on Nineveh, God taught him a lesson. He grew a bush to give Jonah shade, then promptly allowed a worm to destroy it. Jonah became angry, and the Lord pointed out that Jonah's concern for the bush was nothing compared to his concern for "Nineveh, the great city" (Book of Jonah).

Of Interest: The Book of Jonah is considered by most scholars to be an allegory or parable and not factual. Jonas is the Greek form of Jonah.

Famous Namesakes: Jonas Björkman, tennis player; Jonah Lomu, rugby player; Jonas Salk, developer of the polio vaccine.

JONATHAN   *(JON-uh-thuhn)*

Language/Cultural Origin: Hebrew

Meaning: Gift from God

Spiritual Connotation: Faithful Friend

Related Names/Nicknames: John, Jon, Jonatan, Jonny, Jonty, Nat, Natan, Nate, Nathan

Alternate Names: Johnathan, Johnathon, Jonathon

Background Story: Of the fifteen or more Jonathans in the Bible, one deserves special mention. Jonathan, the oldest son of Saul, was a superb archer and a commander in his father's army, which defeated the Philistines in more than one battle. More important, he was a good friend of David "and loved him as much as he loved himself." Jonathan even warned David of Saul's plan to kill him and helped him escape. When Jonathan later died at the hands of the Philistines, David and his friends "mourned and wept." As a tribute to their friendship, David made sure that Jonathan's son, Mephibosheth, was cared for and "ate at David's table just like one of the king's sons" (1 Samuel 13, 18–20; 2 Samuel 1, 9).

Of Interest: Since 1980, Jonathan has been among the top twenty-five names for boys in the United States.

Famous Namesakes: Jonathan Edwards, reporter; Jonathan Swift, writer; Jonathan Taylor Thomas, Jon Voight, actors.

JORDAN ✦ *(JAWR-dn)* or *(JOR-duhn)*

Language/Cultural Origin: Hebrew

Meaning: River of Judgment

Spiritual Connotation: Anointed

Related Names/Nicknames: Giordano, Jared, Jarod, Jarred, Jarrod, Jerad, Jerred, Jerrod, Joord, Jordell, Jordi, Jordy, Jori, Jory, Jud, Judd, Yarden, Yordan

Alternate Names: Jordaan, Jordain, Jorden, Jordin, Jordon, Jordyn, Jourdain, Jourdan

Background Story: Jordan is the name of a river in the Bible and the valley through which it passes. Lot settled in the plain of Jordan, which was "well watered everywhere, like the garden of the Lord" (Genesis 13:10). When the Israelites crossed the Jordan into the Promised Land, the waters rose up and they crossed "on dry ground" (Joshua 3:17). The Jordan also marked the beginning of Jesus's ministry. It was there that John baptized him and "saw the Spirit of God descending like a dove" on him (Matthew 3:16).

Of Interest: The Jordan River flows between Jordan and Israel today and forms much of the boundary between the two countries.

Famous Namesakes: Jordan Bridges, actor; Jordan Knight, singer; Jordan Rudess, musician/composer.

> **JOSEPH** ✦ *(JO-sehf)* or *(JO-suhf)* or *(JO-zuhf)*
>
> *Language/Cultural Origin:* Hebrew/Arabic
>
> *Meaning:* God Will Add
>
> *Spiritual Connotation:* Righteous
>
> *Related Names/Nicknames:* Giuseppe, Iosef, Iosif, Jessop, Jessup, Jo, Jodi, Jodie, Jody, Joe, Joey, Joop, Joos, Jose, Joseito, Josep, Josephus, Josif, Josip, Joss, Josue, Pepe, Pepito, Peppi, Pino, Pipo, Sepp, Seppi, Yosef, Yousef, Yusif, Yussuf, Yusuf
>
> *Alternate Names:* Josef, Josephe, Joszef, Jozef

Background Story: Three men stand out among the Josephs in the Bible. Joseph was Rachel's first son and the favorite of his father, Jacob. His brothers were jealous and sold him into slavery in Egypt, telling their father he had been killed by a wild animal. Joseph, however, could interpret dreams, and Pharaoh had a dream that was puzzling him. Joseph interpreted his dream as a prediction of a future famine and "became a successful man" helping Pharaoh prepare for it. In time, Joseph reconciled with his brothers, reunited with his father, and moved the entire family to Egypt. Joseph's sons, Manasseh and Ephraim, were the ancestors of two of Israel's twelve tribes (Genesis 30, 37, 39–48).

Another biblical Joseph was the husband of Mary, the mother of Jesus. He was a carpenter by trade and a "righteous man" who married the pregnant Mary at the Lord's request and raised Jesus as his own son (Matthew 1, 13:55). The final one is Joseph of Arimathea, a member of the Jewish Sanhedrin and a disciple of Jesus. After Jesus died, Joseph "boldly" asked Pilate for his body. He bought a linen cloth, then took down his body, "wrapped it in the linen cloth, and laid it in a tomb that had been hewn out of the rock" (Mark 15:43–46).

Famous Namesakes: Joseph Biden, Joe Lieberman, U.S. senators; Joseph Campbell, mythologist; Joseph Conrad, Joseph Heller, Joseph Wambaugh, writers; Joseph Fiennes, Josef Sommer, actors; Joseph Priestley, chemist; Joseph Pulitzer, publisher; Joseph Ratzinger, newly elected Pope Benedict XVI; Joseph M. W. Turner, artist.

JOSHUA ✦ *(JAWSH-oo-uh)* or *(JAWSH-yoo-uh)*

Language/Cultural Origin: Hebrew

Meaning: The Lord Is My Salvation

Spiritual Connotation: Bold Leader

Related Names/Nicknames: Hoshea, Jehoshua, Jeshua, Jeshuah, Jesus, Josh, Joshe, Joss, Josua, Josue, Oshea, Yehoshua

Alternate Names: Joshuah, Joshuwa, Joushua, Jozua

Background Story: Joshua, son of Nun, was the man chosen by God to succeed Moses as the leader of the twelve tribes. The Lord commissioned Joshua himself: "Be strong and bold, for you shall bring the Israelites into the land that I promised them; I will be with you" (Deuteronomy 31:23). His past had prepared him for it. He had participated in the Exodus, accompanied Moses on Mount Sinai, and assisted him for forty years in the wilderness. When the Israelites crossed the Jordan into the Promised Land, God gave them a sign that he was with them. The waters from above were "cut off" and the entire nation crossed on dry land. On the other side, Joshua's armies quickly took control, beginning with the famous battle of Jericho. Over the years, he defeated a number of kings and nations until Israel was in charge at last. Joshua then divided the country among the twelve tribes as God and Moses had instructed him (Book of Joshua).

Of Interest: Since 1980, Joshua has been one of the five most popular names for boys in the United States.

Famous Namesakes: Josh Beckett, baseball player; Joshua Bell, violinist; Josh Hartnett, Josh Lucas, actors; Joshua Logan, director; Joshua Reynolds, artist.

JOSIAH *(jo-SAI-uh)* or *(jo-ZAI-uh)*
Language/Cultural Origin: Hebrew
Meaning: Fire of the Lord
Spiritual Connotation: Pious
Related Names/Nicknames: Jed, Josias
Alternate Names: Josia, Josya, Josyah, Joziah

Background Story: Josiah, the son of King Amon and Jedidah, was only eight years old when he began to reign in Judah. He was a religious reformer who discovered Moses's book of the law during the temple restoration. When Josiah read it, he was alarmed to see how far his people had fallen from the Lord and "tore his clothes." After consulting with the prophetess Huldah, he purged the land of its pagan priests and idols and destroyed all their places of worship. He then made a new covenant with God and held the first Passover festival "since the days of the judges who judged Israel." His piety earned him these biblical words of praise: "Before him there was no king like him, who turned to the Lord with all his heart, with all his soul, and with all his might, according to all the law of Moses; nor did any like him arise after him" (2 Kings 22–23).

Famous Namesakes: Josiah Bartlet, character played by Martin Sheen on the television series, *The West Wing;* Josiah Bartlett, signer of the Declaration of Independence; Josiah Wedgwood, British potter.

JOTHAM ✦ *(JOH-thuhm)* or *(JO-thuhm)*

Language/Cultural Origin: Hebrew

Meaning: Perfection of the Lord

Spiritual Connotation: Justice

Related Names/Nicknames: None

Alternate Names: Jothem, Jothym

Background Story: There are two Jothams of note in the Bible. The first was the only one of Gideon's seventy sons to escape death at the hands of their brother, Abimelech, who wanted to be king. Before fleeing, Jotham called out a parable about the bramble who was asked to be king over the trees: "If in good faith you are anointing me king over you, then come and take refuge," the bramble said, "but if not, let fire come out . . . and devour the cedars of Lebanon." His words prophesied the violence to come during Abimelech's unjust reign (Judges 9:1–57). The second Jotham was Uzziah's son, who governed Judah during his father's illness and ruled as king after his death. Like his father, he was an enthusiastic builder and constructed numerous towers, forts, and cities. Jotham was a strong king "because he ordered his ways before the Lord" (2 Chronicles 27:1–9). His name is also found in the genealogy of Jesus (Matthew 1:9).

JUDAH ✦ *(JOO-duh)*

Language/Cultural Origin: Hebrew

Meaning: The Praise of the Lord

Spiritual Connotation: Chosen Leader

Related Names/Nicknames: Jody, Jud, Judas, Judd, Jude

Alternate Names: Juda

Background Story: The first Judah in the Bible is the most prominent. He was Jacob and Leah's fourth son—called Judah because his mother said at his birth, "This time I will praise the Lord." Judah and Reuben were the only ones to speak against killing their younger brother Joseph. Years later, when they encountered Joseph in Egypt, he acted as their spokesperson. Because of his older brothers' sins, Judah received his father's blessing, usually reserved for the firstborn son. Jacob said, "Judah, your brothers shall praise you; your hand shall be on the neck of your enemies; your father's sons shall bow down before you." Judah was the patriarch of the most powerful of Israel's twelve tribes, which eventually became the kingdom of Judah (Genesis 29, 37, 44, 49).

Of Interest: Judah's descendants include David and Jesus, as well as the entire Jewish people (Matthew 1:3).

JUDE ✦ *(JOOD)*

Language/Cultural Origin: Hebrew/Latin

Meaning: The Praise of the Lord

Spiritual Connotation: Standing Firm

Related Names/Nicknames: Jud, Judah, Judas, Judd, Judsen, Judson

Alternate Names: None

Background Story: In his own words, Jude was "a servant of Jesus Christ and brother of James" in the New Testament. He wrote a letter warning Christians to be wary of false teachers "who pervert the grace of our God." According to Jude, these were "worldly people, devoid of the Spirit" and "causing divisions." He urged his readers to "pray in the Holy Spirit" and "look forward to the mercy of our Lord Jesus Christ that leads to eternal life" (Jude 1:1–25).

Of Interest: Jude is considered by some to be Christ's younger brother. Others believe he was the apostle Jude—or Thaddeus—the brother of James. The apostle Jude (*not* Judas Iscariot) is honored as the patron saint of hopeless situations in the Catholic Church.

Famous Namesakes: Jude Cole, singer/songwriter; Jude Law, actor.

JULIUS ✦ *(JOOL-yuhs)* or *(JOO-lee-uhs)*

Language/Cultural Origin: Greek/Latin

Meaning: Soft-haired

Spiritual Connotation: Considerate

Related Names/Nicknames: Giulio, Jolyon, Jule, Julee, Jules, Juley, Juli, Julian, Juliano, Julianus, Julien, Julio, July, Julyan

Alternate Names: Julias

Background Story: A Roman centurion named Julius was placed in charge of Paul when he set sail for Rome as a prisoner. On the voyage, "Julius treated Paul kindly," showing him the respect that was common between Roman citizens. When the ship was run aground by a violent storm, the soldiers on board planned "to kill the prisoners, so that none might swim away and escape." Julius, "wishing to save Paul," stopped them and made certain that everyone was brought to shore (Acts 27).

Famous Namesakes: Julius Axelrod, Nobel Prize winner in medicine; Julius Erving, Hall of Fame basketball player; Jules Feiffer, playwright; Julio Iglesias, Julius La Rosa, singers; Jules Verne, writer.

JUSTUS ✦ *(JUHS-tuhs)*

Language/Cultural Origin: Latin

Meaning: Just

Spiritual Connotation: Safe Haven

Related Names/Nicknames: Giostino, Giusto, Joos, Joost, Just, Justain, Justan, Juste, Justen, Justin, Justinas, Justinian, Justinius, Justino, Justinus, Justo, Justyn

Alternate Names: Justice, Justis, Justyce

Background Story: Three of Christ's followers in the Bible were called Justus. After Jesus's ascension, the apostles considered Joseph Barsabbas, "also known as Justus," a possible replacement for Judas Iscariot (Acts 1:23). Titius Justus was "a worshipper of God" whom Paul visited in Corinth (Acts 18:7); and "Jesus who is called Justus" was a fellow Jew and coworker who had "been a comfort" to Paul (Colossians 4:11).

Of Interest: Justus is the name of a saint in the Catholic Church.

KEDAR ✦ *(KEE-dahr)* or *(KEE-der)*

Language/Cultural Origin: Hebrew/Arabic

Meaning: Blackness

Spiritual Connotation: Spiritual Traveler

Related Names/Nicknames: None

Alternate Names: Kadar, Kadir, Keder, Qadar, Qadir

Background Story: Kedar was the second son of Ishmael, whom Abraham sent away after the birth of Jacob (Genesis 25:13). He was prince of the eastern tribe of Kedar, who lived in tents and were "favored dealers in lambs, rams, and goats" (Ezekiel 27:21). Solomon's bride described herself as "black and beautiful . . . like the tents of Kedar" (Song of Solomon 1:5).

Of Interest: Kedar was an ancestor of the prophet Mohammed. The meaning of the name in Arabic is "strong" or "powerful."

KENAN ✦ *(KEE-nuhn)*

Language/Cultural Origin: Hebrew

Meaning: Acquire

Spiritual Connotation: Accomplished

Related Names/Nicknames: Cain, Cainan, Cian, Kain, Kainan

Alternate Names: Keenan

Background Story: Kenan was the son of Enosh and great-grandson of Adam. "When he had lived seventy years, he became the father of Mahalalel." Kenan had other sons and daughters and died at the age of "nine hundred and ten years" (Genesis 5:9–14). The name Kenan suggests a man with all the qualities necessary for success.

Famous Namesakes: Kenan Derson, Kenan Thompson, Keenen Ivory Wayans, Keenan Wynn, actors; Kenan Malik, writer.

LABAN ✦ *(LAY-ban)* or *(LAY-buhn)*

Language/Cultural Origin: Hebrew

Meaning: White

Spiritual Connotation: Glorious

Related Names/Nicknames: Lavan

Alternate Names: None

Background Story: Laban was Bethuel's son and Rebekah's brother who agreed to his sister's marriage to Isaac. Years later, Isaac's son Jacob went to his uncle's house to avoid the wrath of his twin brother, Esau. Laban's daughters, Leah and Rachel, became Jacob's wives and had eight of his children. Laban took full advantage of his nephew Jacob. He tricked him into marrying his older daughter first and worked him long and hard as manager of his flocks. When Jacob fled with his family, Laban pursued them. But God warned Laban, "Take heed that you say not a word to Jacob, either good or bad." So Laban made a covenant with Jacob and left in peace (Genesis 24, 28–31).

LAMECH ✦ *(LAY-mehk)* or *(LEH-mehk)*

Language/Cultural Origin: Hebrew

Meaning: Powerful

Spiritual Connotation: Strength in the Lord

Related Names/Nicknames: None

Alternate Names: Lemech

Background Story: The two Lamechs in the Bible were as different as night and day. One was a fierce descendant of Cain who bragged he had "killed a man for wounding" him. He was the first man in the Bible to have two wives, Adah and Zillah. His sons—Jabal, Jubal, and Tubal-cain—were the ancestors of shepherds, musicians, and metalworkers (Genesis 4:19–24). The other was the son of Methuselah—the oldest man in the Bible—and the father of Noah. When his son was born, Lamech expressed his prayerful hope for the future: "This one shall bring us relief from our work and from the toil of our hands" (Genesis 5:25–31).

LAZARUS ✦ *(LAZ-uh-ruhs)*

Language/Cultural Origin: Latin/Greek/Hebrew

Meaning: God Is My Help

Spiritual Connotation: New Life

Related Names/Nicknames: Lazar, Lazare, Lazaro, Lazear, Lazer, Lazzaro

Alternate Names: Lazaros

Background Story: The name Lazarus belongs to two men in the Bible, one real and one fictional. In a parable, Jesus told about a rich man "who feasted sumptuously every day" and Lazarus, a poor man "who longed to satisfy his hunger with what fell from the rich man's table." After death, the rich man found—too late—their roles were reversed: While Lazarus was now "comforted," the rich man had to suffer (Luke 16:19–31). The real Lazarus lived in Bethany with his two sisters, Martha and Mary. They were close friends of Jesus, who visited their home often. One day, Jesus received an urgent message from the sisters: "Lord, he whom you love is ill." By the time Jesus arrived, Lazarus was dead and buried. Jesus was moved by the grief of the two women and asked to be taken to the tomb. He ordered the stone turned aside and cried, "Lazarus, come out!" To the amazement of all, Lazarus walked out of the tomb (John 11:1–44).

Of Interest: A poem by Emma Lazarus is inscribed on the pedestal of the Statue of Liberty. Her famous words—"Give me your tired, your poor / Your huddled masses yearning to breathe free"—have inspired generations of immigrants to the United States.

LEVI ◆ *(LEE-vai)* or *(LEE-vee)*

Language/Cultural Origin: Hebrew

Meaning: Joined

Spiritual Connotation: In God's Service

Related Names/Nicknames: Levin, Levon

Alternate Names: Leevi, Levey, Levy

Background Story: In the Old Testament, Levi was Leah's third son by Jacob. Hoping to replace her sister, Rachel, as Jacob's favorite, Leah called him Levi. "Now this time my husband will be joined to me," she said, "because I have borne him three sons." As an adult, Levi reacted strongly when his sister, Dinah, was "defiled" by a Hivite man. He and his brother Simeon killed all the Hivites in revenge. Because his sons had caused trouble for him, Jacob refused them his deathbed blessing (Genesis 29, 34, 49). Levi, however, was redeemed by his descendants, Moses and Aaron. Beginning with them, the Levite tribe would forever serve the house of the Lord (Deuteronomy 10:8). In the New Testament, Levi was Matthew's given name before he became an apostle. When Jesus first saw him, he said, "Follow me." And Levi "got up and followed him" (Mark 2:14).

Famous Namesakes: Levi Coffin, "president" of the Underground Railroad; Levi P. Morton, U.S. vice president; Levi Strauss, clothing manufacturer; Levi Woodbury, U.S. Supreme Court justice.

LINUS ✦ *(LAI-nuhs)*

Language/Cultural Origin: Greek

Meaning: Flax

Spiritual Connotation: True Friend

Related Names/Nicknames: Lino

Alternate Names: Linas, Linos

Background Story: Paul mentioned Linus in his second letter to Timothy from Rome. Linus was a fellow Christian who did not desert Paul, as others had. In the same letter, Paul told Timothy that his end was near. "I have fought the good fight, I have finished the race, I have kept the faith," he said (2 Timothy 4:7, 21).

Of Interest: Paul's friend Linus is often identified with Pope Linus, the saint who was the second pope of the Catholic Church.

Famous Namesakes: Linus Pauling, Nobel Prize winner for chemistry and peace; Linus Roache, actor; Linus Torvalds, developer of the Linux computer operating system.

LOT ✦ *(LAHT)*

Language/Cultural Origin: Hebrew

Meaning: Covered

Spiritual Connotation: Protected

Related Names/Nicknames: None

Alternate Names: Lott

Background Story: Lot was the son of Haran, Abraham's brother. When Haran died young, Abraham took his nephew under his wing. Lot shared Abraham's nomadic life until their herds became so large, they had to separate. Lot chose to live in "the plain of the Jordan" near the city of Sodom. One day, God told Abraham of his plan to destroy the cities of Sodom and Gomorrah for their wickedness. Abraham convinced the Lord to seek the "righteous" first, but Lot was the only man to prove his innocence. God's angels warned him to flee the city with his family, adding this caution: "Do not look back . . . or else you will be consumed." Lot's family escaped, but his wife looked back and "was turned into a pillar of salt" (Genesis 11–13, 18–19).

LUCAS ✦ *(LOO-kuhs)*

Language/Cultural Origin: Greek

Meaning: Luminous

Spiritual Connotation: Radiant

Related Names/Nicknames: Luc, Luca, Lucasta, Luce, Lucius, Lucky, Luka, Lukacs, Luke, Lukey

Alternate Names: Loucas, Loukas, Lucais, Lukas, Lukasz, Luukas

Background Story: Lucas was one of Paul's "fellow labourers" during a period of imprisonment. Paul mentions him in a letter telling Philemon about his runaway slave who became a follower of Christ (Philemon 1:24). The name Lucas suggests a man whose presence brings light to the darkest moments.

Of Interest: It is possible that Lucas is the same man as Luke, the author of the third gospel and the Acts of the Apostles.

Famous Namesakes: Lucas Belvaux, film director; Lucas Black, Lukas Haas, actors; Lucas van Leyden, painter and engraver; George Lucas, writer/director/producer.

LUCIUS ✦ *(LOO-shee-uhs)* or *(LOO-shuhs)*

Language/Cultural Origin: Latin

Meaning: Luminous

Spiritual Connotation: Heaven's Light

Related Names/Nicknames: Lucian, Luciano

Alternate Names: Lucas, Luke

Background Story: Lucius is the name of two early Christians in the Bible. Lucius of Cyrene was among the "prophets and teachers" at Antioch who sent Saul and Barnabas out as missionaries (Acts 13:1). The other Lucius was Paul's "relative" whose greetings he sends from Corinth to the Christian community in Rome (Romans 16:21). The name is a reminder of the early Christians who risked it all to bring God's light into the world.

Famous Namesakes: Lucius Beebe, writer; Lucian Freud, artist; Lucius Quintus Cincinnatus Lamar, U.S. Supreme Court justice; Luciano Pavarotti, singer.

LUKE ✦ *(LOOK)*

Language/Cultural Origin: Greek

Meaning: Luminous

Spiritual Connotation: Enlightened

Related Names/Nicknames: Loukas, Luca, Lucais, Lucas, Lucasta, Luce, Lucian, Lucien, Lucio, Lucius, Luck, Lucky, Luka, Lukacs, Lukas, Lukasz, Lukey

Alternate Names: Luc, Luk

Background Story: Luke is one of the most influential men in the New Testament, though his name is mentioned only twice. Paul wrote that "Luke, the beloved physician," sent his greetings to the "faithful brothers and sisters in Christ in Colossae" (Colossians 1:2, 4:14), and when Paul believed that his end was approaching and other friends had deserted him, he wrote to Timothy from Rome, "Only Luke is with me" (2 Timothy 4:11).

Of Interest: Luke's reputation comes from the tradition that he is the author of the third gospel, as well as the Acts of the Apostles. In the Catholic Church, he is honored as the patron saint of doctors and artists.

Famous Namesakes: Luke Appling, baseball player; Luke Perry, Luke Wilson, actors; Luke Powell, photographer; Luke Skywalker, fictional character in *Star Wars* series.

MALACHI ✦ *(MAL-uh-kai)* or *(MAL-uh-kee)*
Language/Cultural Origin: Hebrew
Meaning: Messenger of God
Spiritual Connotation: Word of the Lord
Related Names/Nicknames: Malaquias
Alternate Names: Malachai, Malachie, Malachy, Malakai, Malaki, Malakia, Malakie, Malechy, Maleki, Malequi

Background Story: Malachi is a minor prophet and the author of the last book in the Old Testament. In his writing, he denounced the priests of his time for neglecting their sacred duties. He urged the Jewish people to obey Moses's law and remain faithful to the Lord's covenant. Malachi also prophesied the coming of John the Baptist and the arrival of the Messiah: "I am sending my messenger to prepare the way before me, and the Lord whom you seek will suddenly come to his temple. The messenger of the covenant in whom you delight" (Book of Malachi).

Famous Namesakes: Malachi Favors, musician; Malachi Martin, writer; Malachy McCourt, writer/entertainer; Malachi Throne, actor.

    MANAEN ✦ *(MAN-ee-uhn)* or *(MAN-ay-ehn)*
    Language/Cultural Origin: Hebrew/Greek
    Meaning: Consoler
    Spiritual Connotation: Compassionate
    Related Names/Nicknames: Manny, Menahem
    Alternate Names: None

Background Story: Manaen, a member of Herod's court, was one of the "prophets and teachers" in Antioch, who ordained Saul and Barnabas to be missionaries for the church (Acts 13:1–2). Manaen is an unusual name, suggesting a man who will never ignore a friend in need.

Of Interest: Manaen is an example of the many educated Gentiles of the first century who were actively involved in the early Christian Church.

    MANASSEH ✦ *(muh-NAS-uh)*
    Language/Cultural Origin: Hebrew
    Meaning: Causing to Forget
    Spiritual Connotation: Soothing Spirit
    Related Names/Nicknames: Manases, Manassas, Manasses, Menashe, Menashi
    Alternate Names: None

Background Story: Manasseh was one of Joseph's two sons and the grandson of Jacob. At his birth, his father said, "God has made me forget all my hardship and all my father's house" and named his son Manasseh (Genesis 41:51). When Jacob was dying, Joseph brought Manasseh and his younger brother, Ephraim, to visit their grandfather. Jacob claimed the boys as his own sons and gave them his deathbed blessing. Manasseh "shall be great," he said, but he added that the "younger brother shall be greater" (Genesis 48:1–24). Manasseh and Ephraim were the patriarchs of two of Israel's twelve tribes.

MANOAH ✦ *(muh-NO-uh)*

Language/Cultural Origin: Hebrew

Meaning: Rest

Spiritual Connotation: Man of Peace

Related Names/Nicknames: None

Alternate Names: Manoa, Manoach

Background Story: Manoah, a native of Zorah, had a wife who was barren. One day, an "angel of the Lord" visited her and said that she would "conceive and bear a son." With the good news came a warning. The angel said, "No razor is to come on his head, for the boy shall be a Nazirite to God from birth. It is he who shall begin to deliver Israel from the hand of the Philistines." A son was born to Manoah and his wife, and they named him Samson (Judges 13:1–25).

Of Interest: Nazirite were people who were consecrated to the Lord. One of the vows they took was not to cut their hair. Samson is the first Nazirite mentioned in the Bible.

MARK ✦ *(MAHRK)*

Language/Cultural Origin: Latin

Meaning: Polite

Spiritual Connotation: Servant of God

Related Names/Nicknames: Marcas, Marcel, Marcello, Marcellus, Marcelo, Marciano, Marcio, Marco, Marcos, Marcus, Marek, Mario, Marius, Marke, Markell, Marko, Markos, Markov, Markus, Marqes, Marques, Marquez, Marqui, Marquis, Martin, Marx

Alternate Names: Marc, Marq, Marque

Background Story: Mark—also known as John—and his mother were active members of the church in Jerusalem. Peter referred to him as "my son Mark" and went directly "to the house of Mary, the mother of John whose other name was Mark" following his miraculous escape from prison. Mark, who was a cousin of Barnabas, joined him and Paul on their first missionary journey. After a while, Mark and Paul parted ways because of a disagreement, and Mark returned to Jerusalem. They apparently reconciled, as Mark became one of Paul's "fellow workers" while he was imprisoned in Rome (1 Peter 5:13; Acts 12:12, 13:13; Colossians 4:10; Philemon 1:24).

Of Interest: Mark is traditionally considered the author of the second gospel. In the Catholic Church, he is the patron saint of Venice; in Eastern and Coptic tradition, he was the first pope of Alexandria. The name peaked in the 1960s, when it was the sixth most popular for boys in the United States.

Famous Namesakes: Mark Hamill, Mark Harmon, actors; Marc Jacobs, fashion designer; Mark McGwire, Mark Prior, baseball players; Mark Morris, choreographer; Marco Polo, explorer; Mark Spitz, swimmer; Mark Twain, pen name of writer Samuel Clemens.

MATTHEW ✦ *(MATH-yoo)*

Language/Cultural Origin: Hebrew

Meaning: Gift of God

Spiritual Connotation: Transformed by the Lord

Related Names/Nicknames: Mat, Mata, Mateo, Mateus, Mateusz, Mathe, Mathian, Mathias, Matias, Matico, Mats, Matt, Mattaeus, Mattaus, Matteo, Matthaios, Matthaus, Mattheus, Matthias, Mattias, Mattie, Mattieu, Matty, Matvey, Matyas, Matz

Alternate Names: Matheu, Mathew, Mathieu, Matthieu, Matthiew

Background Story: Matthew, "the tax collector," was one of Jesus's Twelve Apostles. When Jesus first saw him, he said, "Follow me," and Matthew did. Later, Jesus and his disciples had dinner at Matthew's house, where they were joined by "many tax collectors and sinners." The Pharisees questioned Jesus about the company he kept, and he replied, "Those who are well have no need of a physician. . . . I have come to call not the righteous but sinners" (Matthew 9:9–13).

Of Interest: According to tradition, Matthew—whose original name was Levi—is the author of the first gospel. He is also a saint in the Catholic Church. From 2002 to 2004, it was the fourth most popular name for boys in the United States.

Famous Namesakes: Matthew Arnold, poet; Mathew Brady, photographer; Matthew Broderick, Matt Damon, Matt LeBlanc, Matthew McConaughey, Matthew Perry, actors; Matt Groening, cartoonist; Matthew Sweet, musician; Mats Wilander, tennis player.

MATTHIAS ✦ *(muh-THAI-uhs)*

Language/Cultural Origin: Hebrew

Meaning: Gift of God

Spiritual Connotation: Chosen by God

Related Names/Nicknames: Matias, Matt,
Matthew, Mattias

Alternate Names: Mathias, Matthaios, Matthiaos

Background Story: After the crucifixion, the apostles needed to find a replacement for Judas Iscariot. According to Peter, he had to be selected from a group of men who had been followers of Christ "from the baptism of John until the day when he was taken up from us." Two were proposed: Matthias and Joseph called Barsabbas. The apostles prayed and cast their lots. "The lot fell on Matthias; and he was added to the eleven apostles" (Acts 1:21–26).

Of Interest: The Catholic and Eastern Orthodox Churches honor Matthias as a saint.

Famous Namesakes: Matthias Grunewald, Renaissance painter.

MICAH ✦ *(MAI-kuh)*

Language/Cultural Origin: Hebrew

Meaning: Humble

Spiritual Connotation: Reverent

Related Names/Nicknames: Micaiah, Michael,
Mikal, Mike, Mikey

Alternate Names: Mica, Micha, Michah, Mycah

Background Story: Of the numerous Micahs in the Bible, the most inspired is Micah of Moresheth. Although little is known about this minor prophet and contemporary of Isaiah, his words can still be read. Micah's prophesies foretold the fall of Jerusalem but added that "in days to come" people would once again "stream" to the Lord's house. Micah also predicted the coming of the Messiah: "O Bethlehem . . . from you shall come forth . . . one who is to rule in Israel . . . he shall be great to the ends of the earth; and he shall be the one of peace" (Book of Micah).

Famous Namesakes: Micah Bowie, baseball player; Micah Knorr, football player; Micah Wright, writer/animator.

MICHAEL ✦ *(MAI-kuhl)*

Language/Cultural Origin: Hebrew

Meaning: Who Is Like God

Spiritual Connotation: Defender of God's People

Related Names/Nicknames: Micha, Michaelangelo, Michelangelo, Michele, Mickey, Micky, Miguel, Mihail, Mihaly, Mike, Mikey, Mikhalis, Mikhos, Miko, Miky, Miles, Millo, Milo, Mischa, Misha, Mitch, Mitchell

Alternate Names: Micael, Mical, Michail, Michal, Micheal, Michel, Michiel, Mikael, Mikel, Mikell, Mikhail, Mikkel, Mikol, Miquel, Mychael, Mychal, Mykal, Mykel, Mykell

Background Story: Michael, a popular name in the Old Testament, is best known for the archangel who was Israel's champion. Daniel is told in a vision, "Michael, the great prince, the protector of your people, shall arise" and "your people shall be delivered" (Daniel 12:1); Jude said "the archangel Michael contended with the devil and disputed about the body of Moses" (Jude 1:9); and in John's vision of the end, "Michael and his angels fought against the dragon" who was defeated (Revelation 12:7–8).

Of Interest: Michael is the patron saint of soldiers in the Catholic Church. For half a century, it has been the first or second most popular name for boys in the United States.

Famous Namesakes: Michelangelo Buonarroti, artist; Michael Caine, Michael Douglas, Michael J. Fox, Mike Myers, Mickey Rooney, actors; Michael Faraday, chemist/physicist; Mikhail Gorbachev, former Russian premier; Mick Jagger, singer; Michael Jordan, basketball player; Mickey Mantle, baseball player.

MISHAEL   *(MIHSH-ay-ehl)*

Language/Cultural Origin: Aramaic

Meaning: Who Is Like God

Spiritual Connotation: Supporter

Related Names/Nicknames: Meshach

Alternate Names: None

Background Story: There are three Mishaels in the Bible: Aaron's cousin, ordered by Moses to carry away the bodies of Aaron's sons, who had been consumed by the "unholy fire" they offered the Lord (Leviticus 10:4); a supporter of Ezra as he read aloud "the book of the law of Moses" (Nehemiah 8:4); and one of three Israelite princes in the court of Nebuchadnezzar. Renamed Mesach, Mishael and his companions were thrown into a "furnace of blazing fire" for refusing to worship pagan gods. With the help of an angel, all three walked out unharmed (Daniel 1:7).

MORDECAI ✦ *(MOR-duh-kai)*

Language/Cultural Origin: Hebrew/Aramaic/Persian

Meaning: Contrition

Spiritual Connotation: Integrity

Related Names/Nicknames: Mordy, Mort, Motel, Motke

Alternate Names: Mordechai, Mordikai

Background Story: Mordecai was a Jew living in Susa during the Babylonian captivity. His beautiful cousin Esther, whom he had raised "as his own daughter," was taken into the king's harem and later crowned queen—although she did not reveal she was a Jew. Meanwhile, Haman, the king's highest official, noticed that Mordecai did not show him the proper respect whenever he passed. When Haman learned that Mordecai was a Jew, he "plotted to destroy all the Jews" in the kingdom. News of the plot reached Mordecai, who asked Esther to entreat the king "for her people." The king was happy to grant her request and the Jews were saved. Mordecai was given a position of honor and Haman was "hanged on the gallows that he had prepared for Mordecai" (Book of Esther).

Of Interest: The Jewish feast of Purim commemorates the deliverance of the Jews by Esther and Mordecai.

Famous Namesakes: Mordecai Brown, Hall of Fame baseball player; Mordecai Gorelik, scenic designer; Mordecai Richler, writer.

MOREH ✦ *(MOR-eh)* or *(MO-ray)* or *(MO-ree)*

Language/Cultural Origin: Hebrew

Meaning: Stretching

Spiritual Connotation: Achievement

Related Names/Nicknames: None

Alternate Names: None

Background Story: Moreh was the site of several biblical events in Canaan. It was at "the oak of Moreh" that God appeared to Abraham and promised, "To your offspring I will give this land," inspiring the patriarch to build his first altar there (Genesis 12:6–7); Moses identified "the oak of Moreh" as a landmark in the Promised Land (Deuteronomy 11:30); and "below the hill of Moreh" is where the Midianite army was camped when Gideon attacked them (Judges 7:1). Moreh is an appropriate name for boys who are unafraid to take on new challenges.

Of Interest: Moreh may have derived its name from a Canaanite who once lived there.

MOSES ✦ *(MO-zihz)* or *(MO-zehs)*

Language/Cultural Origin: Hebrew/Egyptian

Meaning: Drawn Out of the Water

Spiritual Connotation: Savior

Related Names/Nicknames: Mioshe, Mioshye, Mo, Moe, Moise, Moisei, Moisis, Mose, Moshe, Mosheh, Mosiah, Mosie, Moss

Alternate Names: Moises, Moyses, Mozes

Background Story: Moses, a descendant of Levi, was born in Egypt during a time of slavery for the Israelites. When Pharaoh decreed that all male Hebrew infants be killed, his mother put him in a basket "and placed it among the reeds on the bank of the river." Pharaoh's daughter discovered him and raised Moses as her own, giving him his name because she "drew him out of the water." As a young man, Moses witnessed an Egyptian beating a Hebrew. He killed the Egyptian and was forced to flee to

Midian, where he met his wife, Zipporah. Also at Midian, God appeared to Moses in a flaming bush and told him to bring the Israelites out of Egypt and take them to "a land flowing with milk and honey." With the help of his brother, Aaron, Moses went to Pharaoh and gave him the Lord's message: "Let my people go." Pharaoh refused at first and treated the Israelites even worse. After a series of plagues were brought down on the Egyptians, however, Pharaoh "summoned Moses" and told him to leave. Moses led his people out of Egypt and into the wilderness, stopping after three months at Mount Sinai, where God delivered his Ten Commandments and the secular and nonsecular orders that became known as "the law of Moses" (Book of Exodus). The Israelites eventually reached their destination. But Moses—their great leader, lawgiver, and prophet—died in the wilderness without ever setting foot in the Promised Land.

Famous Namesakes: Moises Alou, baseball player; Moshe Dayan, Israeli defense minister; Moses Gomberg, chemist; Moses Gunn, actor; Moss Hart, director/playwright; Moses Malone, Hall of Fame basketball player.

NATHAN ✦ *(NAY-thuhn)*

Language/Cultural Origin: Hebrew

Meaning: Given

Spiritual Connotation: Prophetic Vision

Related Names/Nicknames: Jonathan, Nat, Natan, Nate, Nathaniel

Alternate Names: Nathen, Nathon

Background Story: The most notable Nathan in the Bible was a prophet who played a significant role in King David's life. When David wanted to build a temple for the ark of the covenant, Nathan revealed God's prophetic wishes: ". . . your offspring . . .

shall build a house for my name, and I will establish the throne of his kingdom forever." Later, Nathan condemned David for taking Bathsheba from Uriah and prophesied the death of their son as payment for his sin. He also supported David by upsetting Adonijah's attempt to seize the throne and participating in Solomon's coronation (2 Samuel 7, 12; 1 Kings 1).

Of Interest: Nathan has been among the top fifty names for boys in the United States since 1970.

Famous Namesakes: Nathan Clifford, U.S. Supreme Court justice; Nathan Cummings, entrepreneur/philanthropist; Nathan Hale, American Revolution hero; Nathan Lane, actor; Nathan Milstein, violinist.

NATHANAEL ✦ *(nuh-THAN-ee-uhl)* or *(nuh-THAN-yuhl)*

Language/Cultural Origin: Hebrew

Meaning: Gift of God

Spiritual Connotation: Spiritual Reward

Related Names/Nicknames: Nat, Natanael, Nataniel, Nate, Nathan, Natty, Thaniel

Alternate Names: Nathaneal, Nathanial, Nathaniel, Nathanyal, Nathanyel, Nethanel, Nethaniel, Nethanyel

Background Story: Nathanael first learned about Jesus from his friend Philip, who said, "We have found him about whom . . . the prophets wrote." Nathanael was dubious at first, but went to see Jesus for himself. "Here is truly an Israelite in whom there is no deceit!" Jesus said about Nathanael when he saw him. Nathanael accepted Jesus as the Messiah and became one of his Twelve Apostles. He was also with the group of disciples who saw Jesus at the Sea of Tiberias after his Resurrection (John 1:45–51, 21:2).

Of Interest: Most biblical scholars agree that Nathanael and Bartholomew are one and the same apostle.

Famous Namesakes: Nat "King" Cole, musician; Nathaniel Currier, lithographer; Nathanael Greene, American Revolution general; Nathaniel Hawthorne, Nathanael West, writers.

NEHEMIAH ❖ *(nee-huh-MAI-uh)* or *(nee-uh-MAI-uh)*

Language/Cultural Origin: Hebrew

Meaning: Comforted by God

Spiritual Connotation: Consolation

Related Names/Nicknames: Nehemias, Nehmiah, Nemo, Nemos

Alternate Names: Nechemia, Nechemiah, Nechemya, Nehemia, Nehemya, Nehemyah

Background Story: Nehemiah was a cupbearer for King Artaxerxes in Susa when he learned about the poor state of Jerusalem and "those who had escaped" the Babylonian captivity. With the king's permission, he returned as governor to Judea and reconstructed the walls of Jerusalem, which he completed in less than two months—despite opposition. He addressed the social and spiritual well-being of his people by appointing government officials, instructing the people in Moses's law, and creating a new covenant with the Lord for "all who have knowledge and understanding" to observe (Book of Nehemiah).

Famous Namesakes: Nehemiah Broughton, football player; Nehemiah Persoff, actor.

NEREUS ✦ *(NEER-oos)* or *(NEER-ee-uhs)*

Language/Cultural Origin: Greek/Hebrew

Meaning: A Lamp

Spiritual Connotation: Light of Faith

Related Names/Nicknames: Ner, Nereo

Alternate Names: None

Background Story: Nereus was a Christian in Rome who was held in high regard by Paul. In a letter, Paul asked that "Nereus and his sister . . . and all the saints who are with them" greet each other "with a holy kiss" (Romans 16:15–16). The name Nereus brings to mind a man who has faith in God and himself.

Of Interest: Nereus is the name of a first-century saint in the Catholic Church. In Greek mythology, Nereus was the wise "old man of the sea" and the father of the Neriads.

NICANOR ✦ *(nai-KAY-ner)*

Language/Cultural Origin: Greek

Meaning: Conqueror

Spiritual Connotation: Victorious

Related Names/Nicknames: Nicholas, Nick, Nicky

Alternate Names: None

Background Story: Nicanor was an early disciple of the Church in Jerusalem at a time when discipleship was growing. The apostles found it necessary to appoint deacons to attend to practical matters so that they could devote themselves "to prayer and to serving the word." They called all the disciples together and told them to "select from among yourselves seven men of good standing, full of the Spirit and of wisdom." Nicanor was one of seven men elected (Acts 6:1–7).

Famous Namesakes: Óscar Nicanor Duarte Frutos, president of Paraguay; Nicanor Parra, poet.

NICODEMUS ✦ *(nihk-uh-DEE-muhs)*

Language/Cultural Origin: Greek

Meaning: Conqueror of the People

Spiritual Connotation: Born of the Spirit

Related Names/Nicknames: Nick, Nicky, Nicodemo, Nicolas, Nikodem, Nikodema, Nikodim

Alternate Names: Nikodemus

Background Story: Nicodemus, a Jewish leader and a Pharisee, questioned Jesus about being "born again." "How can anyone be born after growing old?" he asked. Jesus explained, "That which is born of the flesh is flesh, and that which is born of the Spirit is spirit" (John 3:1–21). After the crucifixion, Nicodemus came with myrrh and aloes to help Joseph of Arimethea care for Jesus's body. They "bound it in strips of linen with the spices, as the custom of the Jews is to bury" and laid him in a tomb (John 19:38–42).

NICOLAS ✦ *(NIHK-o-luhs)*

Language/Cultural Origin: Greek

Meaning: Victory of the People

Spiritual Connotation: Triumphant Spirit

Related Names/Nicknames: Nic, Nicanor, Niccolo, Nichol, Nicholai, Nichole, Nicholl, Nichols, Nick,

Nickey, Nickie, Nicklas, Nicky, Nicol, Nicola,
Nicolaas, Nicolai, Nicolay, Nicolet, Nicoli, Nicoll,
Nicollet, Nicolls, Nicolo, Nik, Niki, Nikki, Nikkolay,
Nikky, Niklaas, Niklas, Niklos, Nikolai, Nikolay,
Nikos, Nilos, Nils

Alternate Names: Nicholas, Nicholaus, Nickolas,
Nickolaus, Nicolaas, Nicolas, Nicolaus, Nicolis,
Nikkolas, Nikolas, Nikolaus, Nikolos

Background Story: Nicolas—or Nicolaus—was "a proselyte of
Antioch" and an early disciple of the Church. He and six other
men, "full of the Spirit and of wisdom," were chosen from
among the disciples to serve as deacons of the growing Church
in Jerusalem. The apostles "prayed and laid their hands on"
Nicolas and the others, whose work would allow them to focus
on their ministry (Acts 6:1–7).

Of Interest: Nicholas, bishop of Myra, is the patron saint of
Greece, Russia, children, scholars, sailors, and pawnbrokers, as
well as the origin of the legend of Santa Claus.

Famous Namesakes: Nicholas Murray Butler, Nobel Peace Prize
winner; Nicolas Cage, Nicol Williamson, actors; Nicolaus Coper-
nicus, astronomer; Nicolas Flagello, Nicolai Rimsky-Korsakov,
composers; Niccolo Machiavelli, philosopher; Nicholas Sparks,
writer.

NOAH ✦ *(NO-uh)*

Language/Cultural Origin: Hebrew

Meaning: Peaceful

Spiritual Connotation: Source of Comfort

Related Names/Nicknames: Noach, Noak, Noe, Norrie

Alternate Names: Noa

Background Story: Noah was a "righteous man," the only one who "found favor in the sight of the Lord." As a result, God spared him when he sent a flood to destroy the rest of humankind. He told Noah to build an ark for himself and his family—and "two of every kind" of animal and bird. It rained for forty days and nights, destroying everything but Noah and those on the ark. After the flood receded, God told Noah and his sons to "be fruitful and multiply." He also made a covenant with him that "never again shall there be a flood to destroy the earth" and placed a rainbow in the sky as a sign (Genesis 5–9).

Of Interest: Since 1997, Noah has been among the top forty names for boys in the United States.

Famous Namesakes: Noah Beery, Noah Taylor, Noah Wyle, actors; Noah Herron, football player; Noah Webster, lexicographer.

OBADIAH ✦ *(o-buh-DAI-uh)*

Language/Cultural Origin: Hebrew

Meaning: Servant of God

Spiritual Connotation: Humble Protector

Related Names/Nicknames: Obadias, Obed, Obie, Ovadia, Ovadiach, Ovadiah, Oved

Alternate Names: Obadia, Obadya, Obedia, Obediah

Background Story: Of the many Obadiahs in the Bible, two men stand out. The first is the chief of King Ahab's palace, a devout man who "revered the Lord greatly." When Ahab's wife, Jezebel, began to kill the Lord's prophets, Obadiah hid a hundred of them in caves "and provided them with bread and water" (1 Kings 18:3–4). The second Obadiah is a minor prophet whose book— the shortest in the Bible—prophesied the fall of Edom and the restoration of Israel (Book of Obadiah).

OMAR ✦ *(O-mahr)*

Language/Cultural Origin: Arabic/Hebrew

Meaning: Eloquent

Spiritual Connotation: Compelling

Related Names/Nicknames: None

Alternate Names: Omarr, Omer, Ommar

Background Story: Omar was Eliphaz's son and Esau's grandson. He was a chief among the clans of Edom, a kingdom that became prominent before Israel existed as a nation (Genesis 36:11, 15). The name Omar suggests a man with a gift for words.

Famous Namesakes: Omar Bradley, World War II commander; Omar Epps, Omar Gooding, Omar Sharif, actors; Omar Khayyam, poet; Omar Moreno, baseball player; Omar Omidyar, eBay founder.

OREN ✦ *(OR-ehn)*

Language/Cultural Origin: Hebrew

Meaning: Pine Tree

Spiritual Connotation: Standing Tall

Related Names/Nicknames: Orenthal

Alternate Names: Oran, Orin, Oron, Orren, Orrin

Background Story: Oren was one of "the sons of Jerahmeel, the first born of Hezron" (1 Chronicles 2:25). He and his kinsmen were responsible for establishing the tribe of Judah. The name Oren is mindful of the tree that represents it—tall, strong, and flexible.

Famous Namesakes: Oren Fader, classical guitarist; Orrin Hatch, U.S. senator; Oren Williams, actor.

OTHNIEL ✦ *(AHTH-nee-ehl)*

Language/Cultural Origin: Hebrew

Meaning: God's Lion

Spiritual Connotation: Heroic Leader

Related Names/Nicknames: Neal

Alternate Names: None

Background Story: Othniel was the first judge of Israel after Joshua's death. He first distinguished himself by conquering the city of Kiriath-sepher, and he won the hand of Caleb's daughter Achsah as a reward. When the Israelites found themselves oppressed by the king of Aram, they "cried out to the Lord," who "raised up a deliverer"—Othniel. Under Othniel's direction as judge, Israel threw off the yoke of Aram and "had rest for forty years" (Judges 1:12–13, 3:8–11).

Famous Namesakes: Othniel Charles March was a nineteenth-century paleontologist who discovered numerous fossils in the American West, including the first pterosaur remains in America.

PAUL ✦ *(PAWL)*

Language/Cultural Origin: Latin

Meaning: Small

Spiritual Connotation: Humble Servant

Related Names/Nicknames: Pablo, Paolo, Paula, Paulie, Paulin, Pauline, Paulino, Paulinus, Paulo, Paulsen, Paulson, Paulus, Pauly, Pavel, Pavlik, Pavlo, Pawel, Saul

Alternate Names: Pal, Pol, Poll, Poul

Background Story: Paul—whose Hebrew name was Saul—was a key figure in the early Christian Church. At first, he opposed Christianity and persecuted its followers. Then one day on the road to Damascus, "a light from heaven" blinded him and Jesus's voice said, "Saul, Saul, why do you persecute me?" Paul literally saw the light. Within three days his sight was restored, Paul was baptized, and "he began to proclaim" in the synagogues that Jesus was the Messiah. After preaching in Jerusalem, he set out on the first of three missionary journeys, spreading God's word to Jews and Gentiles alike. His trips found success and miracles, but opposition and imprisonment as well. Yet Paul never stopped preaching—even when he was shipwrecked in Malta and imprisoned in Rome. He also wrote numerous letters to his followers, urging them to be strong in their faith. Paul never forgot his experience at Damascus and the mission he had accepted from God: to turn others "from darkness to light . . . so that they may receive a place among those who are sanctified by faith in me" (Acts 8–9, 11–26).

Of Interest: Paul is honored as a saint by the Catholic Church.

Famous Namesakes: Paul Bunyan, folk hero; Paul Cezanne, Paul Gauguin, artists; Paul Krause, football player; Paul McCartney, Paul Simon, Paul Williams, musicians; Paul Newman, Paul Reiser, Paul Scofield, Paul Sorvino, actors; Paul O'Neill, baseball player; Paul Prudhomme, chef; Paul Revere, American Revolution hero; Paul Taylor, dancer/choreographer; Paul Tillich, theologian; Pope John Paul II.

PEREZ ✦ *(PEHR-ehz)*

Language/Cultural Origin: Hebrew

Meaning: Divided

Spiritual Connotation: Spiritual Unity

Related Names/Nicknames: Prez

Alternate Names: Phares, Pharez

Background Story: Perez was one of Judah's twin sons by Tamar. When Tamar was in labor, Perez's twin brother reached out his hand, and the midwife wrapped it with "a crimson thread," indicating which twin came first. Suddenly, his brother "drew back his hand" and Perez came out instead. "What a breach you have made for yourself!" the midwife said, and "he was named Perez." His brother was named Zerah (Genesis 38:28–30). Perez was an ancestor of David and appears in the genealogy of Jesus (Luke 3:33).

Famous Namesakes: Adolfo Pérez Esquivel, Nobel Peace Prize winner; Perez Prado, musician called "the Mambo King."

PETER ✦ *(PEE-ter)*

Language/Cultural Origin: Greek

Meaning: A Rock

Spiritual Connotation: Foundation of Faith

Related Names/Nicknames: Cephas, Kephas, Pearce, Pedro, Pernell, Pete, Peterson, Petey, Petra, Petras, Petros, Petrov, Pierce, Pierre, Piers, Piet, Pietro, Pyotr, Simon

Alternate Names: Peder, Petar, Petr, Pieter

Background Story: When he first met Jesus, Peter was a simple fisherman from Galilee whose name was Simon. Jesus changed his name to Cephas—or Peter in Aramaic (John 1:42). Then he said to Peter and his brother Andrew, "Follow me, and I will make you fishers of men" (Matthew 4:19). As one of Jesus's Twelve Apostles, Peter accompanied Jesus throughout his ministry, witnessed his teachings as well as his miracles, and even walked on water at Jesus's command. One day Jesus said to him, "You are Peter, and on this rock I will build my church. . . . I will give you the keys of the kingdom of heaven, and whatever you bind on earth will be bound in heaven" (Matthew 16:18–19). After Jesus's ascension, Peter became a leader in the young Christian community. Although he was "uneducated and ordinary," he boldly preached to the crowds, baptized new believers, and performed numerous miracles, such as healing a lame man and raising a small girl from the dead. He was arrested, beaten, and imprisoned, but when he was ordered not to speak about Jesus, his answer was simple: "We cannot keep from speaking about what we have seen and heard." Peter was a true "rock" of the church (Acts of the Apostles).

Of Interest: Peter is the author of two letters in the Bible. He is a saint in the Catholic Church and the first bishop of Rome.

Famous Namesakes: Peter Agre, Nobel Prize winner/chemist; Peter Arno, cartoonist; Peter Bogdanovich, Peter Jackson, directors; Peter Falk, Peter Fonda, Peter O'Toole, Peter Sellers, actors; Peter Cetera, Peter Gabriel, Pete Townshend, musicians; Peter Jennings, journalist; Peter Paul Rubens, artist; Pete Sampras, tennis player.

PHILEMON ✦ *(fih-LEE-muhn)*
Language/Cultural Origin: Greek
Meaning: Affectionate
Spiritual Connotation: Brotherhood of Love
Related Names/Nicknames: Phil
Alternate Names: Philimon, Philymon

Background Story: Philemon was a "dear friend and coworker" of Paul. He received a letter from the apostle while he was a prisoner in Rome, explaining to Philemon that he was sending

back his slave, Onesimus, who had run away and become a
Christian. Paul asked that Philemon accept him "no longer as
a slave but . . . a beloved brother . . . both in flesh and in the
Lord" (Philemon 1).

PHILIP ✦ *(FIHL-ihp)* or *(FIHL-uhp)*
Language/Cultural Origin: Greek
Meaning: Lover of Horses
Spiritual Connotation: Messenger
Related Names/Nicknames: Felipe, Filippo, Flip, Phil,
Philipa, Philippa, Philippos, Philippus, Philips, Pip,
Pippa, Pippo
Alternate Names: Filip, Fillip, Fyllip, Philipp, Philippe,
Phillip, Phyllip

Background Story: There are two prominent Philips in the New
Testament. The first was Philip from Bethsaida, one of the
original apostles, whom Jesus named "to be sent out to proclaim
the message." Philip introduced Nathanael to Jesus and was present when Jesus fed a crowd of five thousand with "five loaves
and two fishes" (Mark 3, John 1, 6). The second Philip was one of
Christ's seven disciples who were appointed deacons of the
Church in Jerusalem. In addition, Philip "proclaimed the Messiah" in Samaria, where "the crowds . . . listened eagerly" to what
he said (Acts 6, 8).

Of Interest: The apostle Philip is a saint in the Catholic Church.

Famous Namesakes: Prince Philip, royalty; Philip Barry, playwright; Phil Collins, musician; Philip K. Dick, Philip Roth, writers; Phil Donahue, television personality; Philip Glass, John
Philip Sousa, composers; Philip Seymour Hoffman, actor; Phil
Simms, football player/commentator.

PHINEHAS ✦ *(FIHN-ee-huhs)* or *(FIHN-ee-uhs)*

Language/Cultural Origin: Hebrew/Egyptian

Meaning: Face of Protection

Spiritual Connotation: Zealous

Related Names/Nicknames: Finn, Pinchas, Pinchos, Pincus, Pinhas, Pinkas, Pinkus

Alternate Names: Phinees, Phineas, Phineus, Phinnaeus

Background Story: Phinehas was the son of Eleazar and grandson of Aaron (Exodus 6:25). When he was a young man, he witnessed an Israelite bring a foreign woman into his family. God had declared such behavior unacceptable, as it tempted the Israelites to participate in pagan worship. With great zeal, Phinehas "pierced the two of them" with a spear, earning for him and his descendants a covenant of "perpetual priesthood" from the Lord (Numbers 25:6–13).

Famous Namesakes: Phineas T. Barnum, entertainer; Pinchas Zukerman, violinist.

RAM ✦ *(RAM)*

Language/Cultural Origin: Sanskrit/Hebrew

Meaning: Elevated

Spiritual Connotation: Pleasing to God

Related Names/Nicknames: Aram, Rama, Ramos

Alternate Names: Rahm

Background Story: Ram is the name of three biblical characters, most importantly the second son of Hezron, who appears in the genealogy of Jesus (Matthew 1:3). The name Ram suggests a man who holds high standards for himself.

Of Interest: In Hindu mythology, Rama is the seventh incarnation of Vishnu.

Famous Namesakes: Ram Oren, writer; Ram Singh, philosopher; Ram Gopal Varma, film director.

RAPHA ✦ *(RAY-fuh)*

Language/Cultural Origin: Hebrew

Meaning: Comfort

Spiritual Connotation: Power of Healing

Related Names/Nicknames: Raphu, Rephaiah

Alternate Names: Raphah

Background Story: The name Rapha—or Raphah—appears twice in the Bible, as the fifth son of Benjamin (1 Chronicles 8:2), and a Benjamite, the son of Binea, who was a descendant of Saul through his son, Jonathan (1 Chronicles 8:37).

Of Interest: Jehovah Rapha was one of the seven redemptive names of God in the Old Testament. It means "the Lord who heals" and represents God's physical, emotional, and spiritual healing power.

RAPHAEL ✦ *(RA-fai-ehl)* or *(RAY-fee-ehl)* or
(rah-fee-EHL)

Language/Cultural Origin: Hebrew

Meaning: God Has Healed

Spiritual Connotation: God's Messenger

Related Names/Nicknames: Raf, Rafa, Rafael, Rafaela, Rafaello, Rafaelo, Rafe, Rafel, Rafello, Raffaello, Raphaella, Raphaello, Raphello, Ravel

Alternate Names: Rafaelle, Raffael, Rephael

Background Story: Raphael was an archangel sent by God to help Tobit, a blind Israelite who lived in Nineveh. Disguised as a young man, Raphael accompanied Tobit's son Tobias on a trip to Media to retrieve his father's money and find a wife. On the way, Tobias caught a fish and Raphael told him to remove its gall, heart, and liver for "useful medicines." In Media, Tobias fell in love with Sarah, a young woman who had lost seven bridegrooms because of an evil spirit, and Raphael arranged their marriage. Not only did the "useful medicines" destroy the evil spirit, they later healed Tobit of his blindness. Before he left, Raphael revealed himself as one of God's seven angels who "serve before the Glory of the Lord" (Book of Tobit).

Famous Namesakes: Raphael Mostel, composer; Rafael Nadal, tennis player; Rafael Santana, baseball player; Raphael Sanzio, Renaissance painter; Rafael Yglesias, writer.

REI ✦ *(REE-ai)*

Language/Cultural Origin: Hebrew

Meaning: My Companion

Spiritual Connotation: Constant Friendship

Related Names/Nicknames: None

Alternate Names: Ray

Background Story: Rei supported David during one of his darkest hours, when his son, Adonijah, attempted to replace him on the throne. David saw many of his advisers defect, but Rei, along with Zadok, Nathan, and Benaiah, "did not side with Adonijah." Instead, they supported David's choice of Solomon as the new ruler of Israel (1 Kings 1:8). The name Rei is a reminder that loyalty creates not only good friends but great men.

REUBEN ✦ *(ROO-bihn)*

Language/Cultural Origin: Hebrew

Meaning: Behold, a Son

Spiritual Connotation: Gift from the Lord

Related Names/Nicknames: Reuven, Rouvin, Rube, Rubens, Rubina, Rubino, Ruby

Alternate Names: Reuban, Reubin, Ruben, Rubin

Background Story: Reuben was the firstborn son of Jacob and Leah. Leah knew that Jacob preferred Rachel to her, so when she was able to give Jacob a son, she named him Reuben and said, "Because the Lord has looked on my affliction; surely now my husband will love me" (Genesis 29:32). Reuben's relationship with his father was rocky, perhaps because his younger brother Joseph was Jacob's favorite. Yet it was Reuben who talked his jealous brothers out of killing Joseph, and he "tore his clothes" when he learned they had sold him into slavery (Genesis 37:22–29). Although Jacob denied Reuben his father's blessing, Reuben's descendants became one of the twelve tribes of Israel.

Famous Namesakes: Rubén Blades, Ruben Ramos, Ruben Studdard, singers; Rube Goldberg, political cartoonist; Ruben Patterson, basketball player.

REUEL ✦ *(ree-YOO-uhl)*

Language/Cultural Origin: Hebrew

Meaning: Shepherd

Spiritual Connotation: Friend of God

Related Names/Nicknames: None

Alternate Names: Rauel

Background Story: Of the three Reuels in the Bible, the most prominent is Moses's father-in-law, a Midianite priest with seven daughters. Moses came to the defense of Reuel's daughters, who were driven away by rude shepherds while they were trying to water their flocks. Reuel invited Moses to "break bread" with his family and gave him his daughter Zipporah as a wife. Reuel is also known as Jethro in the Bible (Exodus 2:16–22).

Famous Namesakes: John Ronald Reuel (J. R. R.) Tolkien is the author of *The Hobbit* and the classic trilogy *The Lord of the Rings*.

ROSH ✦ *(RAWSH)*

Language/Cultural Origin: Hebrew

Meaning: Beginning

Spiritual Connotation: Innovative

Related Names/Nicknames: None

Alternate Names: None

Background Story: In the Bible, Rosh was one of Benjamin's ten sons and among the offspring his grandfather, Jacob, "brought with him into Egypt" (Genesis 46:21). The name Rosh suggests a man who has a talent for leading others along new paths.

Of Interest: Rosh Hashanah is a spiritual holiday, usually occurring in September, which celebrates the Jewish New Year.

RUFUS ✦ *(ROO-fuhs)*

Language/Cultural Origin: Latin

Meaning: Red-haired

Spiritual Connotation: Man of Virtue

Related Names/Nicknames: Rufino, Russ, Russell

Alternate Names: Ruffus, Rufous

Background Story: The name Rufus is mentioned twice in the New Testament. Rufus was the son of Simon of Cyrene, a "passerby . . . from the country" who was compelled to carry Jesus's cross to Golgotha, where Jesus was crucified (Mark 15:21). In his letter to the Romans, Paul greets a Christian named Rufus, who is "chosen in the Lord," and his mother, who Paul says is "a mother to me also" (Romans 16:13).

Of Interest: Rufus was the nickname of William II of England, because of his red hair.

Famous Namesakes: Rufus Wheeler Peckham, U.S. Supreme Court justice; Rufus Reid, musician/composer; Rufus Sewell, actor; Rufus Wainwright, singer/songwriter.

SAMSON ✦ *(SAM-suhn)*

Language/Cultural Origin: Hebrew

Meaning: Like the Sun

Spiritual Connotation: Strength from God

Related Names/Nicknames: Sam, Sammie, Sammy, Sansom, Sanson, Sansone, Shem

Alternate Names: Sampson

Background Story: Samson is perhaps the most famous judge in the Old Testament. His birth was foretold by an angel who instructed his parents to raise him as a Nazirite—one who is dedicated to God—allowing "no razor . . . to come on his head." Because of God's blessing, Samson developed a strength that was legendary, and he spent much of his life single-handedly battling the Philistines. His love for the beautiful Delilah, however, was his downfall. At her insistence, he surrendered the secret of his strength. "If my head were shaved, then my strength would leave me," Samson told her. While he slept, Delilah had his hair shaved, then informed the Philistines, who "seized him and gouged out his eyes." While he was in prison, Samson's hair began to grow and God gave him one last opportunity to use his strength. Called to entertain a gathering of Philistine leaders at the temple, the blind Samson asked to "lean against" its two central pillars and "strained with all his might." The temple collapsed, killing all who were inside, including Samson himself (Judges 13–16).

Of Interest: Samson's story—much of which is based on legend—has inspired countless works of art: an oratorio by Handel, an opera by Camille Saint-Saëns, a poem by John Milton, paintings by Rembrandt and Rubens, and an epic film by Cecil B. DeMille.

Famous Namesakes: Samson Abramsky, computer scientist; Samson Raphaelson, playwright/screenwriter; Samson Samsonov, writer/director.

SAMUEL ◆ *(SAM-yoo-uhl)*

Language/Cultural Origin: Hebrew

Meaning: Asked of God

Spiritual Connotation: In God's Heart

Related Names/Nicknames: Sam, Samm, Sammie, Sammy, Samuello, Shem, Shemuel

Alternate Names: Sammuel, Samuele, Samwell

Background Story: Samuel played a major role in the Old Testament as Israel's high priest, last judge, and first prophet. He was born to Elkanah and Hannah, who named him Samuel because she had "asked him of the Lord." Raised by Eli, the high priest of Shiloh, he developed a reputation as "a trustworthy prophet of the Lord" and became Eli's successor. Samuel inspired the Israelites to conquer the Philistines and judged Israel all his life. When his people asked him to appoint a king over them, Samuel looked to the Lord for guidance. At first he anointed Saul, who proved unworthy of the position, then David as Saul's successor, initiating a power struggle that did not end for years. When Samuel died, "all Israel assembled and mourned for him" (1 Samuel 1–31).

Of Interest: Since 2002, Samuel has ranked among the top twenty-five names for boys in the United States. The name has also ranked among the top ten in Britain since 1999.

Famous Namesakes: Samuel Adams, American patriot; Samuel Beckett, playwright; Samuel de Champlain, explorer; Samuel Clemens, Samuel Johnson, writers; Samuel Taylor Coleridge, poet; Sammy Davis Jr., entertainer; Samuel L. Jackson, actor; Samuel Ramey, opera singer; Sammy Sosa, baseball player.

SAUL ✦ *(SAWL)*

Language/Cultural Origin: Hebrew

Meaning: Prayed For

Spiritual Connotation: God's Blessing

Related Names/Nicknames: Sauli, Saulo, Shaul, Sollie

Alternate Names: Sol

Background Story: There are two Sauls of importance in the Bible. The first was Kish's son, chosen by God and ordained by Samuel to be Israel's first king. A "handsome young man," Saul stood "head and shoulders above everyone else" and defended Israel against the Philistines. When he failed to follow God's wishes, however, "the spirit of the Lord departed from Saul" and Samuel anointed David as his successor. David became one of Saul's great warriors, and his popularity with the people increased. Driven by jealousy, Saul tried to have David killed, but Saul's son and daughter, Jonathan and Michal, helped David escape their father's intrigues. For years, Saul and David played a deadly game of cat and mouse, which ended only when Jonathan was killed and Saul "fell upon" his sword after a deadly battle with the Philistines. When David heard of their deaths, he grieved for the men he had loved: "Your glory, O Israel, lies slain upon your high places! How the mighty have fallen!" (1 Samuel 9–31, 2 Samuel 1). Saul was also the Hebrew name of Paul, a Jew from Tarsus whose conversion on the way to Damascus transformed him from Christianity's persecutor into its greatest champion (Acts 9:1–22).

Famous Namesakes: Saul Bellow, Nobel Prize winner in literature; Saul Landau, writer/filmaker; Saul Steinberg, cartoonist; Saul Stokes, musician; Saul Williams, poet/actor/musician.

SERAIAH ⧫ *(suh-RAI-uh)*

Language/Cultural Origin: Hebrew

Meaning: Prince of the Lord

Spiritual Connotation: Noble Follower

Related Names/Nicknames: Sera, Sheva, Shisha

Alternate Names: None

Background Story: Among the notable Seraiahs in the Bible are: the secretary to King David (2 Samuel 8:17); a "chief priest" put to death when Jerusalem was crushed by the Babylonians (2 Kings 25:18–21); a man who read a prophecy of Babylon's doom, tied a stone to it, and threw it in the Euphrates, saying, "Thus shall Babylon sink, to rise no more." Within seventy years, Babylon had fallen (Jeremiah 51:59–64).

SERGIUS ✦ *(SER-juhs)* or *(SER-jee-uhs)*

Language/Cultural Origin: Latin

Meaning: Net

Spiritual Connotation: Seized by God's Power

Related Names/Nicknames: Serge, Sergei, Sergeo, Sergey, Sergi, Sergio, Sergiu, Serjio, Sirgio

Alternate Names: Sergios, Sergiusz, Sirgios

Background Story: Sergius Paulus — the proconsul of Cyprus — was "an intelligent man" who asked to speak to Barnabas and Paul so that he could "hear the word of God." There was a magician with Sergius who opposed what they taught and "tried to turn the proconsul away from the faith." Paul simply caused the magician to go blind for a short time, an act that convinced Sergius of God's power (Acts 13:7–12).

Famous Namesakes: Serge Diaghilev, ballet impresario; Sergei Grinkov, Olympic ice dancing medalist; Sergei Prokofiev, Sergei Rachmaninoff, composers; Sergio Rossi, fashion designer, Sergio Valente, hairdresser.

SETH ✦ *(SEHTH)*

Language/Cultural Origin: Hebrew

Meaning: Appointed

Spiritual Connotation: Placed by God

Related Names/Nicknames: None

Alternate Names: Sheth

Background Story: Adam and Eve had a third son—Seth—who was conceived and born after the death of his brother Abel. Eve named him Seth, saying, "God has appointed for me another child instead of Abel, because Cain killed him" (Genesis 4:25). Seth lived for nine hundred twelve years and was also an ancestor of Noah, connecting the two biblical fathers of mankind (1 Chronicles 1:1). The name Seth also appears in Luke's genealogy of Jesus (Luke 3:38).

Famous Namesakes: Seth Godin, writer; Seth Green, actor; Seth Horan, musician; Seth MacFarlane, writer/cartoonist/producer.

SHADRACH ✦ *(SHAD-rak)* or *(SHAY-drak)*

Language/Cultural Origin: Aramaic

Meaning: Tender

Spiritual Connotation: Earnest Believer

Related Names/Nicknames: Shad

Alternate Names: Shadrack, Shadrick

Background Story: Shadrach was the Babylonian name given to Hananiah, one of four noble youths of Judah appointed to serve in the court of King Nebuchadnezzar. With two of his companions, he refused to worship the "golden statue" the king had set up. "We will not serve your gods," Shadrach and his friends said, and were thrown into a furnace so fiery it killed the men who lifted them. But an angel of the Lord protected them from the flames and they emerged unharmed. The king was amazed and said, "Blessed be the God of Shadrach. . . . There is no other god who is able to deliver in this way" (Daniel 1, 3).

Famous Namesakes: Shadrach Minkins was the first runaway slave to be captured under the Fugitive Slave Law in Boston. Shadrach escaped to Canada and lived as a free man.

SHALLUM ✦ *(SHAL-uhm)*

Language/Cultural Origin: Hebrew

Meaning: Agreeable

Spiritual Connotation: Pleasing

Related Names/Nicknames: Hal

Alternate Names: None

Background Story: Shallum is a popular biblical name. Some of the more notable are: the "keeper of the wardrobe" for King Josiah and husband of the prophetess Huldah (2 Kings 22:14); King Josiah's fourth son, who was called Jehoahaz II when he ascended Judah's throne (1 Chronicles 3:15); and a chief gate-keeper in Jerusalem during David's reign (1 Chronicles 9:17). There were also two Shallums who "made repairs" on the walls of Jerusalem when Nehemiah was governor (Nehemiah 3:12, 15).

Of Interest: In rabbinical literature, Shallum—Huldah's husband—was a respected man who lived during the time of the prophet Elisha. He daily gave help to the poor and needy, for which God rewarded him and his wife with the gift of prophecy.

SHAMIR ✦ *(shuh-MEER)*

Language/Cultural Origin: Hebrew

Meaning: Thorn

Spiritual Connotation: Penetrating

Related Names/Nicknames: Shamira

Alternate Names: Shahmir, Shameer

Background Story: Shamir was the son of Micah and one of the Levites who cast lots for their "appointed duties" to serve the temple during David's reign (1 Chronicles 24:24). Shamir was also a town "in the hill country of Ephraim" from which Tola, one of Israel's judges, "rose to deliver Israel" (Judges 10:1–2). The name Shamir suggests a man who has a penetrating mind and razor-sharp wit.

SHILOH ✦ *(SHAI-lo)*

Language/Cultural Origin: Hebrew

Meaning: His Gift

Spiritual Connotation: God's Abundance

Related Names/Nicknames: None

Alternate Names: Shilo, Shylo, Shyloh

Background Story: Shiloh, a town in the Bible, was a focal point for God's people on more than one occasion. Before entering the Promised Land, Joshua and the Israelites "assembled at Shiloh," where the tribes cast lots for their inheritance (Joshua 18:1–10). Later, the ark of the covenant made its home in Shiloh, which became a sanctuary and place of pilgrimage. At the temple in Shiloh, Hannah dedicated her son, Samuel, to God's service and the Lord "revealed himself to Samuel" while he lived there (1 Samuel 1, 3).

Of Interest: In some translations of the Bible, the name Shiloh appears in Jacob's blessing to Judah, ancestor of the Jewish people: "The scepter shall not depart from Judah, Nor the ruler's staff from between his feet, Until Shiloh comes, And to him [shall be] the obedience of the peoples." Some consider it a prophetic name for the Messiah.

SHIMEA ✦ *(SHIHM-ee-uh)*

Language/Cultural Origin: Hebrew

Meaning: Obeys

Spiritual Connotation: Answers to God

Related Names/Nicknames: Shamma, Shammah, Shammua, Shammuah, Shimma

Alternate Names: Shimeah

Background Story: There are two prominent Shimeas in the Bible: a son of Jesse and David's older brother, who "followed Saul to the battle" with the Philistines at which David slew Goliath (1 Chronicles 2:13, 1 Samuel 17:13), and one of David's sons with Bathsheba (1 Chronicles 3:5). The name Shimea suggests a man who practices God's commandments as a way of life.

SILAS ✦ *(SAI-luhs)*

Language/Cultural Origin: Greek/Latin

Meaning: Forest

Spiritual Connotation: Strength of Character

Related Names/Nicknames: Silvain, Silvan, Silvano, Silvanus, Silvio, Sylvan

Alternate Names: Sylas

Background Story: Silas was an elder of the Church in Jerusalem. The other Christian leaders sent him to Antioch with Paul and Barnabas to reassure the Gentiles they were not required to obey the Jewish law of circumcision. Silas, who was also a prophet, "said much to encourage and strengthen the believers" and was chosen by Paul to accompany him on his second missionary journey. Their task was not easy. People accused Paul and Silas of "disturbing" their cities and "advocating customs that are not lawful." On one occasion, the two men were beaten and imprisoned. Yet they boldly traveled from town to town, converting Jews and Gentiles alike and strengthening the faith of the Church (Acts 15–18).

Of Interest: Silas is the shortened version of Silvanus, the name under which he appears in several epistles from Paul and Peter.

Famous Namesakes: Silas Carson, actor; Silas Griffis, Hall of Fame hockey player; Silas K. Hocking, writer; Silas Marner, title character of a novel by George Eliot.

SIMEON ✦ *(SIHM-ee-uhn)*

Language/Cultural Origin: Hebrew

Meaning: God Is Listening

Spiritual Connotation: Sign of Compassion

Related Names/Nicknames: Shimon, Simon

Alternate Names: Simion, Simyon

Background Story: Four men of distinction are named Simeon in the Bible. The first is Jacob's second son with Leah. His mother saw him as compensation for not being loved by Jacob and named him Simeon. "Because the Lord has heard that I am hated, he has given me this son also," she said. Simeon became the ancestor of the Simeonites, one of Israel's twelve tribes (Genesis 29:33). The next Simeon was a "righteous and devout" man who was promised he would see the Messiah before he died. He was at the temple when Mary and Joseph brought Jesus and held their child in his arms. "Master, now you are dismissing your servant in peace," he said, ". . . for my eyes have seen your salvation" (Luke 2:25–30). Simeon was also a "son of Judah" in the genealogy of Jesus (Luke 3:30) and a prophet and teacher of the early Church at Antioch (Acts 13:1).

Famous Namesakes: Simeon ten Holt, composer; Simeon Lipman, *Antiques Roadshow* appraiser; Simeon Rice, football player.

SIMON ✦ *(SAI-muhn)*

Language/Cultural Origin: Hebrew/Greek

Meaning: God Is Listening

Spiritual Connotation: Loving Companion

Related Names/Nicknames: Peter, Shimon, Si, Sim, Simeon, Simion, Simmons, Simms, Simonson, Simpson, Symms, Syms

Alternate Names: Simen, Simone, Symon, Szymon

Background Story: There is an impressive list of Simons associated with Jesus in the New Testament: Simon, whom Jesus named Peter, the apostle who was close to Jesus during his life and became a leader in the early Christian Church (Matthew 10:2); Simon "the Canaanite," another of the original Twelve Apostles handpicked by Jesus to carry on his message (Mark 3:18); Simon who is mentioned as one of Jesus's "brothers" (Mark 6:3); and Simon of Cyrene, on whom "they laid the cross . . . and made him carry it behind Jesus" (Luke 23:26).

Famous Namesakes: Simon Baker, actor; Simón Bolivar, South American liberator; Simon Dubnow, Jewish historian; Simon Gagne, hockey player; Simon Kuznets, Nobel Prize winner in economics; Simon Rattle, conductor; Simon West, director.

SOLOMON ✦ *(SAWL-uh-muhn)*

Language/Cultural Origin: Hebrew

Meaning: Peaceable

Spiritual Connotation: Wisdom

Related Names/Nicknames: Salman, Salmon, Salomo, Shalmon, Sol

Alternate Names: Salomon, Salomone, Solaman, Soloman

Background Story: Solomon—the son of David and Bathsheba—succeeded his father as king of Israel, but not without fighting his half brother Adonijah for the throne. With David's blessing, however, Solomon was secretly anointed king while his father was still alive. Solomon took David's advice to "Be strong, be courageous, and keep the charge of the Lord your God" and had a peaceful and prosperous reign. He developed alliances with other nations, became involved in trade, and saw to it that his father's plans for a temple in Jerusalem were finally brought to fruition. Known for his wealth, Solomon was better known for the "great wisdom, discernment, and breadth of understanding" that God had given him. "People came from all the nations to hear the wisdom of Solomon," including the queen of Sheba. It was Solomon who settled a dispute between two women claiming the same child. He suggested they divide the child with a sword, then gave him to the woman who said she would rather give up her child than see him die. In his later years, women were Solomon's downfall, as he began to offer sacrifices to the gods of his numerous foreign wives and concubines. God's punishment was swift. After Solomon's death, the kingdom of Israel was divided forever (2 Samuel 12:24, 1 Kings 1–11).

Of Interest: Solomon is historically credited with authorship of the biblical books Proverbs, the Song of Solomon, and Ecclesiastes. *Song of Solomon* is also the name of a book written by the Nobel Prize–winning author Toni Morrison.

Famous Namesakes: Solomon Asch, psychologist; Solomon Burke, singer; Solomon R. Guggenheim, philanthropist; Solomon Jones, writer.

STEPHEN ✦ *(STEE-vehn)* or *(STEHF-uhn)*

Language/Cultural Origin: Greek

Meaning: Crown

Spiritual Connotation: Highest Victory

Related Names/Nicknames: Esteban, Estefan, Estevan, Etienne, Stefan, Stefano, Steffan, Steffen, Steffon, Stefon, Stephanas, Stephano, Stephanos, Stephanus, Stephens, Stephenson, Steve, Stevenson, Stevie, Stevy

Alternate Names: Steeven, Stephan, Stephon, Stevan, Steven

Background Story: Stephen was "a man full of faith and the Holy Spirit," chosen as one of the seven deacons of the early Church. He performed "great wonders and signs" in Jerusalem, and the Christian message continued to spread. Stephen's success angered some Jews, who accused him of "blasphemous words against Moses and God." When Stephen suggested they were not keeping God's law themselves, they stoned him. His last words were to ask the Lord to forgive them (Acts 6–7).

Of Interest: Stephen is considered the first Christian martyr. From 1940 to 2000, the name was in the top one hundred for boys in the United States.

Famous Namesakes: Steve Allen, Steve Martin, entertainers; Stephen Breyer, U.S. Supreme Court justice; Steve Forbes, publisher; Stephen Hawking, physicist; Steve Jobs, Steve Wozniak, entrepreneurs; Stephen King, writer; Steve McQueen, actor; Stephon Marbury, Steve Nash, basketball players; Steve Miller, Steven Morrissey, Stevie Wonder, musicians; Steven Spielberg, Steven Soderbergh, directors.

TABOR ✦ *(TAY-bor)* or *(TAY-ber)*

Language/Cultural Origin: Hebrew

Meaning: A Height

Spiritual Connotation: God's Grandeur

Related Names/Nicknames: Tab, Tabb, Tabbie, Taber, Tayber

Alternate Names: Taibor, Tavor, Taybor

Background Story: Tabor is best known in the Bible as the mountain that stood on the border between northern and southern Israel. From the slopes of Mount Tabor, Deborah and Barak led the Israelites against the Canaanites (Judges 4:6–16); the psalmist sang to God, "Tabor and Hermon joyously praise your name" (Psalms 89:12); and Jeremiah saw it as a metaphor for the power of Babylon: "As I live, says the King, whose name is the Lord of hosts, one is coming like Tabor among the mountains" (Jeremiah 46:18).

TAHAN ✦ (TAH-hahn)

Language/Cultural Origin: Hebrew

Meaning: Merciful

Spiritual Connotation: Forgiving

Related Names/Nicknames: Han

Alternate Names: None

Background Story: Tahan was Ephraim's third son and the grandson of Joseph. He was a patriarch of "the clan of the Tahanites" (Numbers 26:35). Another Tahan was the son of Tela and the father of Ladan (1 Chronicles 7:25). Tahan is a name that brings to mind a kind and forgiving man.

TEMAN ✦ (TEE-muhn)

Language/Cultural Origin: Hebrew

Meaning: Right Hand

Spiritual Connotation: Reaching Out

Related Names/Nicknames: Temani

Alternate Names: None

Background Story: Teman was one of the "kings who reigned in the land of Edom" before the Israelites had kings. The members of his tribe were known as Temani or Temanites, and the town of Teman, whose inhabitants were once known for their wisdom, was named for him (1 Chronicles 1:36, 43; Jeremiah 49:7). The name Teman suggests a man who reaches out to the people around him.

TEMENI ✦ *(TEH-mee-nai)* or *(TEE-mee-nai)*
Language/Cultural Origin: Hebrew
Meaning: From the South
Spiritual Connotation: Spiritual Destiny
Related Names/Nicknames: None
Alternate Names: None

Background Story: Temeni was the son of Ashhur and Naarah. He was also the great-grandson of Judah and a member of the tribe whose descendants were the Jewish people (1 Chronicles 4:6). The name Temeni is a reminder of God's presence in our lives.

TERTIUS ✦ *(TER-shuhs)* or *(TER-shee-uhs)*
Language/Cultural Origin: Latin
Meaning: The Third
Spiritual Connotation: Expressing God's Word
Related Names/Nicknames: Terry
Alternate Names: None

Background Story: Tertius was an early Christian and a scribe who assisted Paul in writing an epistle to the Romans. At the end of the letter, he added his own salutation to them: "I Tertius, the writer of this letter, greet you in the Lord" (Romans 16:22). Tertius is a name indicating a man who has a gift for communicating ideas.

THADDAEUS ✦ *(THAD-ee-uhs)*

Language/Cultural Origin: Aramaic

Meaning: Praises

Spiritual Connotation: Brave Heart

Related Names/Nicknames: Judas, Jude, Lebbaeus, Tad, Tadd, Taddeo, Taddeusz, Tadeo, Tadio, Tadzio, Thad, Thady

Alternate Names: Thaddaos, Thaddaus, Thaddeus, Thaddius, Thadeus

Background Story: In the Bible, Thaddaeus was one of the original Twelve Apostles whom Jesus chose "to be with him, and to be sent out to proclaim the message, and to have authority to cast out demons" (Mark 3:14–18). He is also referred to as "Lebbaeus, whose surname was Thaddaeus," "Judas the son of James," and "Judas (not Iscariot)."

Of Interest: Some Christian writers believe that the use of the surname Thaddaeus in the Bible was an attempt by the gospel writers to separate Judas Thaddaeus from the apostle Judas Iscariot, who brought shame on the name they both shared. In fact, he is often referred to as the "Forgotten Saint" in the Catholic Church, because many people associated him with the Judas who betrayed Jesus. Saint Jude Thaddaeus is honored as the patron saint of hopeless situations.

Famous Namesakes: Thaddeus Hogarth, singer/songwriter; Thad Jones, musician; Thaddeus Kosciusko, American Revolution hero and champion of Polish independence.

THEOPHILUS ✦ *(thee-AHF-uh-luhs)*

Language/Cultural Origin: Greek

Meaning: Lover of God

Spiritual Connotation: Cherished Friend

Related Names/Nicknames: Teofil, Teofilo, Theo, Theophile

Alternate Names: None

Background Story: Theophilus was a respected Christian whom Luke addresses at the beginning of his gospel and the Acts of the Apostles. Luke explains, "I . . . decided . . . to write an orderly account for you, most excellent Theophilus, so that you may know the truth concerning the things about which you have been instructed" (Luke 1:3–4).

Of Interest: Theophilus North is the title of a novel by Thornton Wilder and the name of its principal character.

Famous Namesakes: Théophile Gautier, writer.

THOMAS ✦ *(TAHM-uhs)*

Language/Cultural Origin: Greek/Aramaic

Meaning: Twin

Spiritual Connotation: God Is Patient

Related Names/Nicknames: Thom, Thomason, Thompson, Thomson, Tom, Tomas, Tomaso, Tomasso, Tomey, Tomie, Tomislaw, Tomkin, Tomlin, Tommey, Tommie, Tommy

Alternate Names: Tahmas, Tamas, Tomas, Tomasz, Tomaz, Toomas, Tuomas

Background Story: Thomas, the apostle "called the twin," is best known as the man who doubted Jesus. The story goes that Jesus appeared to the apostles soon after his Resurrection, but Thomas was missing. Although the others told him they had seen Jesus, Thomas said, "Unless I see the mark of the nails in his hands, and put my finger in the mark of the nails and my hand in his side, I will not believe." A week later, Jesus appeared to the apostles again and directed Thomas to touch the wounds in his hands and on his side. Thomas answered, "My Lord and my God!" and Jesus replied, "Have you believed because you have seen me? Blessed are those who have not seen and yet have come to believe" (John 20:24–29).

Of Interest: Thomas Aquinas, Thomas Becket, and Thomas More are three well-known saints in the Catholic Church.

Famous Namesakes: Tom Clancy, Thomas Hardy, Thomas Mann, Thomas Stearns (T. S.) Eliot, writers; Tom Cruise, Tom Hanks, actors; Thomas Edison, inventor; Tom Ford, fashion designer; Thomas Hobbes, philosopher; Thomas Jefferson, third president of the United States; Tommy Tune, dancer/choreographer.

TIMON ✦ *(TAI-muhn)* or *(tee-MON)*

Language/Cultural Origin: Greek

Meaning: Honorable

Spiritual Connotation: Wise Spirit

Related Names/Nicknames: Tim, Timmy, Timo, Timothy

Alternate Names: Tymon

Background Story: Timon was a respected member of the early Christian community in Jerusalem. At the time, discipleship was increasing and some of the physical needs of the community had been neglected. To ease their burden and free themselves "to prayer and to serving the Lord," the apostles gathered together the community to select "seven men of good standing, full of the Spirit and of wisdom" for this task. Timon was one of those chosen (Acts 6:1–5).

Famous Namesakes: Timo Perez, baseball player; Timon of Athens, title character in a play by William Shakespeare; Timon, a hyperactive but loyal meerkat played by Nathan Lane in the animated film *The Lion King*.

TIMOTHY ✦ *(TIHM-uh-thee)*

Language/Cultural Origin: Greek

Meaning: Honoring God

Spiritual Connotation: Child of Faith

Related Names/Nicknames: Tim, Timmo, Timmy, Timo, Timon, Timotheo, Timotheos, Timotheus, Tymon, Tymoteusz

Alternate Names: Timmothy, Timothe, Timothey, Tymmothy, Tymothy

Background Story: Timothy—the son of a Greek man—lived in Lystra, where his faith was nurtured by his mother, Eunice, and grandmother Lois. He began to accompany Paul on his second missionary journey and, over the years, became a trusted disciple. Paul spoke of Timothy repeatedly in his epistles, saying that he was "like a son with a father" to him and calling him "my beloved and faithful child in the Lord." Paul also wrote letters to Timothy, instructing him how to teach Christian doctrine and advising him to "fight the good fight, having faith and a good conscience" (Acts 16:3, 1 Corinthians 4:17, Philippians 2:22, 1 Timothy).

Famous Namesakes: Timothy Busfield, actor/director; Timothy Dalton, Timothy Hutton, Tim Robbins, Tim Roth, actors;

Timothy Ferris, writer; Timothy Goebel, Olympic figure skater; Timothy Zahn, novelist.

TIRAS ✦ *(TAI-ruhs)*
Language/Cultural Origin: Hebrew
Meaning: Desirable
Spiritual Connotation: Originator
Related Names/Nicknames: None
Alternate Names: Tirras

Background Story: Tiras was Japheth's youngest son, born to him after the flood. It was through Tiras and his brothers, Noah's grandchildren, that "the coastland peoples spread," creating the many nations of humankind (Genesis 10:2–5). The name Tiras suggests an innovative man who is full of exciting, new ideas waiting to be born.

TITUS ✦ *(TAI-tuhs)*
Language/Cultural Origin: Greek/Latin
Meaning: Pleasing
Spiritual Connotation: Caregiver
Related Names/Nicknames: Tite, Tito, Ty
Alternate Names: Titos, Tytus

Background Story: Titus—a Greek convert—was one of the few men Paul trusted to assist him with his missionary work. Paul sent him to Corinth when he was concerned about the state of the Christian community there, and he later told the

Corinthians that he "rejoiced . . . at the joy of Titus, because his mind has been set at rest by all of you." While in Corinth, Titus also collected money for the poor in Jerusalem. Later, Paul left Titus to establish the Church at the island of Crete and sent letters with detailed advice, which he summed up in a few words. "Teach what is consistent with sound doctrine," Paul wrote (2 Corinthians 7, 8; Titus 1, 2).

Of Interest: Titus was also a first-century Roman emperor who put down the Jewish rebellion resulting in the destruction of the temple in Jerusalem.

TOBIAS ✦ *(to-BAI-uhs)*

Language/Cultural Origin: Greek

Meaning: God Is Good

Spiritual Connotation: The Lord Provides

Related Names/Nicknames: Tobe, Tobee, Tobey, Tobi, Tobia, Tobie, Tobin, Tobit, Toby, Tobyn

Alternate Names: Tobiah

Background Story: Tobias—or Tobiah in Hebrew—was the son of Tobit, a captive Israelite in the city of Nineveh. When Tobit lost his wealth and his sight, he sent Tobias back to Media to find a wife and reclaim the money he had left behind. In Media, Sarah was equally saddened. She had lost seven bridegrooms on her wedding night because of a "wicked demon." Tobit and Sarah both prayed to the Lord, and he answered them by sending the angel Raphael to Tobias. With Raphael's help, Tobias destroyed the demon, married Sarah, returned with the money, and cured his father of blindness. Tobias and Sarah settled in Media and were spared the destruction of Nineveh (Book of Tobit).

Famous Namesakes: Toby Keith, singer/songwriter; Tobey Maguire, actor; Tobias Picker, composer; Tobias Wolff, writer.

URI ✦ *(YOO-rai)* or *(YOOR-ee)*
Language/Cultural Origin: Hebrew
Meaning: My Fire
Spiritual Connotation: Passion for the Lord
Related Names/Nicknames: Uriah, Uriel, Uril
Alternate Names: Uree, Urey, Urie, Ury, Yuri

Background Story: The name Uri is connected to two men in the Bible: the father of Bezalel, an artisan whom the Lord filled "with divine spirit, with ability, intelligence, and knowledge in every kind of craft" to create the meeting tent and the ark of the covenant for Moses (Exodus 31:1–7); and the father of Geber, one of the twelve officials "who provided food" for Solomon (1 Kings 4:19).

Famous Namesakes: Uri Avneri, journalist/peace activist; Uri Banai, Israeli singer; Yuri Gagarin, Soviet cosmonaut and first man in space; Uri Geller, writer/psychic.

URIAH ✦ *(yoo-RAI-uh)* or *(yer-RAI-uh)*
Language/Cultural Origin: Hebrew
Meaning: The Lord Is My Light
Spiritual Connotation: Man of Integrity
Related Names/Nicknames: Uri, Urian, Urias, Urija, Urijah, Uruah, Yuri
Alternate Names: Uria, Uriyah, Urya, Uryah, Yuria

Background Story: The story of Uriah the Hittite is a dark stain on the otherwise uplifting story of David in the Bible. Uriah was a loyal soldier in King David's army and one of his "mighty men." He was married to Bathsheba, a woman of exceptional beauty, who caught the eye of the king. While Uriah was at war, David surrendered to his lust and "lay with her." When Bathsheba became pregnant, David tried to cover up his sin by calling Uriah from the front and suggesting he visit his family. Uriah refused to go home. "The servants of my lord are camping in the open field," he said. "Shall I then go to my house, to eat and to drink, and to lie with my wife? As you live, and as your soul lives, I will not do such a thing." David then committed an even greater sin. He ordered Uriah back to the front and told his commander to put him in the fiercest of combat, where he was killed. Although Bathsheba lost her child, she eventually became David's wife and the mother of the next king of Israel, Solomon (2 Samuel 11–12).

Famous Namesakes: Uriah Duffy, musician; Uriah Heep, British rock band and a character in the novel *David Copperfield* by Charles Dickens.

URIEL ✦ *(YOOR-ee-uhl)* or *(OOR-ee-ehl)*
Language/Cultural Origin: Hebrew
Meaning: Flame of God
Spiritual Connotation: Heavenly Spirit
Related Names/Nicknames: Uri
Alternate Names: Uriell, Urielle, Uryel, Uryell

Background Story: Uriel was a descendant of Levi's son Kohath. During David's reign he was in charge "of the sons of Kohath" who helped to carry "the ark of the Lord" to the place David had prepared in Jerusalem (1 Chronicles 6:24, 15:3–5).

Of Interest: Uriel is the name of an angel in various traditions. In the Apocrypha, he was an angel sent by God to instruct Ezra; in Jewish mystical tradition, he was the angel who wrestled with Jacob and warned Noah about the flood; and in Muslim tradition, he is the angel who will sound the trumpet on Judgment Day. Uriel is also an angel in John Milton's *Paradise Lost* and the subject of a poem by Ralph Waldo Emerson.

ZACCHAEUS ✦ *(za-KEE-uhs)*

Language/Cultural Origin: Hebrew/Greek

Meaning: Pure

Spiritual Connotation: Cleansed by God

Related Names/Nicknames: Zaccai, Zachariah, Zach

Alternate Names: Zaccheus, Zachaios

Background Story: Zacchaeus, a wealthy tax collector, was in Jericho when Jesus was passing through. Since he was short, he was unable to see Jesus, so he "ran ahead and climbed a sycamore tree." When Jesus saw Zacchaeus up in the tree, he called him down and said, "I must stay at your house today." Zacchaeus was thrilled to have Jesus come to his home and he promised, on the spot, to give half of what he owned to the poor. The people who were watching complained that Jesus was going to the house of a sinner. But Jesus said, "Today salvation has come to this house . . . for the Son of Man came to seek out and to save the lost" (Luke 19:1–10).

ZACCUR ✦ *(ZAK-er)*

Language/Cultural Origin: Hebrew

Meaning: Mindful

Spiritual Connotation: Regard for Others

Related Names/Nicknames: Zach

Alternate Names: Zacchur

Background Story: Three notable Zaccurs in the Old Testament are: one of Asaph's sons, whose service was to "prophesy with lyres, harps, and cymbals" in the temple for David (1 Chronicles 25:1–2); a man who worked on repairing the temple in Jerusalem (Nehemiah 3:2); and a Levite whose name was on Nehemiah's sealed covenant with the Lord (Nehemiah 10:12). The name Zaccur suggests a man who is kind, generous, and mindful of other people's needs and wants.

ZACHARIAS ✦ *(zak-uh-RAI-uhs)*

Language/Cultural Origin: Greek/Hebrew

Meaning: The Lord Has Remembered

Spiritual Connotation: Righteous Before God

Related Names/Nicknames: Zac, Zacary, Zach, Zachariah, Zachary, Zachery, Zack, Zackery, Zackie, Zak, Zakarie, Zakery, Zechariah, Zecheriah, Zekariah, Zekeriah, Zeke

Alternate Names: Zacarias, Zackerias, Zakarias, Zecharias

Background Story: Zacharias, a priest in Judea, was married to a woman named Elizabeth. Although "they were both righteous before God," they had entered their old age childless. One day in the temple, the angel Gabriel visited him. He said, "Do not be afraid, Zacharias, for your prayer is heard; and your wife Elizabeth will bear you a son, and you shall call his name John." When Zacharias dared to doubt the angel's message, he was struck dumb. As Gabriel promised, Elizabeth had a son, and the time soon came to circumcise and name him. Remembering the angel's words, Zacharias wrote on a tablet, "His name is John." At that moment, his voice returned and he praised God. Then he prophesied to his son, "You, child, will be called the prophet of the Highest; For you will go before the face of the Lord to prepare his ways." Zacharias's son was John the Baptist, the man who led the way for Jesus (Luke 1:5–80).

Of Interest: Zacharias is the Greek form of Zechariah and appears in most versions of the New Testament.

Famous Namesakes: Zacharias Hildebrandt, organ builder; Zacharias Janssen, inventor of the compound microscope; Zacharias Topelius, Finnish novelist; Christian Zacharias, pianist/conductor.

ZEBADIAH ✦ *(zehb-uh-DAI-uh)*

Language/Cultural Origin: Hebrew

Meaning: God Has Bestowed

Spiritual Connotation: Gift of Leadership

Related Names/Nicknames: Zabdi, Zabdiel, Zeb, Zebedee

Alternate Names: Zebedia, Zebediah, Zebedya, Zebidia, Zebidiah, Zebydia, Zebydiah

Background Story: A number of Zebadiahs stand out in the Bible: one of David's warriors, who "could shoot arrows and sling stones with either . . . hand" (1 Chronicles 12:2, 7); Asahel's son, a commander of "twenty-four thousand" in David's army (1 Chronicles 27:7); a Levite priest sent by Jehoshaphat to teach the law of Moses "in the cities of Judah" (2 Chronicles 17:8); and a governor of Judah who was chief of the Levite judges "in all the king's matters" (2 Chronicles 19:11). The name Zebadiah suggests a man who takes charge when something needs to be done.

Famous Namesakes: Zeb Turner, musician.

ZECHARIAH ✦ *(zehk-uh-RAI-uh)*

Language/Cultural Origin: Hebrew

Meaning: Remembered by the Lord

Spiritual Connotation: Visions of Triumph

Related Names/Nicknames: Zacarias, Zaccur, Zach, Zacharias, Zachary, Zachery, Zack, Zackary, Zackery, Zak, Zecharias, Zecher, Zichri

Alternate Names: Zacaria, Zaccaria, Zaccariah, Zacharia, Zachariah, Zecheriah, Zekariah, Zekeriah

Background Story: There are no fewer than thirty-one Zechariahs in the Bible, but one stands above the rest. Zechariah, the son of Berechiah and grandson of Iddo, is a minor prophet of the Old Testament. He had a series of visions meant to encourage the Jews who had returned from captivity to rebuild the temple in Jerusalem. "I have returned to Jerusalem with compassion; my house shall be built in it," God said, assuring his people that their enemies had been destroyed. Zechariah also prophesied the coming of the Messiah: "Lo, your king comes to you; triumphant and victorious is he, humble and riding on a donkey . . . and he shall command peace to the nations" (Book of Zechariah).

Famous Namesakes: Zach Braff, Zachery Ty Bryan, Zachary Scott, actors; Zachary Taylor, twelfth president of the United States; Zach Thomas, football player.

ZEDEKIAH ✦ *(zehd-uh-KAI-uh)*

Language/Cultural Origin: Hebrew

Meaning: The Lord Is Mighty and Just

Spiritual Connotation: God Prevails

Related Names/Nicknames: Zed

Alternate Names: Zedechiah

Background Story: There are three prominent Zedekiahs in the Bible: the last king of Judah, placed on the throne after the Babylonians conquered Jerusalem and later taken into captivity himself (2 Kings 24:17); a man whose name was on Nehemiah's sealed covenant with the Lord (Nehemiah 10:1); and one of King Jehoiakim's officials, who warned Baruch to hide from the king after hearing him read Jeremiah's prophecy about the fall of Jerusalem (Jeremiah 36:12).

Famous Namesakes: Zed Nelson, British photojournalist.

ZEPHANIAH ✦ *(zehf-uh-NAI-uh)*

Language/Cultural Origin: Hebrew

Meaning: Treasured by God

Spiritual Connotation: Renewed Faith

Related Names/Nicknames: Zeph, Zephan

Alternate Names: Zephania

Background Story: The most inspiring Zephaniah in the Bible was the son of Cushi and a minor prophet during the reign of King Josiah. Along with the other prophets, he wrote about the impending destruction of Judah because of idolatry and promised that "the day of the Lord" would soon come. Yet Zephaniah tempered his message with a promise of ultimate redemption. To those people who remained and sought "refuge in the name of the Lord," Zephaniah said that God "will renew you in his love" (Book of Zephaniah).

Famous Namesakes: Benjamin Zephaniah, writer.

ZERAH ✦ *(ZEE-ruh)* or *(ZIHR-uh)*
Language/Cultural Origin: Hebrew
Meaning: Brightness
Spiritual Connotation: Bringing Joy
Related Names/Nicknames: Zara, Zarah
Alternate Names: Zerach

Background Story: Of the men named Zerah in the Bible, the twin son of Judah and Tamar is by far the most interesting. When his mother was in labor, Zerah put out his hand first, and the midwife "bound on his hand a crimson thread" to indicate he was the firstborn. Then Zerah "drew back his hand" and his brother, Perez, came out first. Zerah was born later "with the crimson thread" still bound on his hand (Genesis 38:27–30).

Famous Namesakes: Zerah Colburn, child prodigy; Zerah Warhaftig, a founding father of modern Israel.

ZIMRAN ✦ *(ZIHM-ran)*
Language/Cultural Origin: Hebrew
Meaning: Singer
Spiritual Connotation: Song of Praise
Related Names/Nicknames: None
Alternate Names: None

Background Story: Zimran was Abraham's oldest son with his wife or concubine, Keturah. Although Abraham left most of what he owned to Isaac, before he died he "gave gifts" to his other sons and sent them to live in the east country (Genesis 25:1–6). The name Zimran suggests a man who loves music and may have a talent for it.

ZURIEL ⁕ *(ZOO-ree-ehl)* or *(zoo-RAI-uhl)*

Language/Cultural Origin: Hebrew

Meaning: Rock of God

Spiritual Connotation: Responsible

Related Names/Nicknames: None

Alternate Names: None

Background Story: Zuriel was a Levite and chief of the clans of Merari during the Exodus. His clans were responsible for "the frames of the tabernacle" as well as "all their accessories" (Numbers 3:35–36). The name Zuriel suggests a man of faith who shoulders the responsibility of God's work in the world.

Famous Namesakes: Zuriel Smith, football player.

GIRLS' NAMES

A good name is to be chosen rather than great riches.

—Proverbs 22:1

ABANA ❀ *(A-bah-nuh)* or *(uh-BAY-nuh)*

Language/Cultural Origin: Hebrew

Meaning: Constant

Spiritual Connotation: Everlasting

Related Names/Nicknames: Amana, Amanah

Alternate Names: Abanah, Abhanah

Background Story: The Abana was a river in Syria that flowed through the ancient city of Damascus, creating a lush, fertile plain around it. One day, a Syrian called Naaman traveled to the prophet Elisha and asked him to cure his leprosy. The prophet told him to bathe in the Jordan River. Naaman responded angrily, "Are not Abana and Pharpar, the rivers of Damascus, better than all the waters of Israel? Could I not wash in them, and be clean?" After a change of heart, he did as Elisha said— and was cured (2 Kings 5:9–14).

Of Interest: The modern name of this river is Barada. It is considered the "golden stream" by the Greeks. A series of channels fanning out from the main stem give life to the beautiful green oasis that surrounds the city of Damascus today.

ABIGAIL ❀ *(AB-ih-gayl)*

Language/Cultural Origin: Hebrew

Meaning: A Father's Joy

Spiritual Connotation: Understanding

Related Names/Nicknames: Abbe, Abbey, Abbie, Abby, Gael, Gail, Gale, Gayle

Alternate Names: Abagale, Abigael, Abigayle, Abygail, Abygale

Background Story: David had a sister named Abigail in the Bible (1 Chronicles 2:16–17), but another Abigail played an even more significant part in his life. She was the wife of Nabal, a wealthy shepherd whose flocks David and his men protected. Abigail was "clever and beautiful," but her husband was "surly and mean." When David sent his men to Nabal for food and provisions, they were insulted and turned away. An outraged David prepared to destroy Nabal. Without telling her husband, Abigail went to meet David with a generous offering of food. She "fell before David on her face, bowing to the ground" and begged his forgiveness for her husband's behavior. Her graciousness and beauty convinced David not to attack. When Nabal heard what had happened, "he became like stone" and died a few days later. David then took Abigail as his wife (1 Samuel 25:2–42).

Of Interest: From 2001 to 2004 Abigail ranked among the top ten names in the United States.

Famous Namesakes: Abigail Adams was the wife of John Adams, the second president of the United States, and the mother of John Quincy Adams, the sixth president. Also, the popular advice columnist known as "Dear Abby" was Abigail Van Buren.

ABIHAIL ✦ *(ab-uh-HAY-uhl)*

Language/Cultural Origin: Hebrew

Meaning: Father of Might

Spiritual Connotation: Resolute

Related Names/Nicknames: Abbey, Haley

Alternate Names: None

Background Story: Two women are known as Abihail in the Bible. The first was the wife of Abishur, who came from the tribe of Judah. The couple had two sons: Ahban and Molid (1 Chronicles

2:29). The second Abihail was mother to Malahath and mother-in-law to Rehoboam—Solomon's son who succeeded him as king of Judah (2 Chronicles 11:18). Abihail is a bold name that implies a woman with strength of purpose.

ABILENE ✦ *(ab-uh-LEE-neh)* or *(AB-uh-leen)*

Language/Cultural Origin: Hebrew

Meaning: Land of Meadows

Spiritual Connotation: Openness

Related Names/Nicknames: Abila

Alternate Names: Abalene, Abalina, Abilena, Abiline

Background Story: Abilene was a large plain in Israel. Its principal town, Abila, was situated on the Abana River about eighteen miles from Damascus. Lysanias, a Roman, ruled Abilene when John the Baptist began his ministry, "proclaiming a baptism of repentance for the forgiveness of sins" (Luke 3:1–3).

Of Interest: Legend has it that Abilene is the site of Abel's tomb.

Famous Namesakes: In 1857, Eliza Hersey named the frontier village of Abilene in Kansas after the plain described in Luke's gospel. It was the boyhood home of President Dwight David Eisenhower.

ABITAL ✦ *(AB-ih-tal)*

Language/Cultural Origin: Hebrew

Meaning: My Father Is the Night Dew

Spiritual Connotation: Pure

Related Names/Nicknames: Abbey

Alternate Names: Abeetal, Abhital, Avital

Background Story: Abital was one of King David's wives and the mother of his fifth son, Shephatiah. He was born when they lived in Hebron, where David reigned for seven and a half years (1 Chronicles 3:3–4). The name Abital suggests a woman with a fresh and pure spirit.

ACACIA ✦ *(uh-KAY-shuh)*

Language/Cultural Origin: Greek

Meaning: Guileless

Spiritual Connotation: Resurrection

Related Names/Nicknames: Cacia, Cacie, Casey, Casha, Casia, Cassie, Cassy, Caysha, Kacey, Kacia, Kacie, Kasey, Kasi, Kassie, Kassja, Kassy, Keisha

Alternate Names: None

Background Story: The acacia or "shittah" was a thorny hardwood tree abundant in the Holy Land. On Mount Sinai, when God commanded Moses to build a tabernacle, he gave specific instructions: "They shall make an ark of acacia wood" (Exodus 25:10). The ark of the covenant was a constant reminder of God's presence for the Israelites, as they traveled across the desert and into the Promised Land.

Of Interest: The acacia was—and still is—a remarkable desert tree that provides shade from the sun, edible leaves, and wood that is both durable for building and excellent as fuel. The sap that oozes from its bark is known as gum arabic, a useful ingredient in many products today. To the Greeks, this blossoming tree symbolizes rebirth.

ACHAIA ✦ *(uh-KAY-yuh)*

Language/Cultural Origin: Greek

Meaning: Grief

Spiritual Connotation: Remembrance

Related Names/Nicknames: None

Alternate Names: Achaea

Background Story: In the New Testament, Achaia was a Roman province that included the southern half of Greece. Its major cities were Corinth, Athens, and Sparta. Paul the apostle traveled through Achaia on two missionary journeys and spent considerable time in Corinth making converts. In one of his letters, Paul commended the Christians in Achaia who "have been pleased to share their resources with the poor among the saints at Jerusalem" (Romans 15:26). The name Achaia is a reminder to share with those who are less fortunate.

ACHSA ✦ *(AK-suh)*

Language/Cultural Origin: Hebrew

Meaning: Adorned

Spiritual Connotation: Forthright

Related Names/Nicknames: None

Alternate Names: Achsah, Ascah

Background Story: Caleb had one daughter—Achsa—and he offered her in marriage to whoever would take the Canaanite city of Debir. Othniel led a successful attack and won her as his wife. Later, Achsa encouraged Othniel to ask Caleb for the gift of a field. When her father asked if there was anything else she wanted, Achsa said, "Give me a present; since you have set me in the land of the Negeb, give me springs of water as well." Caleb gave her the upper and lower springs, in addition to the land (Joshua 15:16–19).

ADAH ✦ *(AH-duh)* or *(AY-duh)*

Language/Cultural Origin: Hebrew

Meaning: Adornment

Spiritual Connotation: Exalted Nature

Related Names/Nicknames: Adan, Addi, Addiah, Addie, Addy, Adena, Adey, Adi, Adia, Adiah, Adie, Adina, Aida, Dena, Dina

Alternate Names: Ada, Adda, Ade, Aidah, Ayda

Background Story: Two Adahs are mentioned in the Bible. The first was one of Lamech's two wives. Her husband was descended from Cain and bragged that he also had killed for revenge. Adah had two sons: Jabal, "ancestor of those who live in tents and have livestock," and Jubal, "ancestor of all those who play the lyre and the pipe" (Genesis 4:19–24). The second Adah was one of Esau's wives and the daughter of Elon the Hittite (Genesis 36:2).

Of Interest: Adah is the second woman's name to appear in the Bible—after Eve.

ADALIA ✦ *(a-duh-LAI-uh)*

Language/Cultural Origin: Hebrew/Arabic/Old German

Meaning: Noble One

Spiritual Connotation: God Is My Refuge

Related Names/Nicknames: Adal, Adala, Adalee,
Adali, Adalie, Adalley, Addala, Adela, Adelaide,
Adele, Adeline

Alternate Names: Adalya

Background Story: Adalia was the son of Haman, a high-ranking official who plotted to massacre the Jews. He and his brothers were killed and hanged from the gallows when Queen Esther revealed his father's plot to her husband, King Ahasuerus, who allowed the Jewish people to retaliate (Esther 9:8–10). Adalia is primarily a girl's name today and suggests a woman of faith and dignity.

Of Interest: Adalia is the name for the genus of ladybugs.

ADDI ✦ *(AD-ee)*

Language/Cultural Origin: Hebrew

Meaning: Adorned

Spiritual Connotation: In God's Family

Related Names/Nicknames: Ada, Ade, Adelaide

Alternate Names: None

Background Story: Addi—the son of Cosam and the father of Melchi—was an ancestor of Joseph, Mary's husband. His name appears in Luke's genealogy of Jesus (Luke 3:28). The name Addi, which is used for both men and women today, suggests someone who is outgoing and likable.

ADINA ✦ *(uh-DEE-nuh)*

Language/Cultural Origin: Hebrew

Meaning: Delicate

Spiritual Connotation: Gentle

Related Names/Nicknames: Adena, Adene, Adine, Deena

Alternate Names: Adinah

Background Story: Adina—one of David's great warriors—was the son of Shiza. He was a leader of the tribe of Reuben and had thirty men with him (1 Chronicles 11:42). Courageous warriors such as Adina gave David "strong support in his kingdom" and helped him to become king (1 Chronicles 11:10). Adina, a name that suggests quiet strength, is used for both men and women today.

AMARIAH ✦ *(am-uh-RAI-uh)*

Language/Cultural Origin: Hebrew

Meaning: The Lord Promises

Spiritual Connotation: Given by God

Related Names/Nicknames: Amaris, Amarisa, Amarise

Alternate Names: Amaria, Amarihah, Amariya, Amarya, Amaryah

Background Story: Many of the men named Amariah in the Bible dedicated their lives to serving in God's temple. Some notable ones are: a descendant of Moses who worked "in the house of the Lord" during David's reign (1 Chronicles 23:4, 19); Jehoshaphat's chief priest, whose job was to settle religious disputes (2 Chronicles 19:11); and a priest appointed by Hezekiah to apportion the free-will offering to his people (2 Chronicles 31:15).

Amariah—also a lovely name for a woman today—evokes a sense of gratitude and appreciation.

ANNA ✦ *(A-nuh)* or *(AH-nuh)*

Language/Cultural Origin: Greek

Meaning: One Who Gives

Spiritual Connotation: Gracious

Related Names/Nicknames: Anca, Ania, Anica, Anita, Anka, Anne, Annette, Anni, Annice, Anusia, Nan, Nance, Nancy, Nanette, Nanice, Nanita, Nanny, Nansi, Nita, Panni

Alternate Names: Hannah

Background Story: Anna was an elderly widow and prophetess who spent most of her time praying and fasting at the temple in Jerusalem. After Jesus's birth, Mary and Joseph brought their child to the temple as Jewish law required. An old man named Simeon—who had been promised he would see the Messiah before he died—was also there. When Simeon took Jesus in his arms and said, "Master, now you are dismissing your servant in peace . . . for my eyes have seen your salvation," Anna praised God and spoke "about the child to all who were looking for the redemption of Jerusalem" (Luke 2:25–38).

Of Interest: Anna ranked among the top twenty names in the United States from 2001 to 2004.

Famous Namesakes: Anna Kournikova, tennis player; Anna Magnani, Anna Paquin, actresses; Anna Pavlova, Russian classical ballerina; Anna Quindlen, novelist/journalist.

ANTONIA ✦ *(an-TON-ee-uh)*

Language/Cultural Origin: Latin

Meaning: Priceless

Spiritual Connotation: Praiseworthy

Related Names/Nicknames: Antoinetta, Antoinette, Antonella, Antonetta, Antonette, Antonietta, Antonina, Antonique, Antonisha, Nella, Netta, Nettie, Netty, Toinette, Tonette, Toni, Tonia, Tonie, Tony, Tonya

Alternate Names: Antonie, Antonija, Antoniya, Antonya

Background Story: Antonia was a large fortress in Jerusalem, located in a corner of the temple area. Herod, who fortified it with Roman soldiers, named it after his friend Mark Antony. Paul was carried there once by soldiers who were trying to protect him from the violence of a mob. Before going inside, Paul "stood on the steps and motioned to the people for silence." As the crowd quieted, Paul told them the moving story of his conversion on the road to Damascus (Acts 21:27–40).

Of Interest: My Antonia is a famous literary classic written by Willa Cather. Published in 1918, it's the story of a spirited immigrant girl growing up on the Nebraska prairie in the late nineteenth century.

Famous Namesakes: Lady Antonia Fraser, writer; Dr. Antonia Novello, first woman and first Hispanic surgeon general of the United States.

APPHIA ✦ *(AF-ee-uh)*

Language/Cultural Origin: Hebrew/Greek

Meaning: Increasing

Spiritual Connotation: Flourishing

Related Names/Nicknames: Amphia, Appia

Alternate Names: None

Background Story: Apphia lived in Colosse, where she practiced Christianity. Paul mentioned her in a letter he wrote to Philemon and Archippus—who may have been her husband or brother or son. Paul referred to her simply as "our sister" (Philemon 1:2). Apphia, Philemon, and Archippus were stoned to death for their religious beliefs during the first century.

Of Interest: Apphia is a saint and martyr in the Catholic Church.

ARIEL ✦ *(A-ree-ehl)* or *(EHR-ee-ehl)*

Language/Cultural Origin: Hebrew

Meaning: Lioness of God

Spiritual Connotation: Moral Strength

Related Names/Nicknames: Alli, Areille, Ariela, Ariella, Ariellel, Athaleyah, Rel

Alternate Names: Arial, Ariele, Arielle, Aryel

Background Story: When Isaiah spoke the words, "Ah, Ariel, Ariel, the city where David encamped!" he was giving a symbolic name to the city of Jerusalem. The name Ariel had two meanings for Isaiah. He was describing Jerusalem as both the lioness of God and the altar hearth on which sacrifices were made to the Lord (Isaiah 29:1–2).

Of Interest: The brightest moon of the planet Uranus is called Ariel.

Famous Namesakes: Ariel Durant is the coauthor of *The Story of Civilization.* Ariel is also the name of a mischievous sprite in Shakespeare's play *The Tempest,* and the title character in the Disney movie *The Little Mermaid.*

ASA ✦ *(AY-suh)*

Language/Cultural Origin: Hebrew

Meaning: Healer

Spiritual Connotation: Renewal

Related Names/Nicknames: None

Alternate Names: Asah

Background Story: Asa was the third king of Judah and did "what was . . . right in the sight of the Lord." Not only did he rid his kingdom of pagan idols, he also removed his mother, Maacah, as queen mother, because she worshipped them. Asa's faith in God gave him the power to overthrow the enormous Ethiopian army and provide years of peace for his people. Although "the heart of Asa was true all his days," he faltered in his old age and succumbed to a "severe" illness, because he trusted his physicians rather than the Lord (2 Chronicles 14–17). The name Asa is used for both men and women today.

Famous Namesakes: Asa Carlsson, tennis player; Asa Harris, jazz vocalist.

ASIA ✦ *(AY-zhuh)*

Language/Cultural Origin: Greek/Latin

Meaning: Rising Sun

Spiritual Connotation: Life

Related Names/Nicknames: Aisha, Asianne, Aspasia, Asya, Asyah

Alternate Names: Aja, Asiah, Azha, Azia

Background Story: During the time of the New Testament, Asia was a Roman province in the western part of Asia Minor—now called Turkey. Its capital was Ephesus. Paul had many wealthy friends who were "asiarchs," or chiefs of Asia. He also preached there "so that all the residents of Asia, both Jews and Greeks, heard the word of the Lord" (Acts 19:10).

Of Interest: According to the Koran, Pharaoh's wife—the woman who raised Moses as her own son—was called Asia.

ATARAH ✦ *(AT-uh-rah)* or *(uh-TAH-rah)*
Language/Cultural Origin: Hebrew
Meaning: Crown
Spiritual Connotation: Honor
Related Names/Nicknames: Atera, Ateret, Tara
Alternate Names: Atara

Background Story: Atarah was a descendant of Judah and one of Jerahmeel's wives. She was also the mother of Onan who had two sons: Shammai and Jada (1 Chronicles 2:26–28). The name Atarah suggests a woman who carries herself with dignity.

ATHALIA ✦ *(ath-uh-LAI-uh)*
Language/Cultural Origin: Hebrew
Meaning: The Lord Is Exalted
Spiritual Connotation: God is Great
Related Names/Nicknames: Atalee, Atalie, Athalea, Athalee, Athalie, Attalie, Talia
Alternate Names: Atalia, Atalya, Athaliah

Background Story: Athalia's life was filled with intrigue and deception. Her marriage to King Jehoram secured a political alliance between Israel and Judah. Although her husband promoted the worship of Yahweh, Athalia was a devout follower of Baal— like her infamous mother, Jezebel. After Jehoram's death, she acted as counselor to her son Ahaziah, who died a year later. Athalia was determined to hold on to the throne, and she had all her grandchildren executed—all but one. Joash escaped and was hidden by his aunt, Jehosheba, and her husband, Jehoiada. Six years later, Jehosheba revealed Joash to the palace guards, who crowned him king and killed Athalia with a sword. Jehoiada then "made a covenant between the Lord and the king and people, that they should be the Lord's people." The altars to Baal were torn down and his images destroyed. The people rejoiced and "the city was quiet" (2 Kings 11). Athalia was the only woman powerful enough to sit on David's throne.

Of Interest: George Frideric Handel, composer of the well-known *Messiah* oratorio, also wrote an oratorio titled *Athalia,* based on the biblical story of Judah's queen.

AZARIAH   ✦   *(a-zuh-RAI-uh)*

Language/Cultural Origin: Hebrew

Meaning: Helped by God

Spiritual Connotation: Encouragement

Related Names/Nicknames: Azria, Azriah, Zaria

Alternate Names: Azaria, Azaryah, Azeria, Azeriah, Azorya, Azuria, Azuriah

Background Story: Azariah is a popular name for men in the Bible. Some of the better known were: King Amaziah's son who succeeded his father when he was sixteen (2 Kings 14:21–22); a priest in Solomon's temple in Jerusalem (1 Chronicles 6:9–10); and Oded's son, who persuaded Asa to return his people to the Lord

(2 Chronicles 15:1–19). The best known was a young man from Judah who was taken with Daniel and his two friends to King Nebuchadnezzar's palace and had his name changed to Abed-nego. The four young men—who were handsome and "versed in every branch of wisdom"—became advisers to the king (Daniel 1:1–21). Azariah is a name for both boys and girls.

Of Interest: Azariah (Abednego) and his friends were thrown into a fiery furnace for refusing to worship idols. In "The Prayer of Azariah," included in some versions of the Bible, God sends an angel to prevent the men from being harmed, and Azariah gives praise and thanks to God.

BAARA ✦ *(Bay-AY-ruh)*
Language/Cultural Origin: Hebrew
Meaning: Flame
Spiritual Connotation: Zealous
Related Names/Nicknames: None
Alternate Names: None

Background Story: Shaharaim of the tribe of Benjamin had two wives: Baara and Hushim. He sent them away before he left for the country of Moab, where he had seven sons with Hodesh. Hushim had two sons, but no mention is made of Baara having any children (1 Chronicles 8:8–11). Baara is a powerful name, implying a woman who lives life to the fullest.

BATHSHEBA ✦ *(bath-SHEE-buh)*

Language/Cultural Origin: Hebrew

Meaning: Daughter of the Oath

Spiritual Connotation: Promise

Related Names/Nicknames: Batya, Bethsabee, Sheba, Sheva

Alternate Names: Bathseva, Bathshua, Batsheba, Batsheva, Batshua

Background Story: One spring afternoon, King David looked down from his roof and saw a beautiful woman bathing. The woman was Bathsheba, wife of Uriah the Hittite. David had his servants bring her to him, "and he lay with her." When Bathsheba told David she was pregnant, he arranged for her husband Uriah to be killed in battle. After a period of mourning, David took Bathsheba as his wife. The Lord was "displeased" and sent the prophet Nathan to tell David he would pay for his sin with the death of his child. David "pleaded with God," but the child died. Then David "consoled" Bathsheba and "lay with her" again. They had a second son named Solomon. Years later, Bathsheba and Nathan convinced David to name Solomon as his successor (2 Samuel 11–12).

Of Interest: For centuries, the beautiful woman David saw from his roof has intrigued artists. Jan Steen, Rembrandt van Rijn, and Pablo Picasso all painted great works of art with Bathsheba as the subject.

Famous Namesakes: Bathsheba Everdene, a beautiful young woman loved by three men, is the heroine of Thomas Hardy's classic novel *Far from the Madding Crowd*.

BERNICE ✦ *(ber-NEES)*

Language/Cultural Origin: Greek

Meaning: Bringer of Victory

Spiritual Connotation: Victorious

Related Names/Nicknames: Bernelle, Bernetta, Bernette, Berni, Bernie, Berny, Beronica, Berri, Berrie, Berry, Bertrice, Bunni, Bunnie, Bunny, Nixie, Veronica, Veronika, Veronike, Veronique

Alternate Names: Berenice, Berenisa, Berenise, Berenyce, Berneece, Bernice, Bernicia, Bernyce, Berrenice

Background Story: Bernice, Herod Agrippa's oldest daughter, lived with her brother King Agrippa II, with whom she had a relationship. While Bernice and Agrippa were in Caesarea, they heard Paul's defense against those who opposed his teaching and agreed that he had done "nothing to deserve death or punishment" (Acts 26:30).

Of Interest: Most of what is known about Bernice comes from the writings of Flavius Josephus, a famous Jewish historian who witnessed the early years of Christianity.

Famous Namesakes: Berenice Abbott was an American photographer, known for her black-and-white photographs of New York City during the Depression.

BERYL ✦ *(BEHR-uhl)*

Language/Cultural Origin: Greek

Meaning: Precious Stone

Spiritual Connotation: God's Ornament

Related Names/Nicknames: Berillus, Berri, Berrie, Berry,
Bery, Beryla, Berylla, Beryn

Alternate Names: Beril, Berryle, Beryle

Background Story: Beryl is a gold-colored gem of great value; its
brilliant beauty is mentioned throughout the Bible. Beryl, onyx,
and jasper were "set in gold filigree" on Aaron's breastpiece (Exodus 28:20); in one of Ezekiel's visions, the four wheels he saw
appeared "like the gleaming of beryl" (Ezekiel 1:16); and Daniel
described the man in his vision most eloquently: "His body was
like beryl, his face like lightning, his eyes like flaming torches,
his arms and legs like the gleam of burnished bronze, and the
sound of his words like the roar of a multitude" (Daniel 10:6–7).

Of Interest: Pure beryl is a mineral that is colorless, but tinted
with impurities it can become an emerald, an aquamarine, or
even the golden beryl referred to in the Bible.

Famous Namesakes: Dame Beryl Bainbridge, writer; Beryl Fletcher,
novelist; Beryl Markham, pioneer aviator and author; Beryl
Reid, actress.

BETHANY ◆ *(BEHTH-uh-nee)*

Language/Cultural Origin: Hebrew/Aramaic

Meaning: House of Figs

Spiritual Connotation: Fruitful

Related Names/Nicknames: Annabeth, Beth, Bethania,
Bethe, Bethel, Bethuelle, Jobeth, Marybeth

Alternate Names: Bethani, Bethanie, Bethanne,
Bethanney, Betheney

Background Story: Bethany, a village two miles east of Jerusalem,
was the home of Lazarus and his sisters, Mary and Martha. They

were close friends of Jesus, who often visited their home. Several key events in Jesus's life took place in Bethany: He raised his friend Lazarus from the dead (John 11:38–44); he defended Mary when she was criticized for anointing his feet with expensive perfumes (John 12:1–8); and he "lifted up his hands" and blessed his disciples as he "was carried up into heaven" (Luke 24:50–51).

Famous Namesakes: Bethany Dillon, singer; Bethany Hamilton, surfer; Bethany Joy Lenz, actress; Bethany Roberts, writer.

BETHEL ✦ *(BEHTH-uhl)*

Language/Cultural Origin: Hebrew

Meaning: House of God

Spiritual Connotation: Place of Worship

Related Names/Nicknames: Beth, Betheli, Bethuel, Bethuna, Bethune

Alternate Names: Bethell, Bethelle

Background Story: A few miles north of Jerusalem is the town of Bethel, first called Luz. It was there that Abram offered a sacrifice to the Lord (Genesis 12:8) and Jacob stopped to rest. While he slept, Jacob had a dream of a ladder that stretched from earth to heaven with angels walking up and down. When he woke he said, "Surely the Lord is in this place" and named the area Bethel, which meant "house of God" (Genesis 28:11–19). Later, Jacob built an altar at Bethel "because it was there that God had revealed himself to him" (Genesis 35:7).

CAESAREA ✦ *(seh-zuh-REE-uh)*

Language/Cultural Origin: Latin

Meaning: Leader

Spiritual Connotation: Guidance

Related Names/Nicknames: None

Alternate Names: Caesaria, Cesarea, Cesaria, Cesarie

Background Story: Two cities were called Caesarea in the Bible: Caesarea Philippi and Caesarea Palestina. Both cities played important roles in early Christian history. Near Caesarea Philippi, Jesus named Peter the "rock" on which his church would be built (Matthew 16:18) and told his followers he would "undergo great suffering" (Mark 8:31). The city of Caesarea Palestina was where Peter converted Cornelius, the first Gentile to accept Jesus (Acts 10:25–48). Paul was also imprisoned there for two years while he awaited trial (Acts 24:27).

Of Interest: Herod the Great built the city of Caesarea Palestina, which he named after his patron, Caesar Augustus. Today it is one of Israel's major tourist attractions.

CALAH ✦ *(CAY-luh)*

Language/Cultural Origin: Hebrew/Arabic

Meaning: Opportunity

Spiritual Connotation: Open to God's Direction

Related Names/Nicknames: Caila, Cayla, Kaela, Kaelah, Kahla, Kaila, Kailah, Kala, Kalah, Kayla, Kaylah, Keilah, Keyla, Khaila, Khaylah

Alternate Names: Khala

Background Story: Calah—also called Nimrud—is one of four ancient cities of Assyria founded by Nimrod, Cush's son and

Noah's great-grandson, a man with a reputation as a "mighty hunter before the Lord." At one time, Calah was the capital city of Assyria. The name Calah suggests a woman who makes the most of each opportunity.

CANDACE ✦ *(KAN-dis)* or *(kan-DAY-see)*

Language/Cultural Origin: Latin/Greek/Ethiopian

Meaning: Incandescent

Spiritual Connotation: Pure

Related Names/Nicknames: Candi, Candida, Candide, Candie, Candy, Kandee, Kandi, Kandie, Kandy

Alternate Names: Candice, Candis, Candiss, Candyce, Kandace, Kandice, Kandid, Kandiss, Kandyce

Background Story: Candace was a queen of the Ethiopians. One of her high-court officials—a eunuch—met Philip on the road from Jerusalem and asked to be baptized (Acts 8:27). The name Candace implies a woman with a clear and clean heart.

Of Interest: Candace was originally a title given to Ethiopian queens.

Famous Namesakes: Candace Bergen, actress; Candace Lightner, founder of Mothers Against Drunk Drivers (MADD); Candace Pert, biochemist.

CARMEL ✦ *(KAHR-muhl)*

Language/Cultural Origin: Hebrew

Meaning: Vineyard

Spiritual Connotation: Productive

Related Names/Nicknames: Carmela, Carmelina, Carmeline, Carmelita, Carmella, Carmen, Carmia, Carmiel, Carmina, Carmine, Carmita, Karmela, Karmen, Lina, Lita, Melina, Melita, Mell, Melli, Mellie

Alternate Names: Karmel

Background Story: Carmel—a mountain in Palestine—extends twelve miles from the plain of Esdraelon to the sea. The prophets and poets of the Old Testament celebrated its lush wooded beauty: Isaiah referred to Mount Carmel's majesty (Isaiah 35:2); Jeremiah revealed that it would bring Israel prosperity (Jeremiah 50:19); and the bridegroom said to his lover, "Your head crowns you like Carmel" (Song of Solomon 7:5).

Of Interest: The Carmelites, a Roman Catholic religious order, was founded in the twelfth century on Mount Carmel. A Carmelite monastery still stands there today.

CASSIA ✦ *(KASH-uh)* or *(KAS-ee-uh)*

Language/Cultural Origin: Greek

Meaning: Spicy Cinnamon

Spiritual Connotation: Cherished

Related Names/Nicknames: Cass, Cassandra, Cassandre, Cassie, Keziah

Alternate Names: Casia, Casiya, Cassya, Casya, Kasia, Kasiya, Kassia, Kasya

Background Story: Cassia comes from the fragrant inner bark of a tree similar to the cinnamon. In the Bible, people often traded their wares for the treasured spice. Mixed with myrrh and aloes, it created an aromatic scent for clothing. The Lord told Moses to use cassia—together with other spices and olive oil—to make a "sacred anointing oil" for the altars and priests of the Israelites. God said, "This shall be my holy anointing oil throughout your generations" (Exodus 30:22–31).

Of Interest: The Romans frequently used cassia as a salve and a perfume at funerals.

CHARITY ✦ *(CHAR-ih-tee)*
Language/Cultural Origin: Latin
Meaning: Benevolent
Spiritual Connotation: Love
Related Names/Nicknames: Caridad, Carissa, Carita, Charissa, Charisse, Charita, Cherri, Cherry
Alternate Names: Charitee, Chariti, Sharitee, Sharity

Background Story: Charity is the ultimate principal of Christian life taught in the New Testament. Paul encouraged Jesus's followers to live "in faith, hope, and charity," but he made it clear that "the greatest of these is charity." His poetic words to the people of Corinth emphasized his point even further: "Though I speak with the tongues of men and of angels, and have not charity, I am become as sounding brass, or a tinkling cymbal" (1 Corinthians 13:1–13). A woman with the name Charity is a fine reminder of the love and generosity of spirit associated with this great Christian value.

CHLOE ✦ *(KLO-ee)*
Language/Cultural Origin: Greek
Meaning: Tender Shoot

Spiritual Connotation: New Life

Related Names/Nicknames: Chloris, Clo

Alternate Names: Chloé, Cloe, Cloey, Khloe, Khloey, Kloe

Background Story: Chloe was a Corinthian woman—probably a Christian—whom Paul mentioned in one of his letters. Members of her household had reported to him that the Christians in Corinth were quarreling. Paul appealed to the converts to be "united in the same mind and the same purpose" (1 Corinthians 1:10–13).

Of Interest: From 2002 to 2004, Chloe ranked among the top twenty-five names in the United States. In 2002, Chloe was the number one name in England, Scotland, and Wales.

Famous Namesakes: Chloë Sevigny, actress; Chloe Anthony Wofford, birth name of Toni Morrison, African American writer who won the Nobel Prize for literature in 1993.

CILICIA ✦ *(sih-LIHSH-ee-uh)*

Language/Cultural Origin: Hebrew/Latin

Meaning: Which Overturns

Spiritual Connotation: One Who Transforms

Related Names/Nicknames: None

Alternate Names: Cilicea, Salicia

Background Story: Paul came from Cilicia, a province in Asia Minor. He was born in the town of Tarsus, the site of a distinguished school of philosophy. After his conversion, he went to Tarsus to spread the gospel there. On his second missionary journey, Paul returned to "Syria and Cilicia, strengthening the churches" (Acts 15:41).

Of Interest: Cilicia was famous for its coarse cloth made out of goat's hair. The cloth—cilicium—was used to make tents, bags for tools, and clothing for sailors and fishermen.

CLAUDIA ✦ *(KLAW-dee-uh)*

Language/Cultural Origin: Latin

Meaning: Lame

Spiritual Connotation: Dainty

Related Names/Nicknames: Claude, Claudella, Claudelle, Claudetta, Claudette, Claudey, Claudie, Claudina, Claudine

Alternate Names: Klaudia, Klodia

Background Story: Claudia lived in Rome, where she was Paul's friend and a Christian. Paul sent greetings from Claudia to Timothy in a letter he wrote asking him to come to Rome as soon as possible (2 Timothy 4:21). Claudia is a graceful name, implying a woman who is willing to be vulnerable.

Famous Namesakes: Claudia Cardinale, actress; Claudia Cohen, television reporter; Claudia Schiffer, model; Claudia Alta Taylor, name of first lady "Lady Bird" Johnson.

CORIANDER ✦ *(kor-ee-AN-der)*

Language/Cultural Origin: Greek

Meaning: Cooking Plant

Spiritual Connotation: Sustenance

Related Names/Nicknames: Corey

Alternate Names: None

Background Story: Coriander, a plant native to Egypt and the surrounding area, was cultivated for its aromatic seeds. When dried, the seeds had a brown or off-white hue. In the Bible, the manna God dropped from heaven to feed the Israelites in the wilderness "was like coriander seed" (Numbers 11:7–8).

Of Interest: The Romans used coriander in cooking and medicine. Today the seed is used around the world as an ingredient in breads, stews, meats, fish, salads, and curry powder. The leaves of the plant—called cilantro—are a popular herb.

COZBI ◆ *(KOZ-bee)*

Language/Cultural Origin: Hebrew

Meaning: Sliding Away

Spiritual Connotation: Sacrifice

Related Names/Nicknames: None

Alternate Names: Kozbi, Kozvi

Background Story: Cozbi was a Midianite woman who married an Israelite named Zur. At the time "the Lord's anger was kindled against Israel" for associating with people who worshipped pagan gods. God told Moses to have anyone killed who was doing so. When a man named Phinehas saw Zur bring Cozbi "into his family," he grabbed a spear and "pierced the two of them." His actions stopped the "plague . . . among the people of Israel" and God made peace with the Israelites (Numbers 25:1–18).

Famous Namesakes: Cozbi Cabrera has created a line of handmade cloth dolls, which celebrate the beauty of African Americans and are admired by collectors worldwide.

CRYSTAL ✦ *(KRIHS-tuhl)*

Language/Cultural Origin: Greek

Meaning: Clear as Ice

Spiritual Connotation: Pure

Related Names/Nicknames: Christella, Chrystalynn, Cristalyn, Crysta, Crystalann, Crystalina, Kristabelle, Kristalena, Kristalyn, Krystabelle, Krystalyn

Alternate Names: Christal, Christalle, Christel, Christelle, Chrystal, Chrystel, Chrystle, Cristal, Cristalle, Cristel, Cristle, Kristal, Kristel, Kristell, Krystal, Krystle

Background Story: Crystal—the name of a brilliant gemstone—symbolized an object that was splendid and costly in the Bible. Teaching the value of wisdom, Job said, "No mention shall be made of coral or of crystal; the price of wisdom is above pearls" (Job 28:18); Ezekiel had a vision of God sitting on a sapphire throne above a crystal dome (Ezekiel 1:22); and an angel showed John "the river of the water of life, bright as crystal, flowing from the throne of God" (Revelation 22:1).

Of Interest: The Greeks believed that crystal—or crystallized quartz—was actually water formed by intense cold.

Famous Namesakes: Crystal Bernard, actress; Crystal Gayle, Grammy Award–winning singer and sister of Loretta Lynn.

CYRENE ✦ *(sai-REE-nee)*

Language/Cultural Origin: Greek

Meaning: A Wall

Spiritual Connotation: Strength

Related Names/Nicknames: None

Alternate Names: Cyrena, Kyrene, Serena

Background Story: Cyrene was a city in North Africa founded by the Greeks and home to a large number of Jews. Cyrenian Jews were also a common sight in Jerusalem. Some of them were present during the Pentecost (Acts 2:10), and they had their own synagogue (Acts 6:9). Lucius of Cyrene, a convert, was one of the many "prophets and teachers" in the church at Antioch (Acts 13:1). The most notable was Simon of Cyrene. The Roman soldiers pulled him from the crowd and "laid the cross on him, and made him carry it behind Jesus" (Luke 23:26).

Of Interest: According to Greek myth, Cyrene was a beautiful woman who wrestled a lion. Apollo was so impressed, he built the city of Cyrene and named it after her.

DAMARIS ✦ *(DAM-uh-rihs)*

Language/Cultural Origin: Greek

Meaning: Gentle

Spiritual Connotation: Acceptance

Related Names/Nicknames: Damara, Mara, Mari, Maris

Alternate Names: Damaress, Damariss, Damariz, Dameris, Damerys, Dameryss, Damiris, Damris, Demaras, Demaris, Demarys

Background Story: Damaris heard Paul preach about Jesus in Athens. Although many people "scoffed" when Paul spoke about the Resurrection, others said, "We will hear you again about this." Damaris was among those listeners who joined Paul and "became believers" (Acts 17:32–34). The name Damaris suggests a woman who is open-minded.

Famous Namesakes: Damaris Cudworth Masham, seventeenth-century philosopher.

DANNAH ✦ *(DAN-uh)*

Language/Cultural Origin: Hebrew

Meaning: Judging

Spiritual Connotation: Sacred Birthright

Related Names/Nicknames: Danelle, Danette, Dani, Dania, Danice, Danise, Danita, Danitza, Dannalee, Dannee, Dannell, Dannelle, Danni, Dannia, Dannon, Dantina, Dany, Danya

Alternate Names: Dana, Danna

Background Story: In the Bible, Joshua called Dannah part of "the inheritance of the tribe of the people of Judah." It was a city near Hebron and was located in the mountain region of Judah (Joshua 15:49). The name Dannah implies a woman who stands for justice and fair play.

Of Interest: Dannah is also considered a feminine version of the biblical name Daniel.

DAPHNE ✦ *(DAF-nee)*

Language/Cultural Origin: Greek

Meaning: Laurel Tree

Spiritual Connotation: Victory

Related Names/Nicknames: None

Alternate Names: Dafne, Daphnee, Daphney, Daphni, Daphnie, Daphny

Background Story: Daphne was a place of great beauty and a refuge for the citizens of Antioch. The high priest Onias fled there after reproaching Menelaus for a wrongdoing. When an angry Menelaus had Onias lured from his safe haven and killed, Jews and Gentiles alike "grieved for the unjust murder of so great a man" (2 Maccabees 4:33–35).

Of Interest: In Greek mythology, Daphne was a nymph who changed into a laurel tree to escape Apollo's advances.

Famous Namesakes: Daphne du Maurier, writer.

DARDA ✦ *(DAR-duh)*

Language/Cultural Origin: Hebrew

Meaning: Pearl of Wisdom

Spiritual Connotation: Compassionate

Related Names/Nicknames: Dareen, Daria, Darian, Darice, Darissa, Darya

Alternate Names: Dara, Darah, Darra, Darragh, Darrah

Background Story: Darda—also called Dara in the Bible—was a man noted for his wisdom. However, God gave Solomon such great wisdom and discernment that it "surpassed the wisdom of all," including Darda (1 Kings 4:31). Today Darda and Dara are also women's names.

Famous Namesakes: Dara Torres is an American swimmer who won nine Olympic medals and competed in four different Olympic Games. She holds the record for the second-most Olympic medals won by an American woman.

DEBORAH ✦ *(DEHB-er-uh)* or *(DEHB-ruh)* or *(dehb-OR-uh)*

Language/Cultural Origin: Hebrew

Meaning: Bee

Spiritual Connotation: Industrious

Related Names/Nicknames: Deb, Debbi, Debbie, Debby, Debi, Devi, Devri

Alternate Names: Debora, Debra, Debrah, Devora, Devorah, Devra, Dvorah

Background Story: Deborah, a prophetess and a judge, lived at a time when Israel was being oppressed by a Canaanite ruler. "The Israelites called out to the Lord for help" and Deborah gave them God's answer. She summoned a man named Barak and had him raise an army of ten thousand men to assemble at Mount Tabor. The Canaanite army met them there, and Deborah gave the signal for attack. Barak's army rushed down on the enemy, destroying them all. Their leader escaped but was killed soon afterward by a woman to whom he had turned for protection (Judges 4:1–24). A great celebration followed and Deborah was praised for rising up "as a mother in Israel" (Judges 5:7).

Of Interest: Deborah wrote the "Song of Deborah" (Judges 5:1–31) to commemorate the great triumph of the Israelites over the Canaanites. Many scholars believe it is one of the oldest sections of the Bible.

Famous Namesakes: Deborah Gibson, musician; Deborah Kerr, Debra Messing, Debbie Reynolds, Debra Winger, actresses; Deborah Norville, journalist; Debi Thomas, Olympic figure skater.

DELILAH ✦ *(dih-LAI-luh)*

Language/Cultural Origin: Hebrew

Meaning: Delicate

Spiritual Connotation: Hidden Power

Related Names/Nicknames: Lila, Lilah

Alternate Names: Dalila, Delila

Background Story: Delilah was a clever and seductive woman with whom Samson fell in love. The Philistines hated Samson, a man with exceptional strength who had single-handedly won many battles against them, and they bribed Delilah to learn the secret of his power so they could "subdue" him. She tried three times with no success. Finally, she asked Samson how he could say he loved her if he would not reveal what made him so strong. Samson succumbed to her charms and told her he had been raised as a Nazirite and could never cut his hair. "If my head were shaved," he admitted, "then my strength would leave me." As soon as he fell asleep, Delilah called in the Philistines to shave his head. With Samson's strength gone, the Philistines "seized him and gouged out his eyes," then threw him in prison (Judges 16:1–21). Although Samson was blinded, he eventually regained his strength and brought down their temple, killing everyone inside.

Of Interest: Samson and Delilah have inspired artists for centuries. Peter Paul Rubens painted them in 1609, Camille Saint-Saëns wrote an opera about them in 1877, and Cecil B. DeMille told their story in the 1949 epic film.

DINAH ✦ *(DAI-nuh)*

Language/Cultural Origin: Hebrew

Meaning: Judgment

Spiritual Connotation: Justified

Related Names/Nicknames: Adena, Dinora, Dinorah

Alternate Names: Dena, Deena, Dina, Dyna, Dynah

Background Story: Dinah was Jacob and Leah's only daughter. When she was away from home one day, a Hivite named Shechem took her by force. Shechem fell in love with Dinah and said to his father, Hamor, "Get me this girl to be my wife." Hamor approached Jacob, explaining that his son loved Dinah and that his people were willing to share what they had with Jacob's family. Jacob and his sons agreed, on one condition: The Hivite men must all be circumcised. Before they fully recovered, however, Jacob's sons—Simeon and Levi—killed all the men and plundered the city "because their sister had been defiled" (Genesis 34:1–31).

Famous Namesakes: Dinah Manoff, actress; Dinah Shore, actress/singer and first woman to star in a prime-time television variety show; Dinah Washington, singer.

DORA ✦ *(DOR-uh)*

Language/Cultural Origin: Hebrew/Greek

Meaning: Generation

Spiritual Connotation: A Gift

Related Names/Nicknames: Doralea, Doralia, Doralie, Doreen, Dorelia, Dorella, Dorelle, Dorene, Doretta, Dorette, Dorey, Doria, Dorian, Dorie, Dorinda, Dorine, Doris, Dorita, Dorothy, Dory, Theodora

Alternate Names: None

Background Story: The city of Dora is called Dor or Naphath-dor in the Bible. Located on the coast in Palestine, it was occupied by the Canaanites. Joshua defeated the king of Dor with his army and gave his land "to the tribes of Israel" (Joshua 12:7–23). One of the officials responsible for Solomon's food and provisions also lived there (1 Kings 4:11).

Of Interest: When the Greeks arrived at Dor, they Hellenized its name by adding the "a" at the end, changing it to Dora.

DRUSILLA ✦ *(DROO-sihl-uh)*

Language/Cultural Origin: Latin

Meaning: Watered by the Dew

Spiritual Connotation: Refreshing

Related Names/Nicknames: Drisy, Dru, Drucie, Drucy, Drue, Drus

Alternate Names: Drucella, Drucilla, Druesilla, Druscilla, Drusella

Background Story: While Paul was detained in Caesarea, Drusilla accompanied her husband, Felix, to hear him. Drusilla, the youngest daughter of King Herod, was Jewish, but Felix, the Roman procurator of Judea, had convinced her to leave her first husband to marry him. They both were interested in hearing Paul talk about Jesus, until he brought up the subjects of "justice, self-control, and the coming judgment." Felix became so frightened by what Paul said that he told him to leave (Acts 24:22–27).

EDEN ✦ *(EE-dehn)*

Language/Cultural Origin: Hebrew

Meaning: Delightful

Spiritual Connotation: Pleasing

Related Names/Nicknames: Edenia

Alternate Names: Eaden, Eadin, Edan, Edin

Background Story: The name Eden appears often in the Bible. God planted a garden there for Adam and Eve, the first man and woman. He filled it with animals, birds, and trees that were beautiful and fruitful. A river flowed through the garden, and in the middle God placed "the tree of the knowledge of good and evil." Adam and Eve were allowed to eat from any tree but this one (Genesis 2:8–25). The serpent tempted them, however, and they ate from the forbidden tree. When God saw what they had done, he drove them out and placed cherubim at the east of the garden to guard it (Genesis 3:1–24).

Of Interest: John Steinbeck's novel *East of Eden* tells the story of two families who move to the fertile farmlands of California. Three generations of characters reenact the story of Adam and his family who must always live in exile—east of Eden.

EDNA ✦ *(EHD-nuh)*

Language/Cultural Origin: Hebrew

Meaning: Pleasure

Spiritual Connotation: Spirit Renewed

Related Names/Nicknames: Ed, Eddi, Eddy, Edny, Edra, Edrea

Alternate Names: None

Background Story: Edna was Raguel's wife and the mother of Sarah, a young woman who had married seven times but lost her husbands on her wedding night because of an evil spirit. Meanwhile, young Tobias—who was looking for a wife—arrived at Raguel's house in the company of the angel Raphael. A marriage contract was signed and Edna comforted Sarah. "Be brave, my daughter," she said. "May the Lord of heaven grant you joy in place of your grief" (Tobit 7:17–18). With Raphael's help, Tobias drove away the evil spirit, Edna's prayer was answered, and Sarah enjoyed a new life with her husband.

Famous Namesakes: Edna Ferber, novelist; Edna St. Vincent Millay, poet.

ELIADA ◆ *(ee-LAI-uh-duh)*
Language/Cultural Origin: Hebrew
Meaning: God Is Knowing
Spiritual Connotation: Honesty
Related Names/Nicknames: Elle, Ellie, Lia
Alternate Names: Eliadah

Background Story: There are three Eliadas in the Bible: one of David's sons who was born in Jerusalem (2 Samuel 5:14–16); the father of Rezon, the leader of a marauding band and an "adversary against Solomon" (1 Kings 11:23–24); and a "mighty warrior" from the tribe of Benjamin who commanded an army of two hundred thousand men for Jehoshaphat (2 Chronicles 17:17). The name Eliada is also used for women and suggests someone who is not afraid to reveal her true feelings.

ELISHA ✦ *(ih-LAI-shuh)* or *(uh-LEE-shuh)*

Language/Cultural Origin: Hebrew

Meaning: Salvation of God

Spiritual Connotation: Redemption

Related Names/Nicknames: Alicia, Eli

Alternate Names: Elysha, Elyshah

Background Story: Elisha was plowing in the field when the prophet Elijah "passed by him and threw his mantle over him" (1 Kings 19:19). It was a sign from God that Elisha was to succeed Elijah as prophet. The younger man accepted God's call, left his family, and became Elijah's disciple and servant. After Elijah departed from earth in a fiery chariot, Elisha took his place as leader over Israel's prophets. During his sixty years of ministry, Elisha performed numerous miracles. He prophesied that water would appear for Jehoram's thirsty troops (2 Kings 3:9–20), brought the son of a Shunammite woman back to life (2 Kings 4:18–37), turned twenty loaves of barley into food for a hundred men (2 Kings 4:42–44), and cured Naaman the Syrian of leprosy (2 Kings 5:1–14).

Famous Namesakes: Elisha Cuthbert, actress.

ELISHEBA ✦ *(ee-LIHSH-uh-buh)*

Language/Cultural Origin: Hebrew

Meaning: God Is Her Oath

Spiritual Connotation: Sacred Promise

Related Names/Nicknames: Bess, Beth, Elisa, Eliza, Elli, Elsa, Elsbeth, Else, Libby, Lise, Liz, Liza, Lizbeth, Lizzie

Alternate Names: Elisabeth, Elisheva, Elizabeth

Background Story: Elisheba was the wife of Aaron, who was Moses's brother and a descendant of Levi. She had four sons: Nadab, Abihu, Eleazar, and Ithamar (Exodus 6:23). During the exodus of the Israelites from Egypt, Moses appointed Aaron and his sons to the official priesthood, making Elisheba the mother of the priestly tribe of Levi.

Of Interest: Elisheba is the Hebrew form of the name Elizabeth. Elizabeth and Mary, the mothers of John the Baptist and Jesus, were both descendants of Aaron and Elisheba.

ELIZABETH ✦ *(ee-LIHZ-uh-behth)*
Language/Cultural Origin: Hebrew
Meaning: Fullness of God
Spiritual Connotation: Consecrated
Related Names/Nicknames: Bess, Bessie, Bessy, Beth, Betsey, Betsy, Bette, Bettina, Betty, Elisa, Elise, Elissa, Eliza, Elli, Elsa, Elsbeth, Else, Libby, Lilibet, Lilibeth, Lise, Liz, Liza, Lizbet, Lizbeth, Lizzie
Alternate Names: Elisabet, Elisabeth, Elisabetta, Elisheba, Elisheva, Elizabet, Elizabetta, Elsabet, Elsbeth

Background Story: Elizabeth—a Levite woman married to the priest Zacharias—had no children. One day, the angel Gabriel appeared to Zacharias and told him he would have a son named John who would be "filled with the Holy Spirit." Zacharias questioned the angel because he and his wife were "getting on in years," and the angel responded by taking away his power of speech. Elizabeth conceived, and a few months later her cousin Mary came for a visit. Gabriel had also visited Mary and announced that she would be the mother of Jesus. The moment Elizabeth saw Mary, she exclaimed, "Blessed are you among women, and blessed is the fruit of your womb." When Elizabeth later gave birth to a son, they named him John as the angel had told them, and Zacharias's voice returned. Their son grew up to be John the Baptist (Luke 1:5–80).

Famous Namesakes: Queen Elizabeth II of England; Elizabeth Arden, cosmetics entrepreneur; Elizabeth Barrett Browning, poet; Betty Ford, Bess Truman, first ladies; Liza Minelli, Elizabeth Taylor, actresses.

EMERALD ✦ *(EHM-er-uhld) or (EHM-ruhld)*

Language/Cultural Origin: Greek/English/French

Meaning: Green Jewel

Spiritual Connotation: Brilliance

Related Names/Nicknames: Em, Emeraude, Emeroude, Emmie, Esma, Esme, Esmeralda, Esmeraude, Esmerelda, Ezmeralda, Meralda

Alternate Names: Emmarald

Background Story: An emerald is a precious jewel that appears in the Bible. One of the twelve stones on Aaron's magnificent "breast-piece of judgment" was an emerald. Each stone represented the twelve sons of Israel (Exodus 39:8–14). In Revelation, the rainbow around God's throne looked "like an emerald," and the foundation of the new Jerusalem was "adorned" with emeralds (Revelation 21:19).

Of Interest: Cleopatra was famous for wearing emeralds, which came from mines in Egypt—now called Cleopatra's Mines—and Egyptian mummies were buried with an emerald to symbolize eternal life. Today's finest emeralds are found in Colombia. The emerald is the birthstone of those born in May.

ESTHER ✦ *(EHS-ter)*

Language/Cultural Origin: Persian

Meaning: Star

Spiritual Connotation: Triumphant

Related Names/Nicknames: Essa, Essie, Essy, Esterel, Etti, Ettie, Etty, Hadassa, Hadassah, Hettie, Hetty, Starla, Stella

Alternate Names: Asta, Easter, Esta, Ester, Hester, Hesther, Istar

Background Story: Esther—originally named Hadassah—was a Jewish orphan raised by her cousin Mordecai in the Persian city of Susa. After King Ahasuerus divorced his wife for disobeying him, he chose the beautiful Esther as his new queen, not realizing she was a Jew. Meanwhile, Mordecai had managed to incur the wrath of Haman, the king's highest official, who "plotted to destroy all the Jews" in the kingdom. At the risk of her life, Esther told Ahasuerus she was Jewish and pleaded, "Let my life be given me . . . and the lives of my people." When the king learned that Haman had arranged for a massacre of his wife's people, he had Haman hanged on the gallows he had built for Mordecai. The king also wrote a decree allowing the Jews to defend themselves, and they "struck down" their enemies on the same day intended for their annihilation (Book of Esther).

Of Interest: Haman had cast a "pur," or lot, to determine when the Jews would be destroyed: the thirteenth day of the month of Adar. Today the feast of Purim is usually celebrated in March and commemorates the deliverance of the Jews instead.

Famous Namesakes: Hester Prynne, heroine of Nathaniel Hawthorne's book *The Scarlet Letter;* Esther Rolle, Esther Williams, actresses; Esther Singer, Yiddish novelist.

EUNICE ✦ *(YOO-nihs)*

Language/Cultural Origin: Greek/Latin

Meaning: Joyous Victory

Spiritual Connotation: Faithful

Related Names/Nicknames: Eunike

Alternate Names: Unice

Background Story: Eunice lived in Lystra. She was a Jewish woman, married to a Greek man, and an early Christian believer. A woman of "sincere faith," Eunice taught her son Timothy to know "the holy scriptures" (2 Timothy 3:15). Timothy eventually left home to become a disciple and one of Paul's trusted helpers.

Famous Namesakes: Eunice Kennedy Shriver helped found the Special Olympics in 1968. She was also the sister of President John F. Kennedy and the wife of Robert Sargent Shriver Jr., who organized the Peace Corps in 1961.

EVE ✦ *(EEV)*

Language/Cultural Origin: Hebrew

Meaning: Life Giver

Spiritual Connotation: Breath of Life

Related Names/Nicknames: Evaleen, Eveleen, Evelina, Eveline, Evelyn, Evetta, Evette, Evey, Evia, Eviana, Evie, Evika, Evike, Evita, Evonne, Evvie, Evvy, Evy

Alternate Names: Ava, Eva, Ewa, Hava

Background Story: In the Garden of Eden, God created a woman as a partner for the man because it was "not good that the man should be alone" (Genesis 2:18). The couple lived there in innocence until one day the serpent tempted the woman. God had told them they could eat from any tree in the garden except the one in the middle—the tree of good and evil. Encouraged by the serpent, the woman ate from the forbidden tree and gave its fruit to the man. When God saw what they had done, he threw them out of the garden. The couple became the parents of Cain and Abel. The man, now called Adam, named his wife Eve, "because she was the mother of all living" (Genesis 3:20).

Famous Namesakes: Eva Perón—affectionately known as Evita—was the wife of Argentina's president Juan Perón. As first lady, she took a prominent role in his government and created a foundation that built hospitals and orphanages for the poor.

FAITH ✦ *(FAYTH)*

Language/Cultural Origin: Latin

Meaning: Trust

Spiritual Connotation: Belief in God

Related Names/Nicknames: Fae, Fay, Faye, Fayette

Alternate Names: Faithe, Fayth, Faythe

Background Story: Faith is a virtue that Jesus spoke about often in the Bible. He told the disciples, "Whatever you ask for in prayer with faith, you will receive" (Matthew 21:22); he encouraged his disciples by saying, "If you had faith the size of a mustard seed, you could say to this mulberry tree, 'Be uprooted and planted in the sea,' and it would obey you" (Luke 17:6); and he answered the blind man who asked to see again, "Receive your sight; your faith has saved you" (Luke 18:34–42).

Famous Namesakes: Faith Ford, actress; Faith Hill, musician; and Faith Ringgold, textile artist and writer.

GALATIA ✦ *(guh-LAY-shuh)* or *(guh-LAY-shee-uh)*

Language/Cultural Origin: Greek

Meaning: White as Milk

Spiritual Connotation: Purity

Related Names/Nicknames: None

Alternate Names: Galatea, Galatée, Galathea

Background Story: Paul visited Galatia, a Roman province in Asia Minor, on his second missionary journey. An illness kept him there, and he was able to make numerous converts among the Gentiles. On his third journey, Paul revisited Galatia, "strengthening all the disciples" there (Acts 18:23).

Of Interest: In Greek mythology, Galatea was a statue loved by its sculptor, Pygmalion, and brought to life by a goddess. Galatea's story was the source for George Bernard Shaw's play *Pygmalion* on which the musical *My Fair Lady* was based.

GENESIS ✦ *(JEHN-uh-sihs)*

Language/Cultural Origin: Greek/Hebrew

Meaning: Beginning

Spiritual Connotation: Creation

Related Names/Nicknames: Genessa, Genisa, Genisia, Jenny

Alternate Names: Genesies, Genesiss, Genesys, Genisis, Genisys, Gennesis, Gennesiss, Genysis, Genysys, Jenesis, Jenesyss, Jennasis

Background Story: Genesis is the name of the first book of the Bible. Its first words are "In the beginning . . ." (Genesis 1:1), and it tells the early history of the people who became the Israelites.

Genesis includes the stories of Adam and Eve, the fall of man, Cain and Abel, and Noah's flood. The first book also records the lives of the four great patriarchs: Abraham, Isaac, Jacob, and Joseph. The name Genesis is a reminder that life can be full of fresh starts for everyone.

GIAH ✦ *(JEE-uh)*

Language/Cultural Origin: Hebrew

Meaning: To Guide

Spiritual Connotation: One Who Leads

Related Names/Nicknames: None

Alternate Names: Gia

Background Story: Abner stopped at a place called Giah during his escape to Gibeon. As commander of Saul's army, he had just fought a bloody battle with Joab, the leader of David's men. Joab's brother Asahel pursued Abner, forcing Abner to kill him. "As the sun was going down," Joab "sounded the trumpet" to stop the pursuit, and Abner marched on while Joab buried his brother (2 Samuel 2:8–32). The name Giah suggests a woman with leadership qualities.

GRACE ✦ *(GRAYS)*

Language/Cultural Origin: Latin

Meaning: Favor

Spiritual Connotation: Blessing

Related Names/Nicknames: Gracee, Gracella, Gracelynn, Gracey, Graci, Gracia, Graciana, Gracianna, Gracie,

Graciela, Graciella, Gracielle, Gracina, Gray, Grazia, Graziella

Alternate Names: Grayce

Background Story: Grace is a word that appears often in the Bible. It can mean beauty, friendship, a favor, God's mercy, or even a Christian virtue. Paul said his ministry was "by the grace of God" (1 Corinthians 15:10). His letters all began with "Grace to you and peace from God our Father and the Lord Jesus Christ" (Galatians 1:3). And Peter advised his followers to "grow in the grace and knowledge of our Lord and Savior Jesus Christ" (2 Peter 3:18).

Famous Namesakes: Grace Coolidge, first lady; Grace Jones, singer; Grace Kelly, actress; Grace Flores Napolitano, U.S. representative.

HADASSAH *(huh-DAH-suh)*

Language/Cultural Origin: Hebrew

Meaning: Myrtle Tree

Spiritual Connotation: Chaste

Related Names/Nicknames: Asta, Dassah, Essie, Esther, Etty, Hada, Hester, Hesther, Hettie, Hetty, Hodel

Alternate Names: None

Background Story: Hadassah was Esther's name before she married King Ahasuerus of Persia. For a time, she hid the fact that she was Jewish. When she heard that Ahasuerus's highest official, Haman, was scheming to destroy all the Jews, Esther had the courage to speak out. She revealed to her husband that she was also a Jew and pleaded with him to save her people. Ahasuerus allowed the Jews to defend themselves against anyone who "might attack" and they "struck down" their enemy (Book of Esther).

Of Interest: Hadassah is a volunteer women's organization, which runs youth and education programs in the United States and supports health care, education, and child welfare programs in Israel.

HANNAH ✦ *(HA-nuh)*

Language/Cultural Origin: Hebrew

Meaning: Gracious

Spiritual Connotation: Favored by God

Related Names/Nicknames: Anna, Chana, Chanah, Hananiah, Hananiyah, Hanela, Hania, Hannalee, Hanya, Nan, Nana, Nanny

Alternate Names: Hana, Hanah, Hanna

Background Story: Hannah traveled regularly to Shiloh to attend offerings of sacrifice. One year, she went with a special prayerful desire—to have children. Hannah prayed at the temple silently, only moving her lips. At first, the hight priest thought she was drunk and condemned her. When he realized his error, he retracted his accusations and said, "Go in peace; the God of Israel grant the petition you have made." Less than a year later, she gave birth to a son, Samuel. She showed her gratefulness by giving him over to the Lord, even through his name, which means "Heard of God." When the child was three, she brought him back to Shiloh to the house of the Lord and left him with the high priest to minister "before the Lord." Every year, she visited her son and brought him a little robe demonstrating her abiding maternal love. The Lord "took note" and Hannah had three more sons and two daughters after Samuel (1 Samuel 1, 2:18–21).

Of Interest: From 1997 to 2004, the name Hannah ranked among the top five baby names in the United States.

HAVILAH ✦ *(HA-vih-luh)*

Language/Cultural Origin: Hebrew

Meaning: Stretch of Sand

Spiritual Connotation: New Beginnings

Related Names/Nicknames: None

Alternate Names: None

Background Story: In the Old Testament, Havilah was a land rich in gold, bdellium, and onyx stone. One of the four rivers that originated from the Garden of Eden flowed around Havilah (Genesis 2:10–12). There are also two men in the Bible named Havilah: a son of Cush (Genesis 10:7) and a son of Joktan (Genesis 10:29), both descendants of Noah. From their families "the nations spread abroad on the earth after the flood" (Genesis 10:32). Havilah is a name for either a boy or a girl.

HAZEL ✦ *(HAY-zuhl)*

Language/Cultural Origin: Old English

Meaning: Nutbearing Tree

Spiritual Connotation: Clever

Related Names/Nicknames: Haze

Alternate Names: Hazal, Hazell, Hazelle, Hazle

Background Story: The hazel tree flourishes in Syria. In the Bible, Jacob took rods from poplar, hazel, and chestnut trees "and pilled white strakes in them, and made the white appear" (Genesis 30:37).

He placed the rods in front of the watering troughs of Laban's strongest cattle, sheep, and goats so that they would conceive. The name Hazel suggests a smart, resourceful woman.

HELAH ✦ *(HEH-luh)* or *(HEE-luh)*
Language/Cultural Origin: Hebrew
Meaning: Rust
Spiritual Connotation: Wisdom
Related Names/Nicknames: None
Alternate Names: None

Background Story: Helah was one of Ashur's wives. She had three sons—Zereth, Izhar, and Ethnan—who were among Judah's descendants (1 Chronicles 4:5–7). Helah is a name that implies a girl who is wise beyond her years.

HERODIAS ✦ *(hehr-O-dee-uhs)*
Language/Cultural Origin: Greek
Meaning: Watch Over
Spiritual Connotation: Observer
Related Names/Nicknames: Hero
Alternate Names: None

Background Story: Herodias left her first husband to marry his brother, Herod. When John the Baptist said the marriage was unlawful, Herod put him in prison to please his new wife. Herodias wanted him dead, but Herod knew that John was "a righteous and holy man" and was afraid to kill him. An opportunity soon presented itself. On Herod's birthday, Herodias's daughter Salome danced for him and his guests. Herod was pleased and offered to give her whatever she wanted. Herodias told Salome to ask for "the head of John the Baptizer." John was beheaded, and a soldier presented his head on a platter to Salome, who gave it to her mother. Afterward, John's followers took his body and buried it (Mark 6:17–29).

HOPE ✦ *(HOPE)*

Language/Cultural Origin: Old English

Meaning: Expectation

Spiritual Connotation: Trust

Related Names/Nicknames: None

Alternate Names: None

Background Story: Hope is a virtue in the Bible—as essential to the Jews as it was to the Christians. In the Old Testament, the psalmist sang, "Let your steadfast love, O Lord, be upon us, even as we hope in you" (Psalms 33:22), and Proverbs advised, "Hope deferred makes the heart sick, but a desire fulfilled is a tree of life" (Proverbs 13:12). In the New Testament, hope joined faith and love as the keys to Christianity. Paul told his disciples, ". . . in hope we were saved" (Romans 8:24). He also reminded them that "hope does not disappoint us, because God's love has been poured into our hearts through the Holy Spirit" (Romans 5:5).

Famous Namesakes: Hope Cameron, Hope Davis, Hope Lange, actresses.

HYACINTH ✦ *(HAI-uh-sihnth)*

Language/Cultural Origin: Greek

Meaning: A Flower

Spiritual Connotation: Spirit in Bloom

Related Names/Nicknames: Cintha, Cinthia, Cinthy, Giacinta, Hyacintha, Hyacinthia, Jacenia, Jacenta, Jacinda, Jacinta, Jacinth, Jacintha, Jacinthe, Jackie, Jacky, Jacynth

Alternate Names: Hyacinthe

Background Story: Hyacinth—a rich, deep, purplish-blue color—appears only once in the Bible. In the prophetic vision of the second coming, the horsemen with the four angels wore "breast-plates of fiery red, hyacinth blue, and sulfur yellow" (Revelation 9:17).

Of Interest: In Greek mythology, the hyacinth flower sprouted from the blood of Hyacinthus, a boy accidentally killed by Apollo. Hyacinth is also the name of a third-century saint.

IVAH ✦ *(AI-vuh)* or *(EE-vuh)*

Language/Cultural Origin: Hebrew

Meaning: Overturning

Spiritual Connotation: Faith

Related Names/Nicknames: Ivana, Ivane, Ivanka, Ivanna

Alternate Names: Iva, Ivvah

Background Story: Ivah was the name of a city in the Bible that was conquered by the Assyrians. The Assyrian army then confronted Hezekiah and ridiculed the Israelites for believing their God would save them. "Where are the gods of . . . Ivah?"

they called out, but Hezekiah and his men refused to surrender (2 Kings 18:17–37). The name Ivah is a reminder that faith can move mountains.

JAALA ✦ *(JAY-ay-luh)*
Language/Cultural Origin: Hebrew
Meaning: Little Goat
Spiritual Connotation: Renewal
Related Names/Nicknames: Jay
Alternate Names: Jaalah

Background Story: Jaala is the name of a family that returned to Jerusalem and Judah after their exile in Babylon. Their ancestor, Jaala, had been one of "Solomon's servants" (Nehemiah 7:57–58). Jaala is a strong name; it suggests a woman who never gives up.

JACINTH ✦ *(JAY-sihnth)* or *(JAS-ihnth)*
Language/Cultural Origin: Latin
Meaning: Precious Stone
Spiritual Connotation: Splendor
Related Names/Nicknames: Cintha, Cinthia, Cinthy, Giacinta, Hyacinth, Hyacintha, Hyacinthe, Jacenia, Jacenta, Jacinda, Jacinta, Jacintha, Jackie, Jacky, Jacynth
Alternate Names: Jacinthe

Background Story: In the Bible, jacinth was a precious stone, the color of hyacinth and a splendid symbol of what was to come. It was the first stone placed in the third row of the high priest's breastplate (Exodus 28:19) and the eleventh stone in the foundations of the New Jerusalem (Revelation 21:20).

Of Interest: Jacinth is a variety of zircon that has been found in jewelry for centuries. Ancient mystics believed the stone brought wisdom, honor, and peace to the wearer.

JADA ✦ *(JAY-duh)*

Language/Cultural Origin: Hebrew

Meaning: Wise

Spiritual Connotation: Insightful

Related Names/Nicknames: Jade, Jadeana, Jadee, Jaden, Jadine, Jadira, Jadra, Jadrian, Jadrienne, Jady, Jadyn, Jaide, Jaidra, Jayde, Jaydee, Jayden, Jaydon, Jaydra

Alternate Names: Jaeda, Jaida, Jayda

Background Story: Little is known about Jada in the Bible. He was Onam's son and the grandson of Jerahmeel by his wife, Atarah. Jada also had two sons of his own: Jether and Jonathan (1 Chronicles 2:28, 32). Jada is an elegant name and a particular favorite for girls today. It suggests a woman who is clever and observant.

Of Interest: Since 2000, Jada has ranked among the top one hundred names for women in the United States.

Famous Namesakes: Jada Rowland, actress and painter; Jada Pinkett Smith, actress.

JADDUA ✦ *(jad-YOO-uh)*

Language/Cultural Origin: Hebrew

Meaning: Known

Spiritual Connotation: Open Heart

Related Names/Nicknames: Jade

Alternate Names: None

Background Story: There are two men named Jaddua in the Bible: a priest who signed Nehemiah's written covenant with the Lord (Nehemiah 10:21) and the son of Jonathan who returned from captivity in Babylon. He is the last high priest mentioned in the Old Testament (Nehemiah 12:11). Jaddua is a girl's name today, suggesting someone who opens her heart to others.

JAEL ✦ *(JAY-uhl)* or *(JAYL)*

Language/Cultural Origin: Hebrew

Meaning: Climber

Spiritual Connotation: Fearless

Related Names/Nicknames: Yaela, Yaella

Alternate Names: Jaelle, Jahel, Jayel, Jayil, Yael

Background Story: Jael was a courageous woman who helped free the Israelites from years of Canaanite oppression. With the help of the prophetess Deborah, the Israelite army had overcome the Canaanite forces, but their captain, Sisera, had escaped to the camp of Heber the Kenite, who had peaceful relations with the Canaanites. Heber's wife, Jael, hid Sisera in her tent, promising she would not reveal that he was there. As soon as Sisera fell asleep, however, Jael killed him by driving a tent peg through his temple. She then showed the Israelites what she had done (Judges 4:10–22).

Of Interest: The "Song of Deborah" praises the tent-dwelling woman who helped her Israelite neighbors: "Most blessed of women be Jael" (Judges 5:24).

Famous Namesakes: Jael Silliman is a contemporary writer whose book *Jewish Portraits, Indian Frames* tells her story and the story of her foremothers who lived in a Jewish community in Calcutta.

JEMIMA ✦ *(jeh-MAI-muh)*
Language/Cultural Origin: Hebrew

Meaning: Dove

Spiritual Connotation: Serenity

Related Names/Nicknames: Jem, Jemie, Jemmie, Jemmy, Mima, Mimi, Mimma

Alternate Names: Jamima, Jemmima, Jemmimah

Background Story: Jemima was the first of Job's three daughters who were born after his period of suffering ended. The others were called Keziah and Keren-happuch, "and in all the land there were no women so fair as Job's daughters." Job died an old man and divided his inheritance among his sons and daughters (Job 42:10–17).

Famous Namesakes: Jemima Khan is a famous British heiress who became a UNICEF ambassador in 2001 and is a spokesperson for their End Child Exploitation campaign.

JESSE ✦ *(JEH-see)*

Language/Cultural Origin: Hebrew

Meaning: God's Gift

Spiritual Connotation: Source of God's Love

Related Names/Nicknames: Jess, Jessaca, Jessalin, Jessalynn, Jessica, Jessie, Jessika, Jesslyn, Jessye

Alternate Names: None

Background Story: Jesse had eight sons, the youngest of whom was David. One day, God told Samuel he had chosen one of Jesse's sons to succeed him as king and he sent Samuel to anoint him. Jesse introduced his sons to Samuel, beginning with the oldest. One by one, the Lord rejected them. He advised Samuel not to be fooled by outward appearances because "the Lord looks on the heart." Finally, Jesse sent for David, who was watching the sheep. When he arrived, God told Samuel, "Rise and anoint him; for this is the one" (1 Samuel 16:1–13). The name Jesse can be used today for a girl or a boy.

Of Interest: In the Bible, Isaiah referred to David's family as the "stem of Jesse" and to the coming Messiah as the "root of Jesse" (Isaiah 11:1–10).

JOANNA ✦ *(jo-AN-uh)*

Language/Cultural Origin: Hebrew

Meaning: Gift from God

Spiritual Connotation: Grace

Related Names/Nicknames: Gianna, Ivana, Jan, Jana, Janna, Jeanne, Jo, Joan, Joanie, Joann, Jo-Ann, Joanne, Jo-Anne, Johanna, Juana

Alternate Names: Ioanna, Joana, Yoana

Background Story: Joanna was "cured of evil spirits and infirmities" by Jesus and joined the women who "provided for" Jesus and his apostles as they traveled through Galilee (Luke 8:1–3). After Jesus's death, Joanna and the other women brought spices and ointments to the tomb where his body was laid. To their amazement, the tomb was empty. Then two angels in "dazzling clothes" appeared and told them that Jesus had risen from the dead. The women rushed to tell the apostles everything they had seen (Luke 24:1–10).

Famous Namesakes: Joanna Glass, playwright; Joanne (J. K.) Rowling, writer; Joanne Woodward, actress.

JORDAN   ✦   *(JOR-duhn)*

Language/Cultural Origin: Hebrew

Meaning: Flow Downward

Spiritual Connotation: Anointed by God

Related Names/Nicknames: Giordana, Jardina, Jordain, Jordaine, Jordana, Jordane, Jordanka, Jordanna, Jordanne, Jordena, Jordi, Jordie, Jorey, Jori, Jorie, Jorry, Yordan

Alternate Names: Jordann, Jorden, Jordenn, Jordin, Jordyn, Jordynn, Jourdan

Background Story: The Jordan River—mentioned often in the Bible—flowed into the Sea of Galilee and through a deep valley in Palestine down to the Dead Sea. It was the scene of several important biblical events: Lot settled in the plain of the Jordan, which was "well watered everywhere like the garden of the Lord" (Genesis 13:10–12); the Israelites crossed the Jordan River into the Promised Land (Joshua 3:17); John the Baptist conducted his ministry along the Jordan River (Matthew 3:5–6); and Jesus was baptized there (Mark 1:9).

Of Interest: Today the Jordan River flows between Israel and Jordan, forming much of the boundary between the two countries.

Famous Namesakes: Jordan Hill, singer/songwriter.

JUDITH ✦ *(JOO-dihth)*

Language/Cultural Origin: Hebrew

Meaning: Praise of the Lord

Spiritual Connotation: Deliverance

Related Names/Nicknames: Giuditta, Jodie, Jody, Jude, Judeana, Judee, Judeena, Judi, Judie, Judit, Judita, Judite, Juditha, Judy, Judye, June, Jutta, Yehudit, Yudit

Alternate Names: Judithe, Judyth, Judythe

Background Story: There are two Judiths in the Bible: one of Esau's wives, who was the daughter of Beeri the Hittite (Genesis 26:34), and a courageous Jewish widow who saved her people from an invading Assyrian army. The Israelites of Bethulia were about to surrender to the Assyrians when Judith boldly stepped in. Pretending to be an informer, she entered the enemy camp and won over their leader, Holofernes, with her beauty and charm. He invited Judith to a banquet in his tent, and when Holofernes became drunk and fell asleep, she cut off his head and brought it back to Bethulia. Their faith in God renewed, the Israelites drove out the leaderless Assyrian army (Book of Judith).

Famous Namesakes: Dame Judith Anderson, actress; Judy Collins, singer; Judith Guest, novelist; Judith Jamison, dancer/choreographer; Judith Resnik, astronaut; Judith Viorst, humor writer.

JULIA ✦ *(JOO-lee-uh)*

Language/Cultural Origin: Greek/Latin

Meaning: Soft-haired

Spiritual Connotation: Believer

Related Names/Nicknames: Giuliana, Giulietta, Jill, Joleta, Jolette, Jule, Julee, Juli, Juliana, Juliann, Julie, Julienne, Juliet, Julieta, Juliette, Julina, Juline, Julissa, Julita

Alternate Names: Giulia, Yulia, Yuliya

Background Story: Julia is the name of a Roman woman in the Bible who was also a Christian. Paul greeted Julia, Philologus, "and all the saints who are with them" in a letter he sent to the church in Rome. He urged them all to "greet one another with a holy kiss" (Romans 16:15–16).

Of Interest: Julia was one of the top thirty names for girls from 1999 to 2004.

Famous Namesakes: Julia Alvarez, writer; Julia Child, chef; Julia Grant and Julia Tyler, first ladies; Julia Ormond and Julia Roberts, actresses.

JUNIA ✦ *(JOO-nee-uh)*

Language/Cultural Origin: Latin

Meaning: Youthful

Spiritual Connotation: God's Light

Related Names/Nicknames: June, Juniata, Junie, Junieta, Jinina, Junine, Junis, Juno

Alternate Names: Junias

Background Story: Junia lived in Rome and was an early convert to Christianity. Paul "greets" Junia, along with Andronicus, in a letter he wrote to Rome. He called them "my relatives who were in prison with me." Junia and Andronicus were Paul's apostles whom, he says, "were in Christ before I was" (Romans 16:7).

Of Interest: Scholars have debated for centuries whether Junia in the Bible is a woman or a man. If she was female, she was the only woman named as an apostle.

KELAIAH ✦ *(kee-LAY-yuh)*

Language/Cultural Origin: Hebrew

Meaning: Voice of the Lord

Spiritual Connotation: Forgiven

Related Names/Nicknames: Kela

Alternate Names: Keliah, Kelita

Background Story: Kelaiah was a Levite priest who broke God's commandment and married a "foreign" woman. He and other Israelite men mixed their "holy seed" with people who practiced incest and other "abominations." Ashamed of what they had done, they made a new covenant with God and sent the foreign women away with their children (Ezra 10:1–5, 23). Keliah and Kelita—variations of Kelaiah—are usually names for girls.

Famous Namesakes: Kelita Haverland is a Canadian singer/songwriter who inspires audiences with her contemporary Christian music.

KEREN-HAPPUCH ✦ *(KEHR-ehn-HAP-ouk)*

Language/Cultural Origin: Hebrew

Meaning: Horn of Beauty

Spiritual Connotation: God's Radiance

Related Names/Nicknames: Karen, Keran, Keren, Kerena, Kerrin, Keryn

Alternate Names: None

Background Story: Keren-happuch was the last of three daughters born to Job after his suffering ended. She and her older sisters—Jemima and Keziah—were the most beautiful women "in all the land." When Job died, he divided his inheritance among his children—sons and daughters alike (Job 42:13–15).

Of Interest: The name Keren-happuch—horn of beauty—suggests a brilliant black makeup that biblical women applied to the edges of their eyelids to make their eyes appear larger and more attractive.

KERITH ✦ *(KEE-rihth)*

Language/Cultural Origin: Hebrew

Meaning: Cutting

Spiritual Connotation: Retreat

Related Names/Nicknames: None

Alternate Names: Cherith

Background Story: Kerith is the name of a brook that flows into the Jordan River. God told the prophet Elijah to hide there after he prophesied a drought for King Ahab. Elijah followed God's instructions and set up camp next to Kerith Brook. "The ravens brought him bread and meat each morning and evening, and he drank from the brook" (1 Kings 17:1–6).

KETURAH ✦ *(keh-TOOR-uh)*

Language/Cultural Origin: Hebrew

Meaning: Incense

Spiritual Connotation: Holy Offering

Related Names/Nicknames: None

Alternate Names: Katura, Ketura

Background Story: After Sarah died, Abraham took Keturah as his wife or concubine. She had six sons with him: Zimran, Jokshan, Medan, Midian, Ishbak, and Shuah. When Abraham died, all that he had went to Isaac—Sarah's son. But Abraham also gave gifts to his other sons "while he was still living," and he sent them away to the east, where they settled (Genesis 25:1–6). Through Keturah's sons, Abraham soon became "the father of many nations," as God had promised (Genesis 17:4).

KEZIA ✦ *(keh-ZAI-uh)*

Language/Cultural Origin: Hebrew

Meaning: Cinnamonlike

Spiritual Connotation: Fragrant

Related Names/Nicknames: Cassia, Cassie, Kakeshia, Kassia, Kassy, Kazia, Keisha, Keshia, Kessie, Kessy, Ketsia, Ketzia, Ketziah, Keysha, Kezzie, Kisha, Kissie, Kizzie, Kizzy, Lakeisha, Lakisha

Alternate Names: Keziah

Background Story: Kezia was Job's second daughter, born after God returned him to prosperity. Her sisters were named Jemima and Keren-happuch. There were no women "in all the land . . . so fair as Job's daughters." Job also had seven more sons, and he divided his inheritance among all his children when he died (Job 42:13–15).

Of Interest: Kezia is the Hebrew name for Cassia, a tree whose bark produced a spice similar to cinnamon. Mixed with myrrh and aloes, it created a fragrant scent for clothing.

Famous Namesakes: Actress Keshia Knight Pulliam played Rudy Huxtable, the youngest daughter on the popular television comedy *The Cosby Show*.

KINNERET ◆ *(KIHN-uh-reht)*
Language/Cultural Origin: Hebrew
Meaning: Harp
Spiritual Connotation: Spiritual Leadership
Related Names/Nicknames: Kinnette
Alternate Names: Chinnereth, Chinneroth, Kinnereth

Background Story: Kinneret is the Hebrew name for the Sea of Galilee in the Bible. Much of Jesus's ministry took place along its shores: four of his disciples—Peter, Andrew, John, and James—worked as fishermen on the lake until he made them "fishers for men" (Mark 1:16–20); beside the lake, Jesus fed a crowd of five thousand with only five loaves of bread and two fishes (Matthew 14:13–21); and Jesus taught his disciples the power of faith by walking on the waters of Kinneret (Matthew 14:25–33).

Of Interest: Called Kinneret by the Hebrews because it was shaped like a harp, the lake is a popular resort area today. It is also the source of most of Israel's drinking water.

KYRIA ✦ *(KIH-ree-uh)*

Language/Cultural Origin: Greek

Meaning: Ladylike

Spiritual Connotation: Gracious

Related Names/Nicknames: Cyrah, Kaira, Keera, Keira, Kira, Kyra, Kyreena, Kyrene, Kyrha, Kyrie, Kyrra

Alternate Names: None

Background Story: John sent a letter to a Christian woman he called Kyria. In the letter, he greeted her with love and urged her to continue following God's "commands." He also warned her about people who were "leading astray" and advised her not to receive anyone in her house who was "not confessing Jesus Christ" (2 John 1:1–13).

Of Interest: Kyria was a Greek title of respect for a woman.

LAADAN ✦ *(LAY-duhn)* or *(LAY-uh-duhn)*

Language/Cultural Origin: Hebrew

Meaning: For Pleasure

Spiritual Connotation: Delightful

Related Names/Nicknames: Libni

Alternate Names: Ladan

Background Story: There are two men named Laadan in the Bible: an ancestor of Joshua, who led the Israelites into the Promised Land (1 Chronicles 7:26), and a Levite priest from the family of Gershon, one of the divisions that looked after the temple during David's reign (1 Chronicles 23:6–7). Laadan or Ladan, a name suggesting someone who brightens a room with her presence, is primarily used for girls today.

LASHA ✦ *(LAY-shuh)*

Language/Cultural Origin: Hebrew

Meaning: To Anoint

Spiritual Connotation: Comforting

Related Names/Nicknames: None

Alternate Names: None

Background Story: In the Bible, Lasha is a place east of the Dead Sea and in the land of the Canaanites (Genesis 10:19). It was famous for its hot springs. The name Lasha suggests a woman who enjoys helping people.

LEAH ✦ *(LEE-uh)* or *(LAY-uh)*

Language/Cultural Origin: Hebrew

Meaning: Delicate

Spiritual Connotation: Endurance

Related Names/Nicknames: Lee, Leigh

Alternate Names: Lea, Leia

Background Story: Laban had two daughters: Leah and Rachel. Jacob loved Rachel and wanted to marry her, but he was tricked into marrying Leah because she was older. Jacob later married Rachel, and "when the Lord saw that Leah was unloved, he opened her womb." She had six sons—Reuben, Simeon, Levi, Judah, Issachar, and Zebulon—and a daughter, Dinah. With each child, Leah hoped that Jacob would learn to love her, but he never stopped favoring Rachel. God rewarded Leah for her patience, however. Her sons became the forefathers of six of Israel's twelve tribes, and her descendants included some of the most important people in biblical history: Moses, David,

John the Baptist, Peter, Joseph, Mary, and Jesus himself (Genesis 29–30).

Famous Namesakes: Leah Goldberg, poet; Leah Rabin, wife of Israeli prime minister Yitzhak Rabin; Leah Remini, Lea Thompson, actresses.

LEBANA ✦ *(leh-BAH-nuh)* or *(LEHB-uh-nuh)*

Language/Cultural Origin: Hebrew

Meaning: White

Spiritual Connotation: Chaste

Related Names/Nicknames: Levana, Levanah

Alternate Names: Labana, Labanna, Labannah, Lebanah

Background Story: The children of Lebana were a family of Nathinites in the Bible who returned to Judah and Jerusalem, "every man to his city," from exile in Babylon (Ezra 2:45). Lebana is a name that suggests a modest woman.

LILY ✦ *(LIH-lee)*

Language/Cultural Origin: Latin/Greek

Meaning: Flower

Spiritual Connotation: Purity of Heart

Related Names/Nicknames: Leelee, Lil, Lila, Lilas, Lilia, Lilian, Liliana, Liliane, Lilias, Lilibeth, Lilla, Lillia, Lillian, Lillianne, Lillita, Lilyan, Lilyann, Lys

Alternate Names: Lili, Lilie, Lilley, Lilli, Lillie, Lilly

Background Story: The lily—a symbol of innocence and beauty—appears often in the Bible. Solomon used it to describe God's love for Israel: "As a lily among brambles, so is my love among maidens" (Song of Solomon 2:2). Hosea assured an unfaithful Israel that it would "spring as the lily" if it returned to the Lord (Hosea 14:5). And Matthew told his followers to give their concerns to God with the eloquent words: "Why do you worry about clothing? Consider the lilies of the field, how they grow; they neither toil nor spin, yet I tell you, even Solomon in all his glory was not clothed like one of these" (Matthew 6:28–29).

Famous Namesakes: Lily Afshar, classical guitarist; Lily Tomlin, actress/comedian.

LOIS ✦ *(LO-ihs)*
Language/Cultural Origin: Greek
Meaning: More Desirable
Spiritual Connotation: Worthy
Related Names/Nicknames: Heloise, Louise
Alternate Names: Loes

Background Story: Lois lived in Lystra, where Paul converted her and her daughter Eunice to Christianity. Lois's grandson Timothy was taught as a child about the "holy scriptures," and he later became one of Paul's disciples. In a letter to Timothy, Paul praised him for his "sincere faith, a faith that lived first in your grandmother Lois" (2 Timothy 1:5).

Famous Namesakes: Lois Lenski and Lois Lowry, writers of numerous books for young readers, have both received the prestigious Newbery Medal for their work.

LYCIA ✦ *(LIH-shee-uh)* or *(LIH-shuh)* or *(LEE-shuh)*

Language/Cultural Origin: Latin

Meaning: Happy

Spiritual Connotation: Hopeful

Related Names/Nicknames: Alicia, Felicia, Leecea, Leecia, Leesha, Lesia, Lisia

Alternate Names: Licia

Background Story: Lycia was a province in Asia Minor. When Paul was a prisoner, he stopped at Myra, the capital of Lycia, before he boarded a ship to Italy (Acts 27:5–6). A refreshing name such as Lycia suggests someone who is lighthearted and carefree.

Famous Namesakes: Singer Licia Albanese made her debut at the Metropolitan Opera in 1940 and performed there for twenty-six seasons.

LYDIA ✦ *(LIH-dee-uh)*

Language/Cultural Origin: Greek

Meaning: Cultured One

Spiritual Connotation: Spiritual Light

Related Names/Nicknames: Liddie, Liddy, Lidi

Alternate Names: Lidia, Lidie, Lidija, Lidiya, Lydie

Background Story: Lydia was a well-to-do businesswoman who sold purple cloth, a valuable material. She listened to Paul talk about Jesus and "the Lord opened her heart." Lydia was the first person baptized by Paul in Macedonia and became a gracious host to Timothy, Paul, and Silas on their missionary journey (Acts 16:13–15).

Famous Namesakes: Lydia Gueiler Tejada was Bolivia's first female president, serving in an interim capacity from 1979 to 1980.

LYSTRA ✦ *(LIHS-truh)*

Language/Cultural Origin: Greek

Meaning: Free

Spiritual Connotation: Self-reliant

Related Names/Nicknames: Lee

Alternate Names: None

Background Story: Paul and Barnabas visited the town of Lystra to preach the gospel, but the people were not easily persuaded. Then they saw Paul heal a man "crippled from birth" and believed the disciples were gods. Paul and Barnabas insisted they were just men and tried to teach the people about Jesus. Later, a group of Jews from Antioch turned the crowds against Paul and they stoned him (Acts 14:8–20). Paul refused to give up on the people of Lystra. He returned there several times, and asked Timothy, a disciple from Lystra, to accompany him on his missionary journeys (Acts 16:1–5).

MAGDALENE ✦ *(MAG-duh-lehn)* or *(MAG-duh-leen)*

Language/Cultural Origin: Greek

Meaning: Watchtower

Spiritual Connotation: Protector

Related Names/Nicknames: Maddie, Madelaine, Madeleine, Madeline, Magda, Magdala, Maggie, Margaret, Marlena, Marlene

Alternate Names: Magdalen, Magdalina, Magdaline, Magdalyn, Magdelana, Magdelena, Magdelene, Magdelina, Magdeline, Magdelyn, Magdelynn

Background Story: The name Magdalene comes from the village of Magdala on the Sea of Galilee. Mary Magdalene—Mary of

Magdala—was a devout follower of Jesus, who drove seven demons from her (Luke 8:2). She and John were among the few believers who stayed with Jesus until he "breathed his last" on the cross (Matthew 27:50). Mary also watched as Jesus's body was buried in the tomb and, three days later, she was the first to see the risen Savior and to tell the other disciples, "I have seen the Lord" (John 20:14–18). Her name is associated with strength, loyalty, and redemption.

MARA ✦ *(MAHR-uh)*

Language/Cultural Origin: Hebrew

Meaning: Bitter

Spiritual Connotation: God's Healing

Related Names/Nicknames: Amara, Maralina, Maraline, Mari, Mary, Tamara

Alternate Names: Marah

Background Story: The word Mara—meaning bitter—is found twice in the Bible. Mara was the place where Moses led the Israelites after marching through the desert for three days. His people were thirsty but "they could not drink the waters of Mara because they were bitter." The Israelites complained, until the Lord showed Moses a tree to throw into the waters, turning them sweet (Exodus 15:22–25). Mara is also the name Naomi gave herself when she returned to Bethlehem after the deaths of her husband and sons. When her friends asked, "Is this Naomi?" she answered, "Call me no longer Naomi, call me Mara, for the Almighty has dealt bitterly with me" (Ruth 1:19–20).

MARTHA ✦ *(MAHR-thuh)*

Language/Cultural Origin: Aramaic

Meaning: Mistress of the House

Spiritual Connotation: God's Service

Related Names/Nicknames: Mart, Martella, Marth, Marti, Martie, Martina, Marty, Mattie, Pat, Patsy, Patti, Patty

Alternate Names: Marta, Marthe

Background Story: Martha lived in Bethany with her sister and brother, Mary and Lazarus. They were dear friends of Jesus, who frequently visited their home. Martha was often so busy "providing for" Jesus, she did not sit and listen to him as Mary did. On one visit, Martha complained to Jesus that Mary should help more with the housework. Jesus replied, "Mary has chosen the better part, which will not be taken away from her" (Luke 10:38–42). One day, Lazarus became ill and Martha sent a desperate message to Jesus, begging him to come. By the time he arrived, Lazarus was dead and buried. Martha met him and said, "Lord, if you had been here, my brother would not have died." But her faith was so strong she believed Jesus could still save her brother. Moved by her tears, Jesus went to the tomb and told Lazarus to come out. Lazarus came to life again and walked out of the tomb (John 11:1–44).

Famous Namesakes: Martha Graham, dancer/choreographer; Martha Jefferson and Martha Washington, first ladies; Martha Raye, comic actress; Martha Stewart, personality/entrepreneur.

MARY ✦ *(MEIR-ee)*

Language/Cultural Origin: Hebrew/English

Meaning: With Sorrow

Spiritual Connotation: Blessed

Related Names/Nicknames: Mae, Mamie, Mara, Maria, Marian, Marianna, Marianne, Maribel, Marie, Mariela, Marilyn, Marisa, Marissa, Maryann, Marybeth, Maryjo, Marylee, Marylou, Maureen, May, Maya, Mia, Mimi, Moira, Molly, Rosemary

Alternate Names: Mari, Miriam

Background Story: There are several Marys in the Bible. Many of these unique women stood by Jesus during his ministry. Mary, the wife of Cleophas, and Mary Magdalene were present at Jesus's crucifixion (John 19:25). Mary of Bethany "anointed the Lord with perfume and wiped his feet with her hair" (John 11:2). The most prominent Mary was Joseph's wife, chosen by God to be the mother of Jesus. Although she was afraid, Mary accepted God's decision with a few simple words: "Let it be with me according to your word" (Luke 1:26–38). She delivered her child in a humble manger, presented him at the temple, escaped with him to Egypt, asked him to perform his first miracle at the marriage in Cana, and remained by his side during his crucifixion. In every way, Mary was a true "servant of the Lord."

Of Interest: Mary, the mother of Jesus, is the object of great veneration in the Catholic Church, where she is known as the Virgin Mary or Mary Mother of God.

Famous Namesakes: Mary, queen of Scotland; Mary J. Blige, musician; Mary Todd Lincoln, first lady; Mary Martin, Mary Tyler Moore, and Mary Steenburgen, actresses; Mary Pierce, tennis player; Mary Shelley, writer.

MEDEBA ✦ *(MEHD-ih-buh)*

Language/Cultural Origin: Hebrew

Meaning: Waters of Rest

Spiritual Connotation: Serenity

Related Names/Nicknames: None

Alternate Names: Madaba

Background Story: Medeba was the ancient Moabite town assigned to the tribe of Reuben when the Israelites entered the Promised Land (Joshua 15:13–16). Later, during David's reign, the Ammonites sought refuge in Medeba before they were defeated by the Israelites (1 Chronicles 19:6–19). Medeba is a soft, gentle name, suggesting a sense of peace and contentment.

Of Interest: The Madaba Map—formed on the floor of a Byzantine church in Medeba—is one of the oldest detailed maps in the world.

MELEA ✦ *(MEHL-ay-ah)*

Language/Cultural Origin: Hebrew

Meaning: Fullness

Spiritual Connotation: Bountiful

Related Names/Nicknames: None

Alternate Names: Maleah, Malia, Maliah, Maliyah

Background Story: Melea, the son of Menan and the father of Eliakim, was an ancestor of Jesus. Luke mentions him in his genealogy of Jesus—beginning with Jesus as the "son of Joseph, son of Heli" all the way through his ancestry to "son of Adam, son of God" (Luke 3:23–38). The names are a reminder of the long line of faith that led to Jesus. The name Melea is usually given to girls today.

MELITA ✦ *(meh-LEE-tuh)*

Language/Cultural Origin: Greek

Meaning: Honey Sweet

Spiritual Connotation: Industrious

Related Names/Nicknames: Carmel, Carmelita, Lisa, Lissa, Lita, Melissa

Alternate Names: Malita, Malta

Background Story: Paul was shipwrecked on the island of Melita when he was being taken to Rome as a prisoner. The hostile islanders watched as Paul was attacked by a viper and waited for him to "fall down and die." To their amazement, however, Paul survived, and the islanders believed he was a god. Paul's powers were even more evident when he "laid his hands on" and healed the sick father of the island's chief man. Soon, every islander who was sick came to be healed by Paul. For the remainder of their stay, the islanders "honored" Paul and treated him "courteously." After three months, a ship was found and Paul left the island for Rome (Acts 28:1–10).

MERAB ✦ *(MEHR-ab)* or *(MEER-ab)*

Language/Cultural Origin: Hebrew

Meaning: Increase

Spiritual Connotation: Abundant

Related Names/Nicknames: None

Alternate Names: Merav

Background Story: King Saul had two daughters, Merab and Michal. Merab, the older of the two, had the misfortune to become a pawn in her father's plot against David. Saul offered Merab as a wife to David—with one provision: "only be valiant for me and fight the Lord's battles." Saul's motives were far from innocent. He was jealous of David's military success and his overwhelming popularity with the Israelites. Saul hoped that engaging in more battles would ultimately lead to David's death, but David continued to be successful because "the Lord was with him." Saul reneged on his agreement and gave Merab as a wife to Adriel the Meholathite, with whom she had five sons (1 Samuel 18:17–19). Later, all five were put to death by the Gibeonites as expiation for Saul's sins against them (2 Samuel 21:8).

MERARI ✦ *(mih-RAHR-ai)* or *(muh-RAYR-ai)*

Language/Cultural Origin: Hebrew

Meaning: Bitter

Spiritual Connotation: Beloved

Related Names/Nicknames: None

Alternate Names: None

Background Story: In the Bible, Merari was Levi's third and youngest son. He was born before his grandfather Jacob went into Egypt and was one of the seventy members of his family who accompanied him there (Genesis 46:5–27). Merari became the head of the great Levite clan known as the Merarites (Numbers 26:57). The name Merari has a soft, lyrical sound, suggesting a girl or boy with a sweet disposition.

Of Interest: Names of the Israelites often reflected circumstances surrounding their birth. For example, it is possible that Merari was given a name that meant "bitter" because of a difficult childbirth.

MERCY ✦ *(MER-see)*

Language/Cultural Origin: Latin/English

Meaning: Compassion

Spiritual Connotation: Kindness

Related Names/Nicknames: Mercedes, Mercia, Mercilla, Mercina

Alternate Names: Mercee, Mercey, Merci, Mercie

Background Story: Mercy is a fundamental quality of God in the Bible. David said that God's "goodness and mercy shall follow me all the days of my life" (Psalms 23:6), and Paul told his followers that God is not only "the Father of mercies" (2 Corinthians 1:3) but also "rich in mercy" (Ephesians 2:4). God's mercy was also a grace for Christians to imitate. Jesus said to the crowds who were following him, "Blessed are the merciful, for they will receive mercy" (Matthew 5:7).

Of Interest: Mercy Corps is a not-for-profit global relief organization, founded in 1979 to help refugees fleeing the "killing fields" of Cambodia. Every year, it offers assistance to six million people in over thirty-five countries.

MESHA ✦ *(MEE-shuh)*

Language/Cultural Origin: Hebrew

Meaning: Deliverance

Spiritual Connotation: Salvation

Related Names/Nicknames: Lamesha

Alternate Names: Meshah

Background Story: Mesha is a plain in the Old Testament that marks the western boundary of land inhabited by Joktan's descendants (Genesis 10:30). Mesha is also the name of three men in the Bible: Caleb's firstborn son (1 Chronicles 2:42); a son that Shaharaim had with Hodesh (1 Chronicles 8:9); and a Moabite king who rebelled against the king of Israel. Mesha—a name that suggests a free spirit—is given to both men and women today.

Of Interest: Mesha is also a Hindu name that means "born under the sign of Aries."

MICHAL ✦ *(MAI-kuhl)*

Language/Cultural Origin: Hebrew

Meaning: Who Is Like God

Spiritual Connotation: Godliness

Related Names/Nicknames: Mia, Mica, Micayla, Michaela, Michaelina, Michaeline, Michaelyn, Michelle, Mickey, Micki, Mickie, Micky, Micole, Mikaila

Alternate Names: Mical, Mychal

Background Story: Michal was Saul's younger daughter who loved David. Saul gave her to him as a wife, but he was jealous of David's military successes and wished he were dead. One day, Saul tried to kill his son-in-law, but Michal helped him escape, placing an "idol" under David's bed covers to make it appear he was sleeping (1 Samuel 19:11–17). David went into hiding, and Saul gave Michal in marriage to another man. After Saul's death, David asked for Michal and she returned to him. But her love had cooled in the interim. She mocked him for "leaping and dancing" when the ark of the covenant was restored. David said that he was not ashamed to have "danced before the Lord." Michal died childless, and David's line was never mixed with Saul's (2 Samuel 6:20–23).

MILCAH ✦ *(MIHL-kah)*

Language/Cultural Origin: Hebrew

Meaning: Queen

Spiritual Connotation: Good Counsel

Related Names/Nicknames: None

Alternate Names: Malcah, Malkah, Melcha

Background Story: The name Milcah is associated with two women in the Bible. The first Milcah was the wife of Nahor, Abraham's brother. She had eight children, one of whom was Bethuel, who "became the father of Rebekah" (Genesis 22:20–23). Milcah was also one of five sisters who had the courage to ask Moses for their deceased father's land, changing the law of inheritance for the Israelites. The new law allowed for daughters of a man without sons to inherit their father's land and carry on his name (Numbers 27:1–11).

Of Interest: Milcah—Nahor's wife—became an important factor in the lineage of both Israel and Jesus when her granddaughter, Rebekah, married Abraham's son, Isaac.

MIRIAM ✦ *(MIHR-ee-uhm)*

Language/Cultural Origin: Hebrew

Meaning: Rebellious

Spiritual Connotation: Jubilant

Related Names/Nicknames: Mamie, Mariamne, Mariana, Mary, Mimi, Minnie, Mitzi

Alternate Names: Mariam, Maryam, Myriam

Background Story: Of the two biblical Miriams, Moses and Aaron's sister is the more prominent. From a distance she patiently watched over the infant Moses, until he was discovered in the bulrushes by Pharaoh's daughter. Later, she joined Moses and Aaron as they led the Israelites across the Red Sea—which the Lord had parted—with Pharaoh and his army in pursuit. Once they were safe on the other side and the waters of the sea had swallowed up Pharaoh's army, Miriam grabbed a tambourine and led the women in a victory dance, singing, "The Lord . . . has triumphed gloriously; horse and rider he has thrown into the sea" (Exodus 15:20–21).

Of Interest: The "Cup of Miriam" is a modern-day ritual observed during the Passover seder. Filled with water, the cup symbolizes Miriam's Well, a legendary source of water that healed and sustained the Israelites as they wandered through the desert.

Famous Namesakes: Miriam Davenport was an American painter and sculptor who helped European Jews escape the Holocaust during World War II.

MOREH ✦ *(MOR-eh)* or *(MO-ray)* or *(MO-ree)*

Language/Cultural Origin: Hebrew

Meaning: Stretching

Spiritual Connotation: Achievement

Related Names/Nicknames: None

Alternate Names: None

Background Story: Moreh was not only a place in Canaan; it was a biblical landmark. God appeared to Abraham at "the oak of Moreh" and promised "to your offspring I will give this land" (Genesis 12:6–7); Moses later described "the oak of Moreh" as a landmark in the Promised Land (Deuteronomy 11:30); and the Midianite army camped "below the hill of Moreh" from which Gideon made his attack on them (Judges 7:1). Moreh is an appropriate name for girls and boys who are always ready for new challenges.

Of Interest: Moreh probably derived its name from a Canaanite who once lived there.

MORIAH ✦ *(muh-RAI-uh)* or *(maw-RAI-uh)*

Language/Cultural Origin: Hebrew

Meaning: God Is My Teacher

Spiritual Connotation: The Lord Will Provide

Related Names/Nicknames: None

Alternate Names: None

Background Story: The land of Moriah is where God put Abraham's faith to the test. One day, he told Abraham to take his son, Isaac, to a mountain in Moriah and offer him up as a sacrifice. As they approached the place with wood and fire, Isaac said, "Father . . . where is the lamb for a burnt offering?" Abraham answered, "God himself will provide the lamb . . . my son." After they arrived, Abraham built an altar and tied Isaac to it. As he raised his knife to kill his son, an angel stopped him and told him not to harm Isaac. Just then, Abraham saw a ram caught in the bushes, and he offered it as a sacrifice. Because Abraham had such great faith, God promised to bless him and his offspring, who would be "as numerous as the stars of heaven" (Genesis 22:1–18).

Of Interest: Mount Moriah is also a holy site in Islam. According to tradition, it was the place from which the prophet Mohammed rose to heaven.

MYRA ✦ *(MAI-ruh)*

Language/Cultural Origin: Greek/Latin

Meaning: Fragrance of Myrrh

Spiritual Connotation: Generous

Related Names/Nicknames: Mirilla, Moira, Myrah, Myriah, Myrilla, Myrina, Myrna

Alternate Names: Mayra, Mira

Background Story: Myra was a city in Lycia, a few miles from the coast. Paul stopped at Myra on his long journey to Rome as a prisoner. A centurion found a ship there bound for Italy and put him on board (Acts 27:5–6). The name Myra is a reminder of the sweet charms of womanhood.

Of Interest: Saint Nicholas—often associated with gift-giving at Christmas—was the bishop of Myra in Lycia during the fourth century.

MYRTLE ✦ *(MER-tuhl)*

Language/Cultural Origin: Latin/Greek

Meaning: A Plant

Spiritual Connotation: Symbol of Peace

Related Names/Nicknames: Mertice, Mertis, Mirtie, Mirtile, Myrta, Myrtia, Myrtice, Myrtie, Myrtillus, Myrtis, Myrtisa, Myrtos, Myrtus

Alternate Names: Mertle, Mirtle

Background Story: Myrtle is a shrub or small tree with fragrant white flowers. It was seen in the Bible as a symbol of strength and peace. The people of Judah were told to "go out to the hills and bring branches of . . . myrtle . . . and other leafy trees to make booths" as God's law required (Nehemiah 8:15); God promised his people that someday, "instead of the brier shall come up the myrtle; and it shall be . . . a memorial . . . an everlasting sign" (Isaiah 55:13); and Zechariah saw, in a vision, an "angel of the Lord . . . standing among the myrtle trees," who told him, "the whole earth remains at peace" (Zechariah 1:11).

Of Interest: The name Hadassah means "myrtle tree" in Hebrew. In Greek mythology, the myrtle was associated with Aphrodite, the goddess of love, and ancient Greek brides often wore crowns of myrtle on their wedding day.

Famous Namesakes: Myrtle Gonzalez, Myrtle Stedman, silent-film actresses; Myrtle McGraw, psychologist/writer; Myrtle Reed, writer.

NAARAH ✦ *(NAY-uh-rah)*

Language/Cultural Origin: Hebrew

Meaning: Young Girl

Spiritual Connotation: Handmaiden of God

Related Names/Nicknames: Naaran, Naarath

Alternate Names: Naara, Naarai

Background Story: Naarah was one of Ashhur's wives. She had four sons: Ahuzam, Hepher, Temeni, Haahashtari (1 Chronicles 4:5–6). They were from the tribe of Judah.

Of Interest: According to Jewish rabbinical literature, Miriam once took the name of Naarah—after her recovery from a lengthy illness—to signify that she felt like a young woman again.

NAOMI ✦ *(NAY-o-mai)* or *(nay-O-mee)*

Language/Cultural Origin: Hebrew

Meaning: Pleasantness

Spiritual Connotation: Delight in God

Related Names/Nicknames: Naoma, Naomia, Nay, Neoma, Noami, Nomi

Alternate Names: Naomie, Nayomi, Neomi

Background Story: Naomi lived in Bethlehem, a town in Judah. Because of a famine, she left with her family to live in the country of Moab, and her two sons married Moabite women—Orpah and Ruth. After a few years, Naomi's husband and sons died. Saddened by her loss, she returned to Bethlehem with her daughter-in-law, Ruth, who refused to leave her. When Naomi's former neighbors greeted her by name, she said, "Call me Mara, for the Almighty has dealt bitterly with me." Back home, Naomi encouraged Ruth to befriend her kinsman Boaz. Impressed with Ruth's loyalty to Naomi, Boaz married Ruth and purchased the land that belonged to Naomi's husband. They had a son named Obed, and Naomi took care of him in her old age (Book of Ruth).

Famous Namesakes: Naomi Campbell, model; Naomi Judd, singer/songwriter; Naomi Watts, actress.

NEAH ✦ *(NEE-uh)* or *(NAY-uh)*

Language/Cultural Origin: Hebrew

Meaning: Moving

Spiritual Connotation: Inspiration

Related Names/Nicknames: None

Alternate Names: None

Background Story: Neah is the name of a town near Rimmon. In the Bible, it was east of Zebulun and part of the land inherited by the tribe of Zebulon (Joshua 19:13–16). The name Neah suggests a woman who is an inspiration to others.

Famous Namesakes: Neah Lee is a Christian singer/songwriter whose worship music draws from the Bible and is an eclectic mix of folk, jazz, and pop.

NEKODA ✦ *(nee-KO-duh)*

Language/Cultural Origin: Hebrew

Meaning: Painted

Spiritual Connotation: Distinguished

Related Names/Nicknames: None

Alternate Names: None

Background Story: Nekoda was the name of two patriarchs whose families returned from exile in Babylon. The descendants of Nekoda were among "the temple servants to return" (Ezra 2:43–48) and among those who "could not prove their families or their descent, whether they belonged to Israel" (Ezra 2:59–60). Nekoda, more often a girl's name today, suggests a woman who enjoys standing out from the crowd.

NERIAH ✦ *(nuh-RAI-uh)*

Language/Cultural Origin: Hebrew

Meaning: Lamp of the Lord

Spiritual Connotation: Enlighten

Related Names/Nicknames: Neri

Alternate Names: Nereias, Neria, Nerias,
Neriyah, Neriyahu, Nerriah

Background Story: In the Old Testament, Neriah was the father of
Baruch and Seraiah. Baruch was a scribe and Seraiah, a palace
official. Both aided the prophet Jeremiah in his sacred charge to
bring about the restoration of Jerusalem (Jeremiah 32:12). Once a
man's name, Neriah is more popular for women today and suggests a woman who is a born educator.

Of Interest: Every mention of Baruch in the Bible refers to him as
"the son of Neriah." In 1975, an official seal of office was found
near Jerusalem with the following words: "Berekhayahu son of
Neriyahu the scribe"—or, in current language, Baruch son of
Neriah.

Famous Namesakes: Neriah Fox is a former model who is now a
fashion photographer.

NIMRAH ✦ *(NIHM-ruh)*

Language/Cultural Origin: Hebrew

Meaning: Rebellion

Spiritual Connotation: Independence

Related Names/Nicknames: Beth-nimrah

Alternate Names: None

Background Story: Nimrah—also known as Beth-nimrah in the
Bible—was a town east of the Jordan in Gilead. The Reubenites
and Gadites preferred to settle in Gilead—rather than the
Promised Land—because they "owned a very great number of
cattle" and Nimrah was "a land for cattle" (Numbers 32:4). Moses
agreed to their request, provided they first cross the Jordan and

help conquer the Promised Land for the other tribes. Nimrah—a name for both boys and girls today—suggests a free and independent spirit.

NISAN ✦ *(NIH-suhn)* or *(nee-SAHN)*

Language/Cultural Origin: Babylonian/Hebrew

Meaning: Month of Flowers

Spiritual Connotation: Miracle

Related Names/Nicknames: Nisag, Nisannu

Alternate Names: Nican

Background Story: Nisan is the first month of the Jewish sacred year and the month of Passover. In the Bible, the fourteenth of Nisan was when the Lord passed through Egypt and destroyed "every firstborn of the land"—except for any Jews who put blood from a sacrificial lamb on their doorposts. It also marked the day the Israelites began their exodus from Egypt. The Lord said, "This day shall be a day of remembrance for you. You shall celebrate it as a festival to the Lord; throughout your generations you shall observe it as a perpetual ordinance" (Exodus 12:14).

Of Interest: Nisan was also a significant month in Jesus's life. His Last Supper was a Passover celebration; the next day he was crucified and died.

NOA ✦ *(NO-uh)*

Language/Cultural Origin: Hebrew

Meaning: Trembling

Spiritual Connotation: Standing Before God

Related Names/Nicknames: None

Alternate Names: Noah

Background Story: Noa was the youngest of Zelophehad's five daughters. When their father died without leaving any male heirs, Noa and her sisters asked Moses for his land as their inheritance. After consulting with God, Moses agreed that it was their right. Noa and her sisters—Mahlah, Hoglah, Milkah, and Tirzah—all kept their inheritance within the tribe by marrying sons of their father's brothers (Numbers 27:1–11).

Of Interest: Because of Zelophehad's daughters, a new law was established among the Israelites, allowing daughters of a man without sons to inherit their father's land.

Famous Namesakes: Noa Tishby is an Israeli actress, singer, and songwriter, who is a star in her homeland and has also performed in the United States.

NOADIAH ✦ *(no-uh-DAI-uh)*

Language/Cultural Origin: Hebrew

Meaning: Meeting with the Lord

Spiritual Connotation: God's Witness

Related Names/Nicknames: None

Alternate Names: Noadei, Noadhyah, Noadia, Noadya

Background Story: Of the two Noadiahs in the Bible, the more inspiring is the Levite priest who returned from Babylon with

Ezra and was entrusted with the gold, silver, and sacred vessels for the temple (Ezra 8:33). Noadiah—a name given to both boys and girls today—suggests someone who communicates easily with God.

OPHRAH ✦ *(AWF-ruh)* or *(OF-rah)*

Language/Cultural Origin: Hebrew

Meaning: A Place of Dust

Spiritual Connotation: Where the Lord Speaks

Related Names/Nicknames: Ofrit

Alternate Names: Afra, Aphra, Ofra, Ofrah

Background Story: Gideon lived in Ophrah, which was a city of Manasseh. An angel from the Lord appeared to Gideon "under the oak at Ophrah" and commissioned him to "deliver Israel from the hand of Midian" (Judges 6:11–14). To honor the Lord and his angel, Gideon built an altar there and called it "the Lord is peace" (Judges 6:24). Just as God promised, Gideon led the Israelites to freedom and forty years of peace. He died an old man and "was buried in the tomb of his father at Ophrah" (Judges 8:32).

ORPAH ✦ *(OR-puh)*

Language/Cultural Origin: Hebrew

Meaning: Fawn

Spiritual Connotation: Youthful Spirit

Related Names/Nicknames: Oprah, Oreph

Alternate Names: Ofra, Ofrah, Ophra, Ophrah, Orpa, Orpha

Background Story: Orpah and Ruth, two Moabite women, were married to Naomi's sons. Naomi's family had left their home-land of Judah because of a famine and settled in Moab. Sadly, Naomi's husband and sons died, leaving the three women wid-ows. When Naomi decided to return to Judah, Orpah and Ruth chose to remain with their mother-in-law. Naomi was concerned for the well-being of the two younger women. On the trip home, she turned to them and said, "Go back each of you to your mother's house," where she hoped they would find security with new husbands. Weeping, Orpah "kissed her mother-in-law" and turned back, but Ruth stayed with Naomi (Ruth 1:1–18).

Of Interest: Actress and talk-show hostess Oprah Winfrey was originally named Orpah. A clerical error on her birth certificate changed her name to Oprah.

Famous Namesakes: Oprah Winfrey, talk-show hostess.

PEARL ✦ *(PERL)*

Language/Cultural Origin: Latin

Meaning: Gemstone

Spiritual Connotation: Respect

Related Names/Nicknames: Margaret, Pearla, Pearle, Pearleen, Pearlette, Pearlie, Pearlina, Pearline, Perla, Perlette, Perline, Perlita, Perlline, Perna, Purlie

Alternate Names: Pearle, Perl, Perle

Background Story: A pearl is a lustrous gem that was found in oys-ter shells in the Red Sea. It was frequently used as a metaphor in the Bible for something of value. When Job talked about the "price of wisdom," he said it was "above pearls" (Job 28:18), and Matthew warned his followers about judging others, saying, "Do not throw your pearls before swine" (Matthew 7:6). Even Jesus compared the kingdom of heaven to a merchant in search of a fine pearl: "On finding one pearl of great value, he went and sold all that he had and bought it" (Matthew 13:45–46). The name Pearl suggests a girl who is highly regarded.

Of Interest: The pearl is the birthstone of those born in June.

Famous Namesakes: Pearl Bailey, entertainer; Pearl S. Buck, Nobel Prize–winning author.

PERGA ✦ *(PER-guh)*
Language/Cultural Origin: Greek
Meaning: Very Earthy
Spiritual Connotation: Straightforward
Related Names/Nicknames: None
Alternate Names: None

Background Story: Perga—a city in Pamphylia in Asia Minor—was one of the places Paul visited to rally support for the new Church. During his first trip to Perga, one of his companions, John Mark, left him there and returned to Jerusalem (Acts 13:13). Later, Paul returned with Barnabas to speak "the word in Perga" (Acts 14:25).

Of Interest: Apollonius of Perga was a Greek mathematician who influenced later scholars and introduced mathematical terms that are still used today.

PERSIS ✦ *(PER-sihs)*

Language/Cultural Origin: Greek

Meaning: Persian Woman

Spiritual Connotation: God's Worker

Related Names/Nicknames: None

Alternate Names: Persiss, Persys, Persyss

Background Story: Persis—a Roman woman and an early follower of Christ—was one of several Christians Paul "greeted" in a letter to Rome. In the letter, he explained to the new disciples how to live in Christ. Paul speaks well of Persis, calling her "beloved" and observing that she has "worked hard in the Lord" (Romans 16:12).

Famous Namesakes: Persis Khambatta was an actress and former Miss India and Miss World whose most notable role was Lieutenant Ilia in *Star Trek: The Motion Picture*.

PETRA ✦ *(PEH-truh)* or *(PEE-truh)*

Language/Cultural Origin: Greek

Meaning: Rock

Spiritual Connotation: Eternal Strength

Related Names/Nicknames: Peter

Alternate Names: None

Background Story: Petra—called Sela in most versions of the Bible—was an Edomite city located on a plain between the Dead Sea and the Red Sea. Isaiah referred to "Petra of the desert" and prophesied that even the remote "inhabitants of Petra" would one day "give praise" and "cry from the top of the mountains" to the Lord (Isaiah 16:1, 42:11).

Of Interest: The ancient city of Petra was surrounded by hills of pink sandstone with elaborate tombs carved into the cliffs. The ruins of this "rose-red city" still exist today in the country of Jordan.

Famous Namesakes: Petra Berger, singer; Petra Burka, Olympic figure skater; Petra Kelly, peace activist; Petra Nemcova, model.

PHOEBE *(FEE-bee)*

Language/Cultural Origin: Greek

Meaning: Radiant

Spiritual Connotation: Benefactor

Related Names/Nicknames: Febe, Phebe, Phoibe

Alternate Names: Pheabe, Pheby, Pheebe, Pheebee, Pheebey, Pheebi, Pheebie, Pheeby, Phoebee, Phoebey, Phoebi, Phoebie, Phoeby

Background Story: Phoebe was a woman of prominence in the early Church. She was "a deacon of the church at Cenchreae" in Corinth and the first person Paul mentioned in his letter to the Romans. His feelings about her were clear: "Welcome her in the Lord as is fitting for the saints, and help her in whatever she may require from you, for she has been a benefactor of many and of myself as well" (Romans 16:1–2). This high praise from Paul set Phoebe apart as someone who lived her life in Christ through charitable acts.

Of Interest: It is believed that Phoebe herself delivered Paul's epistle to the Christians in Rome.

Famous Namesakes: Phoebe Cates, actress; Phoebe Snow, singer/songwriter; Phoebe Buffay, fictional character on the television series *Friends*.

PHOTINA ✦ *(fo-TEE-nuh)*

Language/Cultural Origin: Greek

Meaning: Enlightened One

Spiritual Connotation: Friend of the Lord

Related Names/Nicknames: Tina

Alternate Names: Photine

Background Story: According to Greek tradition, Photina is the Samaritan woman who met Jesus at Jacob's Well. When he asked her for a drink of water she was surprised, because Jews didn't "share things" with Samaritans. Jesus began to tell her about God's "living water." He said, "Those who drink of the water that I will give them will never be thirsty." Then he revealed that he was the Messiah. Photina returned to the city and told people what Jesus said. Because of her, many Samaritans came to Jesus, heard him for themselves, and believed he was "truly the savior of the world" (John 4:1–42).

Of Interest: Photina is a saint in the Catholic Church. Legend has it she was a Christian missionary in Carthage and was martyred under the Emperor Nero in Rome.

PRISCILLA ✦ *(prih-SIHL-uh)*

Language/Cultural Origin: Latin

Meaning: Long Life

Spiritual Connotation: Venerable

Related Names/Nicknames: Cilla, Pris, Prisca, Prissie

Alternate Names: Pricila, Priscila, Prisila, Prisilla

Background Story: When Paul first met Priscilla and her husband, Aquila, they were living in Corinth. Paul stayed at their home and worked with them, because they shared the same trade—

tentmaking. After a while, Paul left Corinth with Priscilla and Aquila, but the couple stopped in Ephesus. They began their own missionary work when they met an enthusiastic Jew named Apollos who had been "instructed in the way of the Lord." Priscilla and Aquila found they had to explain "the Way of God to him more accurately" (Acts 18:1–26).

Of Interest: For their loyal work, Priscilla and Aquila were regularly remembered by Paul in his epistles. He frequently used her nickname, Prisca.

Famous Namesakes: Priscilla Presley is an actress and only wife of singer Elvis Presley. Priscilla is also the heroine of the Longfellow poem *The Courtship of Miles Standish*.

RACHEL ✦ *(RAY-chuhl)*

Language/Cultural Origin: Hebrew

Meaning: Lamb

Spiritual Connotation: Innocent

Related Names/Nicknames: Rae, Rahel, Rakel, Raquel, Raquela, Ray, Rey, Rochell, Rochelle, Shell, Shelley, Shellie, Shelly

Alternate Names: Rachael, Rachele, Rachelle, Rachil, Raychel, Raychelle

Background Story: Rachel was Laban's younger daughter. She was "graceful and beautiful," and Jacob loved her the moment he saw her tending her father's sheep (Genesis 29:9–11). For seven years, Jacob "served" Laban so he could marry her. But Laban deceived Jacob and switched Rachel with her sister, Leah, on their wedding night. Jacob was allowed to marry Rachel also—in exchange for another seven years of service. To her dismay, Rachel was "barren," while Leah had many sons. Envious of her sister, Rachel cried to Jacob, "Give me children, or I shall die!" Jacob answered, "Am I in the place of God, who has withheld from you the fruit of the womb?" (Genesis 30:1–2). After many years, "God remembered Rachel . . . and opened her womb." She had a son named Joseph, and he was Jacob's favorite. One day, Jacob gathered his family and returned to the land of his father. On the way, his beloved Rachel died giving birth to another son, Benjamin, and was buried.

Famous Namesakes: Rachel Carson was an ecologist whose well-known book *Silent Spring* raised the public's awareness of the effect of pesticides in the natural world.

RAPHA ✦ *(RAY-fuh)*

Language/Cultural Origin: Hebrew

Meaning: Heal

Spiritual Connotation: Purify

Related Names/Nicknames: None

Alternate Names: Raphah, Rephaiah

Background Story: There are two men named Rapha in the Bible: Benjamin's fifth son (1 Chronicles 8:2), and Binea's son, also a descendant of Saul (1 Chronicles 8:37). Rapha is a girl's or boy's name that suggests a gentle, soothing nature.

Of Interest: In Exodus, God revealed himself to Moses as Jehovah Rapha, which means "the Lord is healing."

REBA ✦ *(REE-buh)*

Language/Cultural Origin: Hebrew

Meaning: Stoops Down

Spiritual Connotation: Reverence for God

Related Names/Nicknames: Rebekah

Alternate Names: Reyba, Rheba

Background Story: Reba was one of five Midianite chiefs slain by the Israelites, as God commanded Moses (Numbers 31:8). The Lord was angry at the Midianites for enticing the Israelites to worship pagan gods and for trying to place a curse on them. God said to Moses, "Harass the Midianites, and defeat them; for they have harassed you" (Numbers 25:17–18).

Of Interest: The name Reba is also a shortened form of Rebekah.

Famous Namesakes: Reba McEntire is an award-winning country-music singer, who has acted in films, on the stage, and in her own television series—all to critical acclaim.

REBEKAH ✦ *(rih-BEHK-uh)*

Language/Cultural Origin: Hebrew/Latin

Meaning: To Bind

Spiritual Connotation: Captivating

Related Names/Nicknames: Becca, Becka, Becki, Beckie, Becky, Bekka, Bekki, Bekkie, Reba, Riva, Rivka, Rivqa

Alternate Names: Rebecca, Rebeccah, Rebeckah, Rebekka, Rebekkah, Ribhqah

Background Story: Abraham sent his oldest servant back to his homeland to find a wife for Isaac, his son. After he arrived, the servant saw Rebekah drawing water from a well, which she graciously offered him. Rebekah was not only "fair to look upon," she was related to Abraham through his brother Nahor, her grandfather. Rebekah returned with the servant, and Isaac made her his wife. After twenty years, Rebekah conceived but had a difficult pregnancy. God told her, "Two nations are in your womb . . . the one shall be stronger than the other; the elder shall serve the younger." Rebekah delivered twins: Esau first, and then Jacob. Of the two boys, Rebekah favored Jacob. She even helped him obtain his father's blessing before he died—a blessing that was meant for Esau. When Esau grew bitter and plotted to kill Jacob, Rebekah sent her favorite son away to live with her brother, Laban (Genesis 24–28). She died without seeing Jacob again and was buried with Isaac in the cave at Machpelah.

Of Interest: At its peak in the 1970s, Rebecca was the thirteenth most popular name for girls in the United States.

Famous Namesakes: Rebecca De Mornay, actress; Rebekah Harkness, philanthropist; Rebecca West, writer.

RHODA ✦ *(RO-duh)*

Language/Cultural Origin: Greek

Meaning: Rose

Spiritual Connotation: God's Miracle

Related Names/Nicknames: Rhodie, Rhody, Rodi, Rodie, Rodina, Roe

Alternate Names: Roda

Background Story: Rhoda was a servant of Mary, John Mark's mother. Peter had been thrown into prison, and many of his followers were gathered at Mary's house to pray for him. One night, an angel from God appeared to Peter and led him out of the prison. Peter went straight to Mary's house and "knocked at the outer gate." Rhoda answered. She heard his voice and became so excited she left him "standing at the gate" while she ran to tell the others. No one believed her. They said, "You are out of your mind," and "It is his angel." Peter kept knocking. When they opened the gate at last, they were "amazed" to see Peter and to hear the story of his miraculous escape (Acts 12:5–17).

Of Interest: Rhoda also means "from Rhodes," which is a Greek island originally named for its roses.

Famous Namesakes: Rhoda Morgenstern was a character played by Valerie Harper on two popular 1970s television series, *The Mary Tyler Moore Show* and *Rhoda.*

ROE ✦ *(RO)*
Language/Cultural Origin: Old English
Meaning: Small Deer
Spiritual Connotation: Graceful
Related Names/Nicknames: None
Alternate Names: Ro

Background Story: In the Bible, a roe is a kind of gazelle that was native to the Holy Land. It was known for its beauty, grace, and speed. Asahel was "as light of foot as a wild roe" when he chased Abner (2 Samuel 2:18); Solomon advised his "son" to rejoice in his wife and "let her be as the loving hind and pleasant roe" (Proverbs 5:18–19); and the bride of Solomon described her beloved as "like a roe" who leaped through the hills and mountains (Song of Solomon 2:8–9).

ROSE ✦ *(ROZ)*

Language/Cultural Origin: Latin

Meaning: A Flower

Spiritual Connotation: Perfect Love

Related Names/Nicknames: Rosa, Rosalia, Rosalie, Rosalin, Rosalina, Rosalind, Rosario, Roselia, Roselina, Roseline, Rosella, Roselle, Rosena, Rosetta, Rosette, Rosey, Rosheen, Rosie, Rosina, Rosine, Rosio, Rosita, Roslyn, Rosy, Roza, Rozalie, Rozy

Alternate Names: Roze

Background Story: The rose—a symbol of love and purity—is a flower that appears in several translations of the Bible. Solomon's bride is described as a beautiful "rose of Sharon" (Song of Solomon 2:1); Isaiah prophesied that for those who are faithful to God, one day "the wilderness and the dry land shall be glad; and the desert shall rejoice, and blossom as the rose" (Isaiah 35:1); and Jesus, son of Sirach, encouraged God's "divine offspring" to "bud forth as the rose planted by the brooks of waters" (Ecclesiasticus 39:13).

Of Interest: The rose has long been a symbol of the Blessed Virgin Mary, one of whose designations in the Roman Catholic Church is Mystical Rose.

Famous Namesakes: Rosario Dawson, Rose Marie, Rose McGowan, actresses; Rose Fitzgerald Kennedy, matriarch of the Kennedy family; Rose Maddox, singer; Rosa Parks, civil-rights heroine.

RUBY ✦ *(ROO-bee)*

Language/Cultural Origin: Latin

Meaning: Red Gem

Spiritual Connotation: Treasured

Related Names/Nicknames: Rubena, Rubia, Rubianne, Rubina, Rubinia, Rubyna

Alternate Names: Rubee, Rubey, Rubi, Rubie

Background Story: The ruby was a stone of tremendous value during biblical times, but the Bible points out that some things are even more priceless. Solomon described wisdom as "more precious than rubies" (Proverbs 3:15), and Lemuel found a "virtuous wife" so exceptional that her worth was "far above rubies" (Proverbs 31:10).

Of Interest: The stone sometimes called a ruby in the Bible was either red coral, pearl, or mother-of-pearl. The ruby is the birthstone of those born in July.

Famous Namesakes: Ruby Dee, actress; Ruby Keeler, dancer/actress.

RUTH *(ROOTH)*

Language/Cultural Origin: Hebrew

Meaning: Companion

Spiritual Connotation: Friendship

Related Names/Nicknames: Ruthann, Ruthelle, Ruthellen, Ruthi, Ruthie, Ruthina

Alternate Names: Rhouth, Ruthe

Background Story: Ruth and Orpah were Moabite women who married Naomi's sons after the family moved to Moab. After a few years, Naomi's husband and sons died, and she decided to return to her home country of Judah. When Ruth and Orpah followed, she urged them to turn back. Orpah did, but Ruth said to Naomi, "Where you go, I will go; where you lodge, I will lodge; your people shall be my people, and your God my God."

The two widows settled in Bethlehem, where Ruth met Boaz, a kinsman of her late father-in-law. Boaz was moved by Ruth's devotion to Naomi and allowed her to glean his wheat. At Naomi's prompting, Ruth asked Boaz for his protection. "Spread your cloak over your servant," she said, "for you are next-of-kin." Boaz agreed to marry Ruth and acquire her father-in-law's property. Their son, Obed, became David's grandfather (Book of Ruth).

Of Interest: Ruth was the fifth most popular name for girls from 1900 to 1920.

Famous Namesakes: Ruth Buzzi, Ruth Gordon, actresses; Ruth Bader Ginsburg, Supreme Court justice; Ruth Prawer Jhabvala, screenwriter; Ruth Rendell, writer; Ruth St. Denis, dancer/choreographer.

SAFFRON ✦ *(SAF-ruhn)*

Language/Cultural Origin: Arabic/Old English
Meaning: Yellow Flower
Spiritual Connotation: Precious Spice
Related Names/Nicknames: Saffi, Saffronia, Saffy
Alternate Names: Saffran, Saffren, Saphron

Background Story: Saffron is a spice that comes from a flowering plant that grew in the Holy Land. In the Bible, Solomon described his love as a "garden enclosed," whose "plants are an orchard" filled with "pleasant fruits" and "all the chief spices"—including saffron (Song of Solomon 4:12–14).

Of Interest: Saffron is the most expensive spice in the world today. True saffron comes from the stigmas of the *Crocus sativus* plant, which are handpicked and dried for use. In the ancient world, saffron was also the principal source of yellow dye.

Famous Namesakes: Saffron Aldridge, model.

SALOME ✦ *(SA-luh-may)* or *(suh-LO-mee)*

Language/Cultural Origin: Hebrew/Aramaic

Meaning: Peace

Spiritual Connotation: Welcome

Related Names/Nicknames: Loma, Sally, Salom, Saloma, Salomi, Selima, Shulamit

Alternate Names: Salomea

Background Story: Of the two Salomes in the Bible, one was Herodias's daughter, who pleased Herod with her dancing and was rewarded with the head of John the Baptist (Mark 6:21–28). The other Salome was among the dedicated women who "provided for" Jesus in Galilee. She was Zebedee's wife and the mother of James and John, two of Jesus's apostles. Salome was so moved by Jesus that she asked him to give her sons places of honor in his kingdom (Matthew 20:20–21). With the other women, she witnessed Jesus's crucifixion (Mark 15:40) and brought spices to his tomb "so that they might . . . anoint him" (Mark 16:1).

Famous Namesakes: Salome Jens is a noted stage, film, and television actress.

SAPPHIRA ✦ *(suh-FAI-ruh)*

Language/Cultural Origin: Greek/Hebrew

Meaning: Deep-Blue Gemstone

Spiritual Connotation: Beautiful Jewel

Related Names/Nicknames: None

Alternate Names: Safira, Saphira, Saphire, Sapphire, Sephira

Background Story: Sapphira and her husband, Ananias, belonged to the early Church in Jerusalem. At the time, members of the Christian community had agreed to sell their possessions and give the proceeds to the apostles to be "distributed to each as any had need." With Sapphira's knowledge, however, Ananias "kept back" some of his proceeds and contributed only a part. Peter confronted Sapphira and Ananais and asked how they could "lie to the Holy Spirit." When they heard his words, they fell down and died (Acts 5:1–10).

SARAH ✦ *(SAR-uh)* or *(SEHR-uh)*

Language/Cultural Origin: Hebrew

Meaning: Princess

Spiritual Connotation: Mother of Nations

Related Names/Nicknames: Sadee, Sadie, Sal, Sallee, Sallie, Sally, Sarabeth, Sarahlee, Sarahlynn, Sarajane, Sarajean, Saralee, Saralyn, Saralynn, Sarena, Sarene, Saretta, Sarette, Sari, Sarina, Sarita, Saroya, Soraya, Zahra, Zara, Zarah, Zaria, Zarita

Alternate Names: Saira, Sairah, Sara, Sarai, Sarra, Sarrah

Background Story: Sarah—born Sarai—lived the life of a nomad with her husband and half-brother, Abraham. On two occasions, powerful men were taken by her beauty and tried to acquire her, but the Lord protected her. Although God promised Abraham a son with Sarah, for many years she had no children. Out of desperation, she finally convinced Abraham to have a child with her maid, Hagar, and they named the boy Ishmael. At the age of ninety, Sarah finally conceived. God changed her name from Sarai, meaning "she that strives," to Sarah, meaning "princess," and promised Abraham that she would "give rise to nations" (Genesis 17:16). Through their son, Isaac, and grandson, Jacob, Sarah became the first matriarch of the Jewish people.

Of Interest: Sarah ranked among the top five names for girls in the United States from 1980 to 2000 — except for the year 1991, when it ranked sixth.

Famous Namesakes: Sarah Bernhardt, Sarah Jessica Parker, actresses; Sarah Brightman, singer; Sarah Ferguson, Duchess of York; Sarah Hughes, Olympic figure skater; Sara Teasdale, poet.

SELA ✦ *(SEE-luh)*

Language/Cultural Origin: Hebrew

Meaning: Rock

Spiritual Connotation: Foundation

Related Names/Nicknames: Selena, Seleta

Alternate Names: Selah, Sele

Background Story: In the Bible, the city of Sela—the capital of Edom—was situated in a valley that extended from the Dead Sea to the Red Sea. King Amaziah of Judah "killed ten thousand Edomites in the Valley of Salt and took Sela by storm" (2 Kings 14:7).

Of Interest: Selah is a word frequently found in the Book of Psalms. It was a musical term used by the Hebrews that may mean "silence" or "pause" or "interlude."

Famous Namesakes: Sela Ward is an award-winning actress who is best known for starring roles in two television series: *Sisters* and *Once and Again*.

SERAH ✦ *(SEE-ruh)*

Language/Cultural Origin: Hebrew

Meaning: Morning Star

Spiritual Connotation: Abundance

Related Names/Nicknames: None

Alternate Names: Sarah, Sera

Background Story: Serah was Asher's daughter and Jacob's grand-daughter. She was among the seventy members of Jacob's family who emigrated from Canaan to Egypt and the only grandchild identified as a woman (Genesis 46:17).

Of Interest: According to Jewish tradition, Jacob granted immortality to Serah for revealing that his son Joseph was still alive in Egypt. Serah is known as the "wise old woman" of Jewish legend, and stories about her are still told today.

Famous Namesakes: Serah is an award-winning singer/songwriter. Her melodies cross cultures and her lyrics promote peace, love, and healing.

SHARON ✦ *(SHA-ruhn)* or *(SHEHR-uhn)*

Language/Cultural Origin: Hebrew

Meaning: Fertile Plain

Spiritual Connotation: Land of Plenty

Related Names/Nicknames: Shara, Shareen, Sharelle, Sharena, Shari, Sharla, Sharney, Sharona, Sharonda, Sharone, Sharonna, Sharry, Shaz, Shazza, Sherri, Sherrie, Sherry

Alternate Names: Sharan, Sharen, Sharenne, Sharin, Sharren, Sharrin, Sharyn

Background Story: Sharon is the name of a coastal plain in the Bible that stretched between Joppa and Mount Carmel. It was famous for its forests, beautiful flowers, and rich pastureland. David's herds grazed in Sharon (1 Chronicles 27:29); Solomon's bride compared herself to a "rose of Sharon" (Song of Solomon 2:1); and Isaiah referred to "the majesty of . . . Sharon" (Isaiah 35:2).

Of Interest: The "rose of Sharon" was not a rose, but probably a white narcissus, which flourished in the plain of Sharon. Today the name usually refers to a species of hibiscus.

Famous Namesakes: Sharon Gless and Sharon Stone, actresses; Sharon Lechter, writer; Sharon Osbourne, television personality; Sharon Sheeley, songwriter.

SHEBA ✦ *(SHEE-buh)*

Language/Cultural Origin: Hebrew

Meaning: Solemn Vow

Spiritual Connotation: Search for Wisdom

Related Names/Nicknames: Saba, Sabah

Alternate Names: Scheba, Shebah, Sheeba, Shieba

Background Story: Sheba is best known as the ancient country in southern Arabia where the queen of Sheba lived. Having heard about Solomon's great wisdom, the queen of Sheba went to Jerusalem to see for herself. When she realized that there was "nothing hidden from the king that he could not explain to her," she showered Solomon with gold, spices, and precious stones. In turn, he gave her "every desire that she expressed." Before she returned to Sheba, the queen said to Solomon, "Blessed be the Lord your God, who has delighted in you and set you on the throne of Israel!" (1 Kings 10:1–13).

Of Interest: According to some traditions, the queen of Sheba had a son by Solomon. To this day, many Ethiopian Christians claim to be his descendant.

SHELAH ✦ *(SHEE-luh)*
Language/Cultural Origin: Hebrew
Meaning: Request
Spiritual Connotation: Quiet Prayer
Related Names/Nicknames: Shaya, Shea, Sheya
Alternate Names: Sheela, Sheila, Shela

Background Story: Of the two Shelahs in the Bible, one was the father of Eber and grandson of Shem. His name also appears in the genealogy of Jesus (Genesis 11:10–14, Luke 3:35). The other was Judah's third son, whom he promised to Tamar after she was widowed by his two older sons. Afraid that Shelah would also die, Judah failed to follow through on his promise. Tamar then tricked Judah into helping her conceive. Judah said she was justified because he "did not give her to . . . Shelah" (Genesis 38:5–26).

Of Interest: Although Shelah is a name for a biblical man, it is used as a girl's name today, perhaps because of its similarity to other women's names: Sheela means "gentle" in Hindi, and Sheila is "blind" in Gaelic. Sheila is also Australian slang for "woman."

SHERAH ✦ *(SHEE-ruh)*
Language/Cultural Origin: Hebrew
Meaning: Kinswoman
Spiritual Connotation: Love of Family

Related Names/Nicknames: None

Alternate Names: Sheerah, Shera

Background Story: Sherah, Ephraim's granddaughter, makes a short but impressive appearance in the Old Testament. Although she was a woman, she founded two cities—Lower and Upper Beth-horon—and a third was named after her—Uzzen-sherah (1 Chronicles 7:24). The name Sherah suggests a woman who builds good relationships.

SHILOH ✦ *(SHAI-lo)*

Language/Cultural Origin: Hebrew

Meaning: Bringer of Peace

Spiritual Connotation: God's Bounty

Related Names/Nicknames: None

Alternate Names: Shilo, Shylo, Shyloh

Background Story: Shiloh—a Hebrew town situated in the territory of Ephraim—is often named in the Bible. Joshua and the Israelites "assembled at Shiloh" to cast lots for the seven tribes who had not yet received their inheritance in the Promised Land (Joshua 18:1–10). For many years, the ark of the covenant resided at Shiloh, and the town became a sanctuary and place of pilgrimage. Hannah dedicated her infant son, Samuel, to God's service there (1 Samuel 1:24), and he grew up in Shiloh, where, from time to time, the Lord "revealed himself to Samuel" (1 Samuel 3:21).

Of Interest: The name Shiloh is associated by some with the coming of the Messiah. In several versions of the Bible, the name appears in Jacob's blessing to Judah, ancestor of the Jewish people: "The scepter shall not depart from Judah/ Nor the ruler's staff from between his feet/ Until Shiloh comes/ And to him (shall be) the obedience of the peoples."

SHUSHAN ✦ *(SHOO-shan)*

Language/Cultural Origin: Hebrew

Meaning: City of Lilies

Spiritual Connotation: God's Presence

Related Names/Nicknames: Shushanah, Susa, Susan

Alternate Names: None

Background Story: Shushan, more commonly known as Susa, was a city that was home to many Jews during the Babylonian captivity. Nehemiah was living in Shushan when he first learned of the poor state of Jerusalem and made plans to return (Nehemiah 1:1); it was in "Shushan the citadel" that Esther became queen and helped Mordecai save the Jewish race from destruction at the hands of its enemies (Esther 8:11–14); and Daniel had one of his prophetic visions in Shushan (Daniel 8:2).

SIVAN ✦ *(SIHV-uhn)* or *(see-VAHN)*

Language/Cultural Origin: Assyrian/Hebrew

Meaning: Thorn

Spiritual Connotation: Liberation

Related Names/Nicknames: None

Alternate Names: None

Background Story: Sivan—a spring month—is the ninth month of the Jewish year. At his wife Esther's tearful request, King Ahasuerus sent an edict to all of his provinces in "the month of Sivan" (Esther 8:9). His prime minister, Haman, had planned an attack against the Jews. The royal edict countermanded Haman's orders and allowed the Jews to defend themselves against any forces who might attack them.

SUSANNA ✦ *(soo-ZAN-uh)*

Language/Cultural Origin: Hebrew/Greek

Meaning: Lily

Spiritual Connotation: Virtuous

Related Names/Nicknames: Shanna, Shannah, Su, Suann, Sue, Sueann, Suellen, Sukie, Susan, Susanita, Susann, Susanne, Susette, Susie, Suzan, Suzanne, Suzette, Suzi, Suzie, Suzy, Zanna, Zsazsa, Zsuzsa

Alternate Names: Shoshana, Shoshannah, Susana, Susanah, Susannah, Suzanna, Suzannah, Zuzana, Zuzanna

Background Story: There are two Susannas in the Bible. The first was a woman who "provided for" Jesus as he traveled around "proclaiming . . . the good news" (Luke 8:1–3). Susanna was also Joacim's wife and "a very fair woman." Her beauty incited the passion of two elderly judges, who plotted to seduce her. One day they approached Susanna, who was alone in her garden. When she refused to submit to them, they falsely accused her of adultery with a young man and condemned her to death. But the Lord "raised up the holy spirit" of the young prophet Daniel. He questioned the judges separately and trapped them in their lies. The two accusers were put to death, Susanna's honor was vindicated, and Daniel earned a "great reputation in the sight of the people" (History of Susanna).

Famous Namesakes: Susan B. Anthony, suffragette; Susan Cheever, Susanna De Vries, writers; Susan Sarandon, Susannah York, actresses; Suzanne Vega, singer/songwriter.

TABITHA ✦ *(TAB-ih-thuh)*

Language/Cultural Origin: Aramaic

Meaning: Clear-sighted

Spiritual Connotation: Discerning

Related Names/Nicknames: Beth, Dorcas, Tab, Tabbi, Tabbie, Tabby, Tabi

Alternate Names: Tabatha, Tabetha, Tabita, Tabotha, Tabytha

Background Story: Tabitha was the name of a Christian woman in Joppa, whose Greek name was Dorcas. As a disciple, she "was devoted to good works" and made clothing for the poor. Tabitha became ill and died while Peter was nearby in Lydda. Her friends begged him to come at once. As soon as he arrived, Peter "knelt down and prayed" next to her body, then told her to "get up." To everyone's amazement, she did. The news of her recovery traveled around Joppa, and many people were converted (Acts 9:36–42).

Of Interest: Tabitha is a saint in the Catholic Church.

Famous Namesakes: Tabitha Soren is a journalist, television news anchor, and political commentator.

TABOR ✦ *(TAY-bor)* or *(TAY-ber)*

Language/Cultural Origin: Hebrew

Meaning: Purity

Spiritual Connotation: The Glory of the Lord

Related Names/Nicknames: Tabora

Alternate Names: None

Background Story: Mount Tabor is an object of poetry in the Bible as well as the site of a historic battle. Deborah and Barak courageously led the Israelites "down from Mount Tabor" to conquer the Canaanite army (Judges 4:6–16); the psalmist told the Lord with enthusiasm that even "Tabor and Hermon joyously praise your name" (Psalms 89:12); and Jeremiah compared its majesty to that of the king of Babylon, who he prophesied "is coming like Tabor among the mountains" (Jeremiah 46:18). Tabor is a name given to both girls and boys today.

TALITHA ✦ *(TAL-ih-thuh)*

Language/Cultural Origin: Aramaic

Meaning: Young Girl

Spiritual Connotation: Born Again

Related Names/Nicknames: Taletta, Talicia, Talisha, Talita

Alternate Names: Taleetha, Taletha

Background Story: Talitha was a word spoken by Jesus during one of his miracles in the Bible. While he was preaching, Jesus met a man named Jairus, a synagogue leader whose daughter was dying. Jairus asked Jesus to heal his daughter, and they walked to Jairus's house. On the way, some people ran up to them with tragic news—his daughter had died. Jesus said to Jairus, "Do not fear, only believe." He continued to the house, where he found the girl, took her hand, and said, "Talitha cumi," which meant, "Little girl, get up!" At once, the girl rose from her bed and began to walk around (Mark 5:22–43).

TALMAI ✦ *(TAL-mai)*

Language/Cultural Origin: Hebrew

Meaning: My Furrow

Spiritual Connotation: Passionate

Related Names/Nicknames: None

Alternate Names: Talma

Background Story: Of the two men named Talmai in the Bible, the more prominent is Talmai, the king of Geshur. His daughter, Maacah, married David and had two children, Absalom and Tamar. Talmai provided refuge for his grandson, Absalom, after he killed David's other son for raping Tamar. Absalom lived with Talmai for three years before David allowed him to return (2 Samuel 13:22–39). Talmai is also a woman's name today and suggests someone with a passion for justice.

TAMAR ✦ *(TAY-mahr)* or *(TAY-mer)*

Language/Cultural Origin: Hebrew

Meaning: Palm Tree

Spiritual Connotation: Righteous

Related Names/Nicknames: Mara, Tama, Tamara, Tamarah, Tamarra, Tamarria, Tamera, Tami, Tamia, Tammara, Tammee, Tammi, Tammie, Tammy, Tamra, Taye

Alternate Names: Tamarr

Background Story: There are three biblical Tamars. The first was married to Judah's two oldest sons, who died. When Judah prevented Tamar from having children with his third son, she tricked her father-in-law into helping her conceive. Judah later admitted he had wronged Tamar, who bore his twins, Perez and Zerah, and Perez became an ancestor of Jesus (Genesis 38:6–30). The second Tamar was David's daughter and Absalom's sister. Tamar's half-brother, Amnon, was "tormented" by her beauty and lured her to his chambers by pretending to be ill. Despite her pleas, he forced himself on her, then sent her away "desolate" (2 Samuel 13:1–20). Absalom hated Amnon for violating his sister and ordered his servants to "kill him." He later named his own daughter Tamar (2 Samuel 14:27).

Famous Namesakes: Tamar Braxton, singer and sister of Toni Braxton; Tama Janowitz, novelist; Tamara McKinney, championship skier.

TARAH ✦ *(TAH-ruh)* or *(TA-ruh)*
Language/Cultural Origin: Hebrew
Meaning: Wanderer
Spiritual Connotation: Seeker of Truth
Related Names/Nicknames: Taralyn, Taralynn, Terach
Alternate Names: Tara, Tarra, Tera, Terah, Terra

Background Story: Tarah was one of the many places the Israelites "pitched" their tents as they wandered through the desert for forty years (Numbers 33:27–28). It was a difficult time for God's people who were searching for the Promised Land.

Of Interest: The name Tara in Gaelic means "hill" or "star."

Famous Namesakes: Tara was the name of Scarlett O'Hara's home in Margaret Mitchell's 1936 novel *Gone with the Wind*.

TEKOA ✦ *(tuh-KO-uh)* or *(tee-KO-uh)*
Language/Cultural Origin: Hebrew
Meaning: Trumpet
Spiritual Connotation: Mighty Protector
Related Names/Nicknames: None
Alternate Names: Tekoah

Background Story: Tekoa—a town in Judah near Bethlehem—is mentioned frequently in the Old Testament. It was a "woman of Tekoa" who convinced David to reconcile with his son Absalom (2 Samuel 14:1–21); King Rehoboam built up Tekoa "for defense in Judah" (2 Chronicles 11:5–6); the people of Jerusalem stood "in the wilderness of Tekoa" as they watched the Lord rout their enemies (2 Chronicles 20:20); and Jeremiah called for a trumpet to be blown in Tekoa to warn Judah of God's wrath (Jeremiah 6:1).

TEMA ✦ *(TAY-muh)*

Language/Cultural Origin: Hebrew

Meaning: A Palm Tree

Spiritual Connotation: Safe Refuge

Related Names/Nicknames: Temah

Alternate Names: None

Background Story: Tema was one of Ishmael's twelve sons, "twelve princes according to their tribes" (Genesis 25:15–16). His tribe of descendants and the place where they lived were also called Tema. Isaiah described its oasis-like setting in the desert when he wrote, "Bring water to the thirsty, meet the fugitive with bread, O inhabitants of the land of Tema" (Isaiah 21:14). Tema is a name used for boys and girls today.

TERAH ✦ *(TEER-uh)*

Language/Cultural Origin: Hebrew

Meaning: To Breathe

Spiritual Connotation: God Breathes Life

Related Names/Nicknames: Tarah, Terach

Alternate Names: None

Background Story: Terah was Nahor's son and the father of Abraham, Nahor, and Haran. After Haran died, Terah left his home "in Ur of the Chaldeans," also known as Babylon, and set out with his sons, their wives, and Haran's son, Lot, toward the land of Canaan. On the way, they stopped at Haran, where they settled for a while. Tera "died in Haran," and Abraham continued toward Canaan with his family (Genesis 11:24–32). Terah's name is found in the genealogy of Jesus (Luke 3:34) and is more common as a girl's name today.

TIMNA ✦ *(TIHM-nuh)*

Language/Cultural Origin: Hebrew

Meaning: Restraint

Spiritual Connotation: Prudent

Related Names/Nicknames: None

Alternate Names: Timnah

Background Story: Timna was the concubine of Eliphaz, who was Esau's son. Her own son was Amalek—ancestor of the Amalekites (Genesis 36:12). The name Timna suggests a woman who thinks before acting.

Of Interest: The village of Timna is also mentioned in the Bible. It was where Tamar conceived her two sons with her father-in-law, Judah (Genesis 38:12–18).

Famous Namesakes: Timna Brauer is a singer and musician who fuses the sounds of jazz, classical, and Middle Eastern music.

TIRIA ✦ *(TEER-ee-uh)* or *(TEER-yuh)*

Language/Cultural Origin: Hebrew

Meaning: Searching Out

Spiritual Connotation: Instrument of Justice

Related Names/Nicknames: None

Alternate Names: Tirya

Background Story: Tiria was one of Jehallelel's four sons in the Bible. His brothers were Ziph, Ziphah, and Asareel. They were members of the tribe of Judah (1 Chronicles 4:16). Tiria—a name for boys or girls today—implies someone who is fair and impartial.

TIRZAH ✦ *(TER-zuh)*

Language/Cultural Origin: Hebrew

Meaning: Pleasing

Spiritual Connotation: Favorable to God

Related Names/Nicknames: None

Alternate Names: Terza, Thirza, Thyrza, Tirza, Tyrza

Background Story: Tirzah was the youngest of five sisters in the Bible whose courage changed the law of inheritance for the Hebrews. When Moses divided Canaan among the tribes, Tirzah and her sisters stood outside the meeting tent and protested. Their father had died but left no sons to inherit. "Why should the name of our father be taken away from his clan because he had no son?" they argued. Moses consulted with the Lord, who agreed. The law was rewritten; Tirzah and her sisters received their father's inheritance (Numbers 27:1–11).

Of Interest: Tirzah was also the capital city of Israel's northern kingdom, where several kings reigned.

TOI ✦ *(TO-ai)*

Language/Cultural Origin: Hebrew

Meaning: Who Wanders

Spiritual Connotation: Gratitude

Related Names/Nicknames: None

Alternate Names: Tou

Background Story: Toi, the king of Hamath, was a contemporary of David. When David defeated King Hadadezer's army, "Toi sent his son Joram to King David, to greet him and to congratulate him." Hadadezer was also Hamath's enemy, and Toi expressed his gratitude by sending David "articles of silver, gold, and bronze" (2 Samuel 8:9–10). Toi is a name for girls as well as boys today.

Famous Namesakes: Toi Derricotte, poet; Toi Keon Parham, rap artist.

TOLA ✦ *(TO-luh)*

Language/Cultural Origin: Hebrew

Meaning: Scarlet

Spiritual Connotation: Bold Justice

Related Names/Nicknames: None

Alternate Names: None

Background Story: There are two men named Tola in the Bible: Puah's son "from the hill country of Ephraim," a judge "who rose to deliver Israel" for twenty-three years (Judges 10:1–2), and Issachar's oldest son and Jacob's grandson, whose own sons were "mighty warriors of their generations" (1 Chronicles 7:1–2). The name Tola, suggesting a bold spirit tempered by common sense, is found among women and men today.

Of Interest: The name Tola means "priceless" in Polish.

Famous Namesakes: Tola Lewis, musician.

TOPAZ ✦ *(TO-paz)*

Language/Cultural Origin: Greek/Latin

Meaning: Golden Gem

Spiritual Connotation: Quiet Strength

Related Names/Nicknames: Topaza

Alternate Names: None

Background Story: Topaz is a precious golden yellow or green gemstone found in the Bible. The "first row" of the high priest's breastplate was set with "a sardius, a topaz, and an emerald" (Exodus 39:10); Job told his friends that the price of wisdom was so great that "the topaz of Ethiopia cannot equal it" (Job 28:18–19); and in John's vision, the "ninth" foundation of the new Jerusalem was made of topaz (Revelation 21:20).

Of Interest: The Romans associated topaz with the god of the sun. Topaz is the birthstone of those born in the month of November.

VASHTI ✦ *(VASH-tai)* or *(VASH-tee)*

Language/Cultural Origin: Persian

Meaning: Beautiful

Spiritual Connotation: Self-respect

Related Names/Nicknames: Ashti, Astin, Vashtia, Vastha, Vasthia, Vasti, Washti

Alternate Names: Vashtee, Vashtie

Background Story: Queen Vashti was married to the great King Ahasuerus, who ruled from India to Ethiopia. To display his wealth, the king gave a seven-day banquet. He lavished his officials with wine and they did what they wanted. On the last day, the king was "merry with wine" and sent for his wife to show off her beauty. When Vashti refused to come, the king's anger "burned within him." He consulted with his sages, who warned that Vashti's behavior could have serious consequences. Other women would disobey their husbands and there would be "no end of contempt and wrath." As a result, the king sent a decree into his kingdom stating that Vashti could never come before him again and that "every man should be master in his own house" (Esther 1: 1–22). Ahasuerus found a new queen—Esther—the Jewish woman who became famous for saving her people from genocide (Esther 2:17).

Famous Namesakes: Vashti Bunyan, English folksinger; Vashti Farrer, children's author; Vashti McKenzie, first female bishop of the AME (African Methodist Episcopal) church.

VERONICA ✦ *(vuh-RON-ih-kuh)*

Language/Cultural Origin: Latin

Meaning: True Image

Spiritual Connotation: Compassionate

Related Names/Nicknames: Rana, Ranna, Roni, Ronica, Ronika, Ronna, Ronnee, Ronni, Ronnica, Ronnie, Ronny, Veera, Veira, Vera, Verna, Verona, Veronice, Vonnie

Alternate Names: Veronicka, Veronika, Veronike, Veroniqua, Veronique, Veronka

Background Story: Veronica is a woman who appears in the Apocrypha of the New Testament. She was one of several Jews who defended Jesus before Pilate. Veronica claimed that she "touched the edge" of Jesus's garment and was cured of a disease she had suffered for ten years (Acts of Pilate, 7).

Of Interest: Veronica—the woman who wiped Jesus's face with her veil—never actually appears in the Bible. According to legend, her veil retained the image of Jesus's suffering face as he carried the cross. She brought it to Rome, where it was venerated. The name Veronica is derived from the two Latin words that described the veil: "vera icon," which means "true image." Veronica's story is also told in the Catholic Stations of the Cross.

Famous Namesakes: Veronica Campbell, Olympic track-and-field medalist; Veronica Guerin, Irish journalist; Veronica Lake, actress; Veronica Tennant, Canadian ballerina.

ZACCAI ✦ *(ZAK-ai)* or *(zuhk-AY-ai)*
Language/Cultural Origin: Hebrew
Meaning: Just
Spiritual Connotation: Seeker of Justice
Related Names/Nicknames: Zachy
Alternate Names: None

Background Story: Zaccai was the ancestor of a clan of seven hundred sixty people who "returned to Jerusalem and Judah, all to their own towns" following their captivity in Babylon (Ezra 2:1, 9). Zaccai is considered a girl's name today and suggests a person whose sense of purpose drives her to seek justice in the world.

ZEMIRAH ✦ *(zeh-MAI-ruh)*

Language/Cultural Origin: Hebrew

Meaning: Joyous Melody

Spiritual Connotation: Praised

Related Names/Nicknames: None

Alternate Names: Zemira

Background Story: Zemirah was Becher's first son and the grandson of Benjamin, the head of one of Israel's twelve tribes. He had eight brothers: Joash, Eliezer, Elioenai, Omri, Jeremoth, Abijah, Anathoth, and Alemeth (1 Chronicles 7:8). Zemirah—a name for boys and girls today—suggests someone who enjoys music.

Of Interest: A zemirah is a Hebrew religious song sung at Sabbath meals.

ZIA ✦ *(ZEE-ah)*

Language/Cultural Origin: Hebrew/Arabic/Latin

Meaning: Light

Spiritual Connotation: Radiant Splendor

Related Names/Nicknames: None

Alternate Names: Zea

Background Story: Zia was a kinsman of Joel, who was a chief of the Gadite clan in Bashan (1 Chronicles 5:12–13). Zia, a powerful name for boys and girls today, suggests a person whose inner light is never hidden.

Of Interest: The distinctive Zia sun symbol on New Mexico's flag originated with the ancient Indians of Zia Pueblo and reflects their philosophy of harmony among all things.

Famous Namesakes: Zia Jaffrey, writer; Khaleda Zia, first woman prime minister of Bangladesh.

ZIBIAH ✦ *(ZIHB-ee-uh)*

Language/Cultural Origin: Hebrew

Meaning: Gazelle

Spiritual Connotation: The Lord Dwells

Related Names/Nicknames: None

Alternate Names: Civia, Tzivia, Zibia, Zivia

Background Story: Zibiah from Beersheba was the mother of Jehoash—also known as Joash—who reigned as king for forty years (2 Kings 12:1). Her son narrowly escaped death when he was an infant. After Jehoash's father died, his grandmother murdered all her grandchildren, because they stood between her and the throne. Zibiah's son was hidden by his aunt, Jehosheba. A few years later, his grandmother was overthrown and Jehoash began his reign.

ZILLAH ✦ *(ZIHL-uh)*

Language/Cultural Origin: Hebrew

Meaning: Shade

Spiritual Connotation: Protected

Related Names/Nicknames: None

Alternate Names: Zila, Zilla

Background Story: In the Bible, Zillah was Lamech's second wife. She was the mother of Tubal-cain, "who made all kinds of bronze and iron tools," and Naamah, a daughter. Her husband, Lamech, was a descendant of Cain. Proud of his heritage, Lamech bragged to his wives that he, too, had killed a man for "striking" him (Genesis 4:19–24). The name Zillah implies a woman who faces problems calmly and confidently.

ZION ✦ *(ZAI-uhn)*

Language/Cultural Origin: Hebrew

Meaning: Sign

Spiritual Connotation: Monument to God

Related Names/Nicknames: None

Alternate Names: Ziona, Zionah, Zyona, Zyonah

Background Story: Zion is a symbolic name for Jerusalem in the Bible, the center of worship for God's chosen people. David marched to Jerusalem and "took the stronghold of Zion," changing its name to "the city of David" (2 Samuel 5:7–9); "Mount Zion" was the site of a temple that housed the ark of the covenant (Isaiah 8:18); and the prophets often referred to the city of Jerusalem—and its people—as "daughter Zion" (Micah 4:10). The name Zion suggests a woman of hope, courage, and great faith.

Of Interest: Mount Zion was actually the name for the southeastern hill of the city around which Jerusalem was built.

ZIPPORAH ✦ *(zih-PO-ruh)* or *(ZIHP-uh-ruh)*

Language/Cultural Origin: Hebrew

Meaning: Bird

Spiritual Connotation: Gift of the Spirit

Related Names/Nicknames: Tippi, Tippie, Tzippa

Alternate Names: Tsipporah, Zipora, Ziporah, Zippora

Background Story: Zipporah and her sisters were watering their father's sheep when she met Moses. Some ill-mannered shepherds had driven the women away from the water trough, and Moses "came to their defense." Zipporah's father, Reuel—also known as Jethro—invited Moses to stay with his family and gave him Zipporah as a wife. Zipporah had two sons, Gershom and Eliezer (Exodus 2:16–22). When Moses returned to Egypt, his family accompanied him. Zipporah later returned to her homeland until Moses led the Israelites out of Egypt. After hearing about "all that God had done for Moses," Jethro brought Zipporah and her sons to Moses in the wilderness (Exodus 18:1–6).

ZORAH ✦ *(ZO-ruh)* or *(ZAWR-uh)*

Language/Cultural Origin: Arabic/Latin/Slavic

Meaning: Dawn

Spiritual Connotation: Source of Light

Related Names/Nicknames: Zarya, Zorana, Zoraya, Zoreen, Zorina, Zorine, Zorya

Alternate Names: Zohra, Zora, Zorrah

Background Story: Zorah is the name of a town in Judah, best known as the birthplace of Samson, son of Manoah. Manoah's wife was barren, but an angel of the Lord appeared to her. He told her she would have a son—Samson—who would "begin to deliver Israel from the hand of the Philistines" (Judges 13:2–5). The angel's words came true. After he died, Samson was buried in the tomb of his father near Zorah (Judges 16:31).

Famous Namesakes: Zora Neale Hurston was a noted novelist and short-story writer, whose best-known book, *Their Eyes Were Watching God*, was published in 1937.

ABOUT THE AUTHOR

Judith Tropea is the author of two children's books. She takes great pride in having found the perfect name for several expectant family members and friends and hopes to continue the tradition with this book. She has two sons, Matthew and Daniel.